Y0-AUZ-374

Girls into Science and Technology

Girls into Science and Technology: the story of a project

Judith Whyte

Routledge & Kegan Paul
London, Boston and Henley

First published in 1986
by Routledge & Kegan Paul plc

14 Leicester Square, London WC2H 7PH, England

9 Park Street, Boston, Mass. 02108, USA and

Broadway House, Newtown Road,
Henley on Thames, Oxon RG9 1EN, England

Set in Times, 10 on 11 pt.
by Columns of Reading
and printed in Great Britain
by T.J. Press (Padstow) Ltd
Padstow, Cornwall

Library of Congress Cataloging in Publication Data

Whyte, Judith.

Girls into science and technology.
Bibliography: p.
Includes index.
1. Girls into Science and Technology Project.
2. Sex differences in education—Great Britain.
I. Title.
Q183.4.G7W48 1986 507'.1041 85-10756

British Library CIP data also available

ISBN 0-7102-0364-0

Contents

Figures

Tables

Acknowledgments

Funding for the 'Girls into Science and Technology' project was provided by a joint panel of the Equal Opportunities Commission and the Social Science Research Council, the Schools Council, the Department of Industry Education Unit and Shell UK.

As readers of this book will become aware, the 'Girls into Science and Technology' project was a team effort involving the cooperation of ten schools and well over 100 teachers. I am grateful to my colleagues on the team, Alison Kelly, Barbara Smail and John Catton for entrusting this account to me, and for four years of stimulating discussion, reflection and action. Their energy and dedication to the task of action research was unfailing. Comments on the book from them, and from Chris Byrne and Diana Kealey have helped me, but any errors of fact or interpretation, any deficiencies of reporting are my own responsibility.

Thanks are also due to the schools and teachers who allowed us to work with them, and often gave generously of their time, despite the pressure of many other concerns. Last, but certainly not least, I would like to pay tribute to the tireless patience and professional accuracy of Vera Ferguson and Dolores Donegan who typed drafts of this, and other writings from the project.

Introduction

Girls into Science and Technology (GIST) was an innovative action research programme with the twin aims of investigating the causes of female underachievement in science and technology, whilst simultaneously trying to change the situation.

We wanted to know more about why girls do less well than boys in scientific and technical subjects at school, and we expected the GIST intervention would produce some ideas about how girls might be encouraged to take up options in physical science and technical subjects and consider careers in science, applied science and technology.

Our initial hope that GIST could actually bring about these changes for the cohort of girls in the action schools was not to be fully realized, although we did learn a great deal about what actually happens to discourage girls from science and technology in the mixed comprehensive. Instead our tangible success was to be seen in the increased interest, awareness and understanding of the 'problem' by schools and authorities all over the country, rather than just in the eight schools where we worked. Our very existence as a project seems to have had quite an impact on science educators and those who wished to see more women succeed in previously all-male fields. The year in which the project was completed, 1984, was designated WISE (Women into Science and Engineering) Year, a title obviously rather closely modelled on GIST.

The GIST project was based at Manchester Polytechnic, but was a joint university-polytechnic venture, directed by lecturers from the two institutions. It lasted for just over four years (1979-84), in order to follow a cohort of approximately 2000 girls and boys who entered secondary school in September 1980. Ten coeducational comprehensive schools were involved in the project, two 'control' schools and eight 'action' schools (see below for an explanation of these terms). Although not a random sample, they served a wide variety of socio-economic catchment areas and there is every reason to suppose them typical of such schools in general.

At the end of the third year of the secondary school, children are required to choose a limited number of subjects they will continue to study. If girls drop from physical science or technical crafts at this stage it is difficult if not impossible for them to re-enter science and technology at a later stage. Chapter 1 explains the background to the 'problem' of girls and science and technology and the rationale for planning the GIST action research in the way the team did. As most girls are now offered the opportunity to study physical science, and at least in the last ten to fifteen years technical crafts as well, direct discrimination is no longer, as it may have been in the past, the main reason for female underachievement. It is rather a matter of the choices girls make.

Nowadays the lower years of secondary education offer the only opportunity for most girls to study science or technology, yet most opt to abandon these subjects at the end of third year. The causes of girls' underachievement in science and technology are complex; the perceived difficulty of physics, the absence in science studies of social or human implications, girls' relatively lesser experience with scientific and technical toys and games, the expectations for girls' future lives, and the paucity of role models of women in science and engineering have all been cited as possible causal factors. In school, traditional assumptions and expectations are translated into informal mechanisms of discouragement. After school, girls' relative lack of scientific and technical qualifications effectively bars them from science-based courses in further or higher education, and from jobs and careers outside the sphere of traditional female employment. A range of investigatory instruments and interventions was chosen for the GIST 'experiment' in order to explicate further the complex causes of girls' choices. The research design, with a group of eight 'action' schools in which interventions were to happen, along with the measurement of attitudes and knowledge, and two 'control' schools where only testing was to take place, was to allow us to compare the effects of active change efforts on girls in the control and action schools.

Chapter 2 uses data collected during the project to describe the hidden curriculum of teacher and pupil expectation, and the atmosphere in school labs and workshops which subtly and inexorably leads the majority of girls to opt out of subject areas which seem to present so many formidable though invisible barriers. The sexes, divided in almost every aspect of schooling, diverge even further in the science and craft departments; boys dominate discussions and 'hog' available resources.

Chapter 3 briefly describes the schools, which were mostly urban comprehensives, all in the Greater Manchester area, and the preparatory in-service workshops for teachers with which the project began.

Interventions in the GIST action schools were designed to deal with some of the barriers to girls, both formal and informal. The VISTA scheme, described in Chapter 4, brought working women scientists and technical workers into the schools, to bring science and technology 'alive' in a way that girls would find sympathetic, and to demonstrate by their presence as role models that women can be feminine, competent and rewardingly employed in traditionally 'masculine' jobs. The 'roadshows' (see Chapter 8) went a little further, and presented children with examples of men in women's jobs as well as the reverse. It was the first direct contact between members of the team and pupils themselves; the reactions of both girls and boys filled out for us the picture of their attitudes, their likes and dislikes, collected in the GIST initial survey. Many boys and some girls revealed very traditional and rigid attitudes about the separate roles of men and women in society, but they appeared to enjoy the discussion of alternative views and possibilities. The roadshows were timed to coincide with the weeks in which children were preparing to make their option choices. The effects of the roadshow experiences also showed up in the second attitude survey, and are discussed in Chapter 8.

As soon as it was available, material collected from the initial survey was fed back to the schools, and often provided a motivation and justification for further interventions originating from schools and teachers as well as ourselves. This information, together with an evaluation of the impact of VISTA, taught all of us more clearly what a 'girl friendly' science would look like. The emphasis and pedagogical approach would be rather different from some current methods of teaching science, but probably ultimately more appealing to boys, as well as girls. Chapters 5 and 6 draw together some of the lessons of the project and will be of special interest to science educators.

Chapter 7 is a description and interpretation of some of the findings from cognitive and attitude testing on the GIST children. The results are more fully discussed elsewhere, in a number of articles published in academic journals (see page 278); this chapter links the more important findings to the behaviour and response of the GIST cohort in the schools.

The decision to confront the most stereotyped aspects of the school curriculum – 'girls' and boys' ' crafts as they are still frequently termed – was a difficult one and a novel approach at the time. It turned out to be even more complicated than we had expected because of rapid changes in the definitions of craft subjects. The recent renaming of the old technical crafts as 'craft, design and technology' (CDT) represents a demand on teachers to move away from the traditional teaching of handicrafts or preparation for trades such as plumbing and carpentry towards a broader, design-based or problem-solving approach to technology. Actual practice in the schools varies tremendously. Some retain the old craft syllabus and match it uncomfortably with the unaccustomed presence of girls as well as boys. Others have radically revised the whole craft syllabus to accommodate both sexes and new curriculum needs. Chapter 9 describes the process of encouraging schoolgirls to participate in the new subject of craft, design and technology.

Chapter 10 examines the GIST experience of single-sex clubs and groups within formal classes. The issue of mixed or single-sex schooling is still a live and controversial one, and this evidence contributes food for thought about what can be achieved in coeducational schools, and shows that, without attentive awareness from teachers and others, mixed schools are in danger of becoming boys' schools with girls in them.

The interventions in schools were mainly implemented by the teachers. The project team did not have the staff or resources to work directly with pupils to any great extent. Nor would we have wanted to even if it had been possible, because if any lasting changes could be brought about, they would be continued by teachers who appreciated the need for change. Chapters 11 and 12 describe how our relationship with teachers worked in practice and interprets their response to the aims of GIST, using data from the report of a team of independent evaluators. The report highlights teachers' doubts and hesitancies, and shows up some of the problems we encountered which were compounded in the GIST project by the attitudes and prejudices associated with aims which were perceived as 'feminist'.

Evaluation of the effects of GIST was built into the design of the programme. At the crudest level, numbers of girls opting for science or crafts are compared with the choices for previous years in each school. The more refined measure is the shift in children's attitudes to science, to occupations defined as men's or women's work, and to sex role stereotypes in general. Comparisons were made between the action schools, where interventions were mounted, and control schools, where only testing took place. They indicate in more detail the influences on girls' choices, and the possibilities for change. There are interesting differences between individual schools, and Chapter 13 relates some of the effects of the GIST programme to features of the eight action schools.

The failures perhaps more than the successes of GIST illuminate the barriers to innovation, and the problems associated with work on sex differences and stereotyping. Chapter 14 attempts to identify points of resistance as well as transferable recommendations and implications for schools and teachers.

GIST was innovative in a number of ways, and was the first major project in this country to use an 'action research' approach to address the problems of sex bias and sex-related underachievement. Appendices 1 and 2 contain documents from the project and Appendix 3 explores, for those who are interested, the theoretical and practical aspects of GIST as action research.

The GIST team

GIST originally received funding from a joint panel formed by the Equal Opportunities Commission and the Social Science Research Council, which had the task of promoting research on 'women and underachievement'. The Schools Council, the Department of Industry and Shell UK Ltd funded later parts of the project, including the appointment of a CDT specialist, and the costs of the fourth and fifth year. The bulk of the funding went on staffing costs. Because of the later sponsorship from other sources, and our growing realization of the breadth of the task we had taken on, the team grew from three women and our Project Secretary in 1979 to six people, including an additional full-time secretary, in 1982, the fourth member of the research team being a man. Although we were united in our commitment to the general aims of the project, our backgrounds, experience and expertise differed considerably. In many ways this was an excellent feature of the project; not only are two minds better than one, but four, five or six can be better than two. However the differences of emphasis which were inevitable because of differences in our training, and therefore perceptions, also brought difficulties, especially when priorities had to be discussed. *Girls Into Science and Technology* is the only comprehensive account of the GIST project, written by one member of the team, so the perspective reflects one rather than four viewpoints (but see Endpiece, p. 268). It also seems important, if only to help the reader identify any potential bias, to describe all the members of the GIST team and indicate where their main interests as individuals lay.

Alison Kelly and I were co-directors of GIST, each of us during the life of the project in permanent employment as lecturers in our respective institutions. Given the purposes of GIST, our different backgrounds provided an ideal combination. Alison is a former physicist, who took an MSc in Astrophysics and then taught maths and science for two years in Swaziland. During this time she became interested in the science education of girls and subsequently pursued this interest for a PhD in Education. In 1979 she was a lecturer in Sociology at Manchester University, teaching courses on women in society, sociology of education, and research methods. We were already working together, as Alison had asked me to contribute two chapters (eventually I wrote only one) for her book *The Missing Half*, on girls and science education. I graduated with an MA in Philosophy and English Literature from Glasgow University, and taught in a variety of primary, secondary and special schools in Glasgow and London. Later I became Education Organizer for Oxfam where part of my job was to provide material and advice for teachers on education about the Third World, then I worked in adult education, where I had a variety of responsibilities: teaching, research, publicity and communications, and finally, before joining the Polytechnic, worked as a Research Fellow for the Health Education Council, looking at attitude and behavioural change in relation to health education. In between two of these jobs I took a post-graduate teaching certificate at Oxford, where it was possible to do one's teaching practice in a college of further education rather than a school. The dramatic sexual divide between boys, mainly on day release from engineering employment, and girls (on the whole reluctantly) training to be secretaries struck me at once, and I chose sex difference in occupational choice as the topic for my student dissertation. This is where my interest in the determinants of the sexual division of labour began. In 1979, I was a Lecturer at Manchester Polytechnic, where I taught Philosophy on the BA degree, and several courses on sex differences and sex typing for both pre-service and in-service teachers. Both Alison and I were married, with young children, and had continued to work, breaking off only for the statutory maternity leave. We had both belonged to a variety of women's groups during the previous few years, and consciously regarded ourselves as feminists, although our other political beliefs affected our views of feminism.

At the beginning of the GIST project, in September 1979, Barbara Smail was appointed as Research Fellow and Schools Liaison Officer for Science. A chemistry graduate, she had worked in the microelectronics industry in the States in the late 1960s, taken a break to have two children, and had several years of experience as a chemistry teacher when she joined the team. At the same time, Vera Ferguson began work as the part-time Project Secretary. In the period September 1981 to August 1983, a grant from the Schools Council enabled the further appointment of John Catton, a CDT teacher (also married, with two children), to develop the technical craft side of the project. As a CDT Head of Department in a mixed comprehensive school he was actively involved in new developments in craft, design and technology, and was Chief Examiner for 'O'-level CDT with the Associated Examining Board. Neither Barbara nor John would previously have described themselves as conscious theoretical 'feminists' but both had been particularly successful in teaching girls in their respective subject areas. The opportunity to visit schools with an 'observer' rather than a teacher status revealed the extent of existing bias in classrooms other than their own. In August 1982, Dolores Donegan became Assistant Project Secretary, initially under the Work Experience Employment project (WEEP) scheme.

This book is written for teachers, teacher trainers and educationists, feminists, and the general public interested in the striking pattern of sex differences between boys' and girls' achievement in the secondary school. Sex role expectations, translated into a 'hidden curriculum' of sex and gender divisions in the social context of the school, interactions in the classroom, and differences between boys and girls as learners, apparently exercise a very powerful influence on subject choice and are among the major causes of female underachievement in science and technology.

As an account of a project which set out to change teachers' and pupils' attitudes it may also be of use to anyone who is interested in the more general issues of innovation, evaluation and barriers to change in education.

A number of other publications have arisen from the GIST project. Two sourcebooks, for teachers of science and CDT respectively, were produced by Barbara Smail and John Catton, and are published by Longman for the Schools Council. They describe in greater detail than this book the curricular aspects of the GIST initiative, and provide ideas and recommendations of a practical nature, for teachers. *The Missing Half: Girls and Science Education* is a collection of papers edited by Alison Kelly, the Co-Director of the project. It evaluates competing theories of the sources of girls' underachievement in science, offers short research reports illuminating the problem as it presents itself in schools, and suggests some strategies to improve girls' performance. Published in 1981, it has already become an indispensable classic for those who wish to understand the range of explanations for sex differences in science achievement.

Part I

The need for GIST

Chapter 1

The need for GIST

We had identified a problem: the entry of women into scientific and technical careers is blocked by girls' avoidance of options in physical science and technology at secondary school. We also had a number of ideas for intervention at school which might begin to alter the trend. This chapter describes the background to the problem and the way the GIST team chose to tackle it, with a combination of research and 'action' or 'intervention' in a group of schools.

British schools are committed in the broadest terms to 'equality of opportunity' reflected in the general move towards comprehensivization in the late 1960s and early 1970s. Yet there remains considerable inequality of outcome between girls and boys, comparable to the inequalities between children of different social classes or ethnic groups.

Girls' relative underachievement in comparison with boys was well established before the start of the GIST project in 1979. In the early 1970s, it was still the case that some girls had no opportunity at all to study physical sciences after the third year at secondary school. But even those who were offered the choice tended to opt for biology or human biology, or even to opt out of science altogether where that was still possible. The DES survey carried out in 1973 showed that only 71 per cent of girls compared with 90 per cent of boys were offered the chance to take physics in the fourth and fifth forms. But the sex differences in choosing the subject were much greater. Only 17 per cent of the girls who were offered the choice took physics, compared with 52 per cent of the boys. The same pattern, in a milder form, shows up in chemistry and the reverse is true in biology, the 'girls' ' science.

The DES Education Survey 21, *Curricular Difference for Boys*

TABLE 1.1 *Subject choices of fourth and fifth formers*

		% of pupils being offered	% of those offered choosing
Physics:	Girls	71	17
	Boys	90	52
Chemistry:	Girls	76	22
	Boys	79	35
Biology:	Girls	95	52
	Boys	88	31

Source: Dept of Education and Science, 1975

and Girls, had drawn attention to considerable sex differences in examination entries for science subjects. Boys predominated in physics and chemistry while girls were overrepresented in biology at CSE and 'O'-level entrance. More boys than girls gained 'O'-level maths, while almost all those holding technical qualifications at school were male. At 'A'-level and beyond the underrepresentation of girls in science and technology was even more marked.

Jan Harding's study for the Nuffield Foundation (Harding, 1981) showed that girls in girls' schools were significantly more successful in science than girls in mixed schools of the same selectivity. She also showed that boys tend to achieve higher marks in multiple choice papers and girls in essays, while structured questions appeared to show the least bias.

Up until the age of 11, girls were known to perform at least as well as boys, with a relative decline in achievement in the early years of the secondary school. The attitudes to science of both sexes also deteriorated during this period (Goodwin *et al*., 1981).

A good deal has been written about the way social class background or belonging to an ethnic minority can disadvantage the schoolchild: comprehensivization was intended to minimize some of these differences in educational outcome. The comprehensive philosophy assumed that coeducation – teaching boys and girls together – would also be 'a good thing'. The classic study of the relative benefits of mixed or single-sex education was written by R.R. Dale between 1969 and 1974, that is, during the years when most local authorities were moving towards comprehensivization. Dale's surveys of teacher and pupil attitudes showed

TABLE 1.2 *Percentage of pupils choosing a subject when offered it (in 1981)*

		Mixed schools	Single-sex schools
'Male' subjects			
Physics	Girls	16	37
	Boys	55	57
Chemistry	Girls	26	41
	Boys	36	50
Technical drawing	Girls	1.9	–
	Boys	38	40
Woodwork	Girls	1	–
	Boys	31	32
Design and technology	Girls	1.5	–
	Boys	33	–
'Female' subjects			
Biology	Girls	53	62
	Boys	29	48
Home economics (Cookery)	Girls	38	30
	Boys	6	–
Needlecraft	Girls	20	12
	Boys	0.1	–
Childcare	Girls	30	–
	Boys	0.5	–

Source: Pratt *et al.*, 1984

that coeducational schools were 'happier' and more 'natural' and 'life-like' than single-sex schools. The emphasis was on *social* atmosphere, but Dale also revealed that boys benefited in *academic* terms from the presence of girls in the school. He did not investigate much further as to why this was so, nor did it occur to anyone at the time to ask if the implication was that girls suffered academically from the presence of boys (Dale, 1969, 1971, 1974). Over the next few years a growing body of evidence demonstrated two truths: subject choice is more polarized in mixed schools, and girls are more likely to continue with a study of physical science in an all-girls school, especially if it is, or has been, a selective grammar school.

Subject choice in the mixed school

In 1975 Ormerod investigated the subject preferences and choices of a national sample of children in nineteen secondary schools. By looking both at the subjects *preferred* by boys or girls, and the subjects they actually *chose*, he showed that maths, physics, chemistry and geography were 'male' subjects while biology, languages and arts were 'female' subjects. This divide across the curriculum was even more marked in coeducational schools. For instance a survey carried out by the Inspectorate in 1973 showed that even though fewer girls actually had the opportunity to study physics in girls' schools, when it *was* available, nearly a quarter of them took it in fourth and fifth year (HMI, 1979).

A postal survey carried out in 1981 showed a similar pattern and confirmed the finding that the choices of boys and girls in single-sex schools seem to be somewhat less affected by the 'masculine' or 'feminine' image of a subject than those of their contemporaries in coeducational schools (see Table 1.2) (Pratt *et al.*, 1984).

In single-sex schools *girls* were much more likely to take physics or chemistry and *boys* to take biology. For instance 37 per cent of girls from all-girls' schools chose to do physics, compared with only 16 per cent in mixed schools. The proportion of boys choosing physics was approximately the same in each kind of institution (57 per cent and 55 per cent respectively). On the other hand only 29 per cent of boys took biology in mixed schools compared with almost half the age group (48 per cent) in boys' schools. The same was not true for craft subjects because on the whole the 'non-traditional' craft is not on offer in single-sex schools, which are specifically excluded from the Sex Discrimination Act.

In the decade before, the majority of schools had become comprehensive. Britain now has only 767 single-sex maintained schools compared with 3,885 coeducational establishments (Hall, 1983).

The available evidence suggested that girls in single-sex schools were more likely to succeed in the physical sciences than girls in coeducational schools. The GIST action programme therefore focused on the first three years of the comprehensive coed secondary school in order to create maximum impact in relation to the moment of subject choice. The move to coeducation provided in theory for a common craft curriculum for both sexes, but although a small percentage of boys (6 per cent) took advantage of the new system to learn cookery or home economics, only a minute fraction of those taking technical craft courses were girls (less than 2 per cent in all craft subjects) (see Table 1.2).

Science, technology and career opportunities for girls

It was clear by 1978 that the impact of the Equal Pay Act was negligible in comparison with what had been hoped for by some. Comparisons with men in the same job, a key facet of the law, were rarely possible. This was largely because so many women work in distinct 'feminine' sections of the economy, or at levels in a mixed workforce where no men were employed. One of the crucial determinants of sex segregation in the labour force is the different qualifications with which girls and boys leave school, and in particular, girls' lack of technical and scientific qualifications.

It is generally agreed that as an industrial nation Britain's prosperity depends on an adequate supply of able scientists, technologists and skilled workers in the scientific and engineering industries. Since half the young people in school are female, and an estimated 80 per cent of the most able girls leave school with only one scientific/technological qualification, usually biology, the underrepresentation of women in these types of employment represents a waste of one of the country's most valuable resources. It also deprives women of the means to enter a large range of occupations, and confines them to the lowest paid and least secure jobs and sectors in the economy. Most of the jobs that women do can be seen as an extension of the traditional roles of the housewife, for example, women work in the service sector (catering, nursing, social work), certain parts of manufacturing where they deal with 'food, textiles, clothing, shoe or glove industries', para-medical or social jobs and teaching (Sartin, 1978). Apart from employment in manufacturing industries, often in contracting areas such as textiles, female life chances are effectively reduced to six main possibilities:

Teaching (especially at primary level)
Nursing
Catering
Office work
Employment in retail organizations
Hairdressing
Source: Sharma and Meighan, 1980

The division of the labour market by sex is partly due to cultural assumption about 'men's' and 'women's' work. But it is reinforced by the different qualifications with which boys and girls leave school, and the separate occupational routes they then follow. The 'gender spectrum' of school subjects – arts, languages, domestic subjects for girls, mathematics, physics and technical subjects for boys – not only reflects labour market divisions, it reconstructs them, fitting boys and girls into their future corresponding positions in the male or female labour market.

Improving job prospects for women was not our only concern. Female exclusion from science and technology, even if it is apparently by girls' own choice, means that they have missed out on an important component of general education.

At a personal level, women are bound to experience a sense of incompetency and ignorance about many facets of a technological industrial society; driving a car, and even in the kitchen, where she is surrounded by labour-saving machinery, a woman often feels she does not control or understand these artefacts sufficiently to carry out simple repairs, and thus female dependence on male expertise continues. Lacking a fundamental education in the physical sciences, girls are without the basic intellectual tools required for a critical understanding of nuclear power, fluoridization of water, the dangers of food additives, information technology and a host of other contemporary issues. And on a deeper level the sense of incomprehension of an overwhelmingly male world that is engendered by the limited and biased education most girls receive undermines their self-confidence and their ability to make a genuinely female voice heard in the broader arena of economics and politics. In short, the virtual exclusion of the female sex from the most powerful sources of social, economic and technological change has profound implications for the power and position of women in general.

Efforts to retain girls' interest in science and technology beyond the end of third year were therefore also related to their perceived relevance for future occupational choice. Children's stereotypes about suitable jobs for men and women were investigated, and the VISTA programme (see Chapter 4) and other activities were designed to open up new opportunities for girls especially and to demonstrate to both sexes the possible benefits of making a non-traditional career choice.

Causal factors in girls' underachievement

The phenomenon of girls' poorer achievement in science is so well known that a large number of theories and hypotheses have been put forward to explain it.

Biological and innate differences

The question of whether sex differences in intellectual functioning result from heredity or environment is an aspect of the more general nature/nurture controversy and is an area of research with a long history (see Griffiths and Saraga, 1979). A considerable range of biological theories claims to account for sex differences in ability, and particularly in spatial ability. In a typical visuo-spatial task, subjects have to perceive and manipulate two- or three-dimensional spatial figures. Males usually perform better than females on such tasks. The biological link is said to be, according to the genetic theory, a recessive gene for superior spatial ability carried on the X chromosome and therefore inheritable only by men. This idea is sometimes combined with the theory that hormonal differences between the sexes also produce spatial ability differences. For instance, it has been contended that there is a recessive gene which determines spatial ability and is activated by the operation of androgens (male hormones). A third line of argument is based on the finding that the two halves of the brain are specialized to control different functions. The rest of the hypothesis, i.e. that spatial ability is one of these specialized functions and that female brains are different in this respect from males, has yet to be proven.

Biological arguments, then, are still inconclusive. They are also controversial because they can be used to justify conservative views of sex roles on the grounds that hereditary differences are largely unchangeable. Different explanations, for example, boys' greater experience of games and play which may assist the development of spatial ability, could equally well account for male superiority on spatial tests.

GIST devised two tests of spatial and mechanical ability for use with the children on entry to secondary school. Our testing hypothesis was that spatial/mechanical differences *would* be found to exist between the sexes, but might be shown to be alterable as a result of concrete experiences which the school could conceivably offer, perhaps as part of the intervention.

We envisaged that craft, design and technology (CDT) or science departments might set up special clubs or classes where girls could acquire greater spatial and mechanical competence by making models, designing in three dimensions or 'playing' with Meccano and Lego.

A Science Knowledge test was also administered in the first week of September 1980 when the children had just arrived, to find out if there were sex differences in the amount of science knowledge boys and girls had acquired, either formally or informally, during the primary years. Different versions of the test were made so that we could test the effect of either multiple choice questions or structured questions requiring a one-line answer, on girls' and boys' results. There was also an essay question with a choice of title, to see whether boys and girls would display different preferences and we tried to write some questions in a masculine context in one version and a feminine in the other to see if this affected children's scores (for example, letting air into a can of evaporated milk in the kitchen or into a can of oil in the garage to allow the liquid to pour out (see Chapter 6 for fuller details of cognitive and attitude testing).

Early socialization

Early socialization and childhood experiences have frequently been put forward as key factors in girls' avoidance of physical science and technical activities. If girls have considerably less opportunity than boys to acquire skills and knowledge informally, then they may be relatively handicapped at the outset in practical laboratory and workshop sessions. The Scientific Activities scale told us that girls had participated more in biological activities such as collecting flowers and watching birds, while boys were more likely to be involved in working out inventions, reading science magazines or talking about scientific discoveries. (These rather academic pastimes were uncommon in both sexes, however.) By far the largest sex difference was in 'tinkering activities'. Boys had much more experience of using tools such as a saw or screwdriver, helping to maintain a car or bicycle and playing with constructional and electrical toys.

One of the interventions suggested to schools was the idea of compensatory play sessions where girls could catch up on the experiences they lacked because of stereotyping at home. (See Chapter 8 for further details.)

Prevailing social norms and attitudes

Social norms and attitudes are also said to be determinants of girls' beliefs, opinions and choices concerning science and sex roles. A comprehensive 'background' questionnaire provided us with a data base on social class and ability and parental attitudes and roles, as reported by pupils.

Eighty per cent of fathers and 66 per cent of mothers were employed. A third of the fathers were in non-manual jobs and two-thirds were in manual jobs, proportions which approximate to the national distribution. Most of the children's homes seemed to reflect traditional sex roles. The mothers shopped for food, cooked meals, washed clothes and cleaned and dusted while the fathers mended things when they were broken and decorated the house.

A postal questionnaire sent to the parents of first year children in one school (reported in Kelly *et al.*, 1982) showed that parents' aspirations for their children in school were remarkably egalitarian but that there were strong divisions along sex lines outside school. Parents' estimates of the suitability of various occupations for their children showed a marked preference for traditional jobs. There were also notable differences in the household jobs girls and boys were expected to do, and the way the children used their leisure time. We were interested to know whether girls from 'non-traditional' homes would also be less subject to conventional stereotypes and therefore more likely to choose 'masculine' subjects such as physics or metalwork.

Research into the effects that mothers' attitudes have upon their daughters has shown that mothers who work outside the home are more likely to have daughters with active careers, particularly in non-traditional fields (Hartley and Klein, 1959; Hoffman, 1974). We hoped to test this idea further and see whether the girls with employed mothers would respond more to the GIST interventions than others.

It is frequently suggested that women science teachers may act as role models for girls, but in most of the schools, physical sciences were taught by men. An exception was New Hall, a control school where most of the physics and chemistry staff were female although the Science Department was headed by a male chemist. The VISTA programme was designed to bring into the schools women scientists and technical workers to talk about their work – and their home lives – and to act as positive role models.

The need for GIST

These questionnaires were to be used again when the children were in their third year of secondary school, to determine whether the GIST interventions had altered their attitudes to science or sex roles, in comparison with the children in the control schools who had not experienced interventions (see Chapter 13).

Pupils' attitudes in the years between ages 11 and 14

Attitudes to school subjects and school in general were investigated by the School Questionnaire. At 11, girls seem to enjoy school more and just as many gave science as their favourite subject. More girls than boys gave maths. A considerable body of psychological research has looked at children's self-confidence. Despite the fact that at this age girls are usually doing better in school than boys, more boys than girls claimed to be 'above average'.

Children were also extensively questioned, again by pen and paper tests, about their attitudes to and curiosity about science (Image of Science and Science Curiosity) and their gender role and occupational stereotypes (Gender Stereotype Inventory and Occupational Stereotype Inventory).

The 'masculine image' of science

Perhaps the greatest discouragement to girls arises from the image of science and technology as masculine, both in the sense that masculine characteristics are supposed to be desirable for success in these areas, and because the vast majority of existing scientists and technologists seem to be men.

The personality characteristics associated with the 'typical scientist' – independent, rather cold, single-minded in his work, interested in things rather than people, avoiding complex human emotions, a 'stander-back' from social relationships and encounters – are dramatically opposed to the stereotype of the way women in Western society are expected to behave – with warmth and emotion and showing concern and involvement with people. For adolescent girls, in the process of defining their femininity, the image of the scientist is in conflict with society's ideal of womanhood.

The VISTA programme was intended to counter the stereotype of the hard, cold male scientist and to suggest that femininity and scientific or technical competence are not necessarily mutually exclusive.

Changes in curriculum materials, and the introduction of biographical information about successful women scientists, were also designed to redress the balance. Because most of the people already in scientific and technical occupations are men, girls, their teachers and their parents may feel that even qualified girls will not find training opportunities. Careers education, linked to option choice, were part of the longer-term intervention plan.

Of course a few girls and women have already broken through into the traditional male preserves, but they may be those who have more ability and determination than any of the others. We hoped that amongst the GIST cohort sufficiently large numbers of girls would choose to go ahead with physical science and technical crafts to ensure substantial groups of girls, rather than individuals, going into classes in upper school and eventually together joining training courses or applying to higher education institutions, supporting each other and less likely to drop out because of isolation.

Technology

A good deal has been said and written about girls and science, but from the earliest stage, GIST was not simply a programme of science education, hence the additional phrase in the project's title, 'and Technology'. Technology as such was in 1979 and is still not really specifically taught in schools, but the educational basis for entry to occupations in applied science and technology, and for the ordinary citizen's comprehension of technological matters, is acquired at school. Girls' exclusion from this broader sphere of technology is reflected in the dramatic differences of choice in the crafts subjects which are the most visible and symbolic focus of 'masculine' or 'feminine' areas of the curriculum. In 1979, and the situation is the same at the time of writing, very few girls obtained an O-level in technical drawing and few boys took O-level cookery. Of course the opportunity for boys or girls to take crafts traditionally associated with the opposite sex has received a push in this country from the introduction of the Sex Discrimination Act in 1975. Most schools interpreted the Act to mean that boys and girls should be offered the same curriculum at least in the first year of secondary education. Some schools have a broader interpretation and offer an integrated crafts curriculum for the first three years of secondary school. Five or six years after the passing of the Act, it was estimated that only 25 per cent of schools were not complying with its provisions (Pratt *et al.*, 1984).

In order to accommodate two craft subjects in half the time most schools have a rotating crafts timetable which permits girls and boys to take both home economics and technical crafts. But the impact on take-up of these subjects after third year has been negligible.

The system of crafts circuses appeared to be regarded by schools as a socially rather than educationally valuable experience. That is, they seem to feel that boys and girls should work together, especially in the younger age groups, but fail to perceive any possible educational advantages of home economics or technical crafts, no doubt because of the history of the subjects as being appropriate handwork for the less able. We thought that some sort of design-based technical crafts should be an integral part of education up to 16, because of the intellectual developments the subjects could potentially foster. While straightforward woodwork and metalwork may not be highly significant for mathematical or visuo-spatial skills the newer approach of craft, design and technology with its emphasis on problem solving and elements of design seemed to have the potential for supporting skills and understanding which would be required in maths and physics. It seems likely that girls' poorer performance in visuo-spatial tests during the adolescent years could be modified by more experience of three-dimensional activities where these were offered in craft education. A second reason for our decision to challenge the sexual split in the craft curriculum at school was the fact that home economics and technical studies (or 'girls' and boys' crafts' as they are still termed in many schools) seem to enshrine the separate values of masculinity and femininity, as subjects at the extreme ends of the gender spectrum (see Figure 1.1). If attitudes and choices to girls' and boys' crafts could be changed, it was likely that there would be a knock-on effect to the division between physical and biological science, if only because of the reduction in stereotyping of subjects with the strongest masculine or feminine image. Any opportunity for breaking down barriers between subjects considered suitable for girls or boys was seen as a desirable goal for the aim of the project. It was also possible in a genuinely design-based problem solving CDT course that girls could begin to

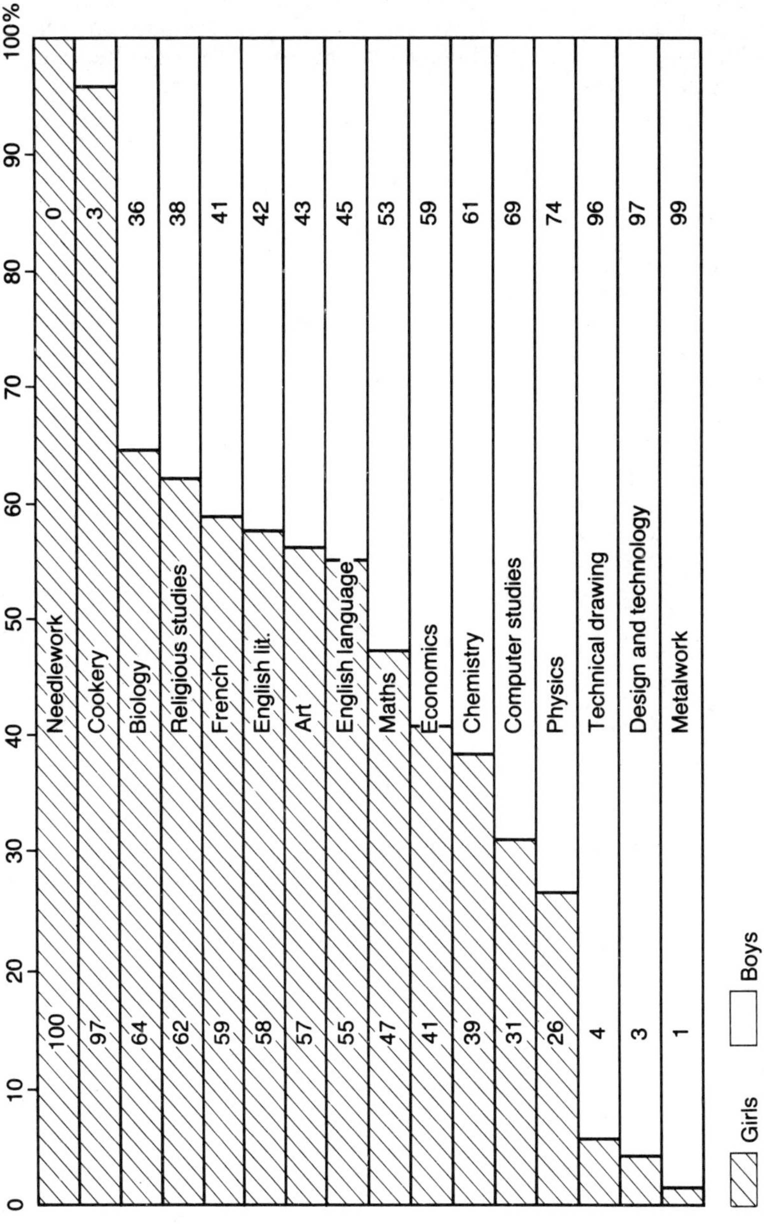

Subject	Girls	Boys
Needlework	100	0
Cookery	97	3
Biology	64	36
Religious studies	62	38
French	59	41
English lit.	58	42
Art	57	43
English language	55	45
Maths	47	53
Economics	41	59
Chemistry	39	61
Computer studies	31	69
Physics	26	74
Technical drawing	4	96
Design and technology	3	97
Metalwork	1	99

0 10 20 30 40 50 60 70 80 90 100%

Girls Boys

Figure 1.1 Gender spectrum of O-level entrance

Source: Compiled from *DES Statistics of School Leavers CSE and GCE, England, 1981*, Tables C28 and C29, Examination Boards Survey and Sample Survey

acquire, in a way they could not outside school, the sort of technical expertise which would be a real preparation for technological work. For all these reasons, the crafts issue became a central concern.

Chapter 2

Edging girls out

Eleven-year-old children are socialized creatures; that is, they have learned norms of behaviour which they know how to apply in social situations. For example, pupils know the unwritten classroom rule that you cannot speak publicly to the teacher without first raising your hand above your head. In addition they may have realized that chances of being permitted to speak are increased when you wave your arm about wildly and say, 'Miss, Miss!' in a sibilant whisper. Boys and girls are also aware of the behaviour and attitudes appropriate to their respective gender roles. Mixed schools offer plenty of opportunities for this kind of learning and school experience seems daily to reinforce and confirm the traditional sex role stereotypes.

This chapter is based on our observations, formal and informal, during four years of visiting the eight GIST action schools. The schools have been given fictitious names to preserve the confidentiality of staff and pupils. (A full description of the schools, social class catchment areas, numbers of boys and girls on the roll, etc. appears on p. 44-5). These visits, accompanying VISTA visitors (see Chapter 4), going to speak to teachers, or actually carrying out classroom observation, revealed several themes of gender differentiation:

the sexes constantly divide and are divided at school;
boys dominate classroom discussion;
boys insist on more of the teacher's attention;
boys and teachers 'masculinize' the lesson content in science and crafts;
boys 'hog' resources;
girls 'fetch and carry' for the boys.

Sex divisions

Because of our interest in sex divisions we were undoubtedly highly aware of the significance of daily observed incidents and patterns of school life. Separation by sex is an endemic feature of every aspect of movement around the school. At Edgehill, for instance boys and girls lined up separately outside the building and used separate staircases. When we asked why this was necessary, the staff blamed the architects for building male and female lavatories at opposite ends of the school. In every school, boys and girls lined up separately outside workshops or science labs, boys on the left of the door, girls to the right, or vice versa.

> On entering the classroom, the pupils were told by their teacher to sit wherever they wished. This immediately led to a segregation between boys and girls which the design of the classroom seemed to reinforce . . . a partition ran down the centre of the room which enabled boys to sit on one side and girls on the other . . . pupils arranged themselves in such a way as to create exclusively male and female units. (MR)*

> Seating in the metalwork room was by pupil choice. As there were three large workbenches, and pupil inclination to segregate the sexes, there was a problem. This had been solved by the girls herding as much as possible on one table and the boys sprawling over two. (GB)

Boys' initial assertion of dominance in the lab or workshop appears to be primarily physical. Nearly all observers remarked on the consistent way boys and girls voluntarily segregated themselves into distinct, but sometimes unequal gender zones in the room:

> Each week when they entered (the workshop) the boys charged in and sat on the front benches with their backs to the teacher. (BH)

* Initials after extracts from observation notes refer to the person who carried out the observation. AK, JW, BS, and JC refer to Alison Kelly, Judith Whyte, Barbara Smail and John Catton; GB, BH, PH, CH, MR and LW refer to postgraduate students then at Didsbury School of Education, Manchester Polytechnic, who also carried out observations: Gwen Baker, Beverley Harris, Pamela Herbert, Catherine Holland, Marie Roberts and Lynn Wakefield; GW is Glenys Ward, one of the GIST teachers who carried out observations in her own school.

> The seating plan meant that girls had no reason or need to infiltrate the boys' territory although boys constantly crowded the girls' area as more of the practical work got under way. The application of the enamel glazes [was] done on the girls' table, which left the girls more tidying away at the end of the lesson. (GB)

Occasionally teachers would ask the children to mix – mainly for our benefit. Usually sex divisions are accepted as unproblematic, and even firmly reinforced. There is seldom any difficulty in distinguishing the sexes, because of differential rules about clothing. At Sutton Hill in 1982 the uniform colour was black for boys and grey for girls, and in the Home Economics department, boys wore plain blue aprons and girls pink patterned ones! (MR)

The gender division of pupils created by separate seating arrangements is frequently exploited by teachers as a mild form of control:

> [In Home Economics] the teacher said to the boys [in a separate part of the room], 'Look at the girls over there, they've finished!' (MR)

Yet as a means of persuading children to do something, a teacher's instructions weighted with a 'gender signal' can have the opposite effect. By accentuating the behavioural difference between the sexes she is inadvertently teaching the boys not to tidy up, i.e. not to be 'like the girls'.

A craft teacher jocularly called curly-headed boys 'Matilda', ridiculing them in effect for looking like girls. In another school, a misbehaving girl was told off for her 'boyish' behaviour. Here the unintended message is that such behaviour will in fact be tolerated from boys, but not from girls.

Sex stereotypes extend to class work: a craft teacher tried to make the task of colouring isometric cubes more appealing to girls by suggesting they use 'marriage and love' colours (LW), thus dragging in gender quite gratuitously. Boys and girls are being warned of the teacher's expectation that one sex, but not the other, will be interested in a particular task. Dividing the sexes as a means of control or motivation is ultimately ineffective: if something is said to be 'for the boys' it is automatically assumed to be of no interest to the girls, and vice versa. So every topic labelled as 'gender appropriate' is likely to be immediately rejected by half the class, presumably not the teacher's first intention. Gender divisions constantly rebound on the teacher, by reinforcing boys' naughtiness and girls' unwillingness to participate.

Teachers' attempts to be friendly and create rapport often involve calling attention to gender, even when it is clearly irrelevant to the task in hand:

> Teacher helping girls in the workshop says jokingly, 'I don't often get the chance to put my arms round a pretty girl.' The girl blushes.
>
> (To girl giving good answer) 'You're beautiful, you!' (JC)
>
> While rebuking the girls, the metalwork teacher adopts a softer more pleading tone of voice 'go and do what you're told' with a rising inflection at the end of the sentence. This contrasts with the monotone exclamation 'Stop it, lad!' directed towards boys, in a more abrupt and aggressive tone. (MR)
>
> 'Isn't she a neat writer!' (JC)
>
> When girl asks why she has to wear safety goggles, teacher replies, 'You want to stay beautiful, don't you?' (AK)

These well-meant asides make children more conscious of gender, and incidentally, of the associated differential expectations that the teacher has for boys and girls: boys must be dealt with firmly, even aggressively: girls can be flirted with, to 'encourage' them along. Boys will be messy and careless, girls are 'neat writers'. The expectations quickly become self-fulfilling prophecies.

Boys dominate classroom discussion

In a large study of science teachers, staff were categorized according to the number and nature of questions directed to pupils by the teacher (Galton, 1981). By far the most popular style amongst physical science teachers was Style 1, the 'problem solving' approach, distinguished by a relatively high frequency of teachers' questions combined with relatively greater use of teachers' statements. (Style 2, the 'informers', used fewer questions except those demanding recall and application of facts and principles to problem solving, while Style 3 depended more on pupil-initiated behaviour.) Science teachers rightly feel that there are advantages to using a 'brainstorming technique' or posing a problem and getting the children to think out the answers for themselves. The potential danger, often unrecognized, is the tendency for teachers to direct more questions at pupils they perceive as more able. Consequently, other pupils may begin to become uninterested and unresponsive. With our heightened perception of sex differences in response, we noticed that these other pupils were often girls.

> The big sex difference in this lesson was in calling out behaviour. In class discussion round the front the boys were falling over themselves to give the answer and the girls were sitting back. At one point teacher says: '[girl's name], are we going to sleep?' Boys sometimes complete teacher's sentences: 'What I'd like you to do is. . . .' Boys: 'draw them in', i.e.rays of light. (AK)

> Question and answer session about different ideas sparked off by the word 'energy'. All the answers came from boys. (BS)

> Brainstorming session on the shape of the letter 'T' and drawing, with reference to shadows. Boys dominate discussion. Boys frequently the only pupils offering answers. (JC)

One teacher who was observed on a number of occasions and then went on to observe her colleagues remarked: 'I was rather surprised at the small number of girls who actually answered questions. . .' [and think it's because] 'they don't want to appear stupid' (GW, taped conversation). A science teacher, writing about the unwillingness of girls to answer questions even when they are equally able to do so, suggests, 'they are already conscious that it is not considered "their subject" and also perhaps . . . they prefer to offer answers only if they are confident they are correct' (Samuel, 1981, p. 254). Certainly, the boys are likely to jeer if a girl gives the wrong answer:

> When girls ask questions in class discussion, boys tend to groan [this happened three times] . . . . [Teacher's name] controls them. 'No, it's a good question.' (AK)

But girls may be equally afraid of appearing too bright!

> '[girl's name] worried that people would make fun of her because she always knew the answer, and tended not to put up her hand because people would say, "Oh no, it's her again." ' (GW)

Girls seem quite reluctant to take part. One observer describes their evasive techniques:

> In order to prevent the teacher pressing them for an answer, they would pretend they were still working, or else they would busily turn through the book looking for the answer, but never quite finding it in time to answer the question. (PH)

Question and answer sessions seem to benefit pupils who are willing to shout out answers, many of them 'wrong', or at least off the point, at the expense of pupils who are not risk-takers:

> In general [teacher's name] did not invite a specific child to answer. On four occasions when he did pick a girl, boys called out the answer before she had spoken. (AK)

> Boys call out answers more often than girls. On several occasions a question was directed at a girl [by name] but the boys shouted out the answer before the girl replied. (AK)

The hands-up rule can limit the tendency of boys to shout out spontaneously, but if a teacher seems to want an accurate answer quickly, girls can again be 'shown up':

> Hands up rule in asking questions ensures that girls get a fair share of discussion . . . when named girls didn't reply . . . teacher did well always to move on to another girl, so didn't get position of boys giving correct answers after girls had failed. One example when this did happen was discussion of hinge joint. Girl said that it 'makes things move' and teacher commented 'not quite right'. Moved to boy who said that it 'moves only one way' and was rewarded with 'good lad'. Girl could probably have got this if she had been encouraged to expand her answer, e.g. 'yes, but what's special about a hinge joint? Which way does it move?' (AK)

The hands-up rule can, however inadvertently, exclude all those pupils who are unwilling to look foolish for making a mistake:

> Maths revision lesson: teacher and class are together obeying an unspoken convention that the child who first raises her/his hand wins the right to answer. As the lesson goes on, it is clear that pupils who have already answered are more likely to do so again, so that precedence has effectively been handed over to a small group of pupils. Fewer girls than boys participate. (JW)

Girls in mixed classes are apparently self-conscious about speaking up at all, while boys, in contrast, revel in the limelight, happily, if wrongly, guessing at answers to questions and probably learning a good deal in the process.

Boys demand more of the teacher's attention

When discussion is over, and practical work begins, boys seem to be much more demanding of the teacher's attention. Several research studies have shown that boys in mixed classes are successful in taking up more of the teacher's time. Girls are more likely to obey the unwritten classroom rules for gaining teacher help or attention. A girl would raise her hand, wait patiently for the teacher to see her, and, as likely as not, give up if she wasn't noticed.

> Some girls and boys raised their hands but remained sitting in their seats when seeking teacher's attention. This device generally worked, but required patience (1-3 minutes' wait). Other children called out without leaving their seats. This technique was particularly used by Darren [not his real name], e.g. the second he had finished Darren put up his hand, called out loudly, 'Miss! Finished!' At one point the teacher said, 'Darren, I'm not your servant, come here.' (JW)

Teachers' differential treatment of girls and boys may only be a function of their response to sex-typed behaviour. Boys demand more attention than girls:

> Boys would frequently expect the teacher to ignore the girl who was in front of them and deal with his query. One boy, for instance, held up his design sheet in front of the girl and as close as it could be positioned to the teacher's nose! (JC)

> In the jewellery class the pupils followed the teacher around asking for his advice. If there was a queue the boys would always push in front of the girls to get the teacher's attention. One boy in particular was constantly asking the teacher's advice. (CH)

Girls' greater conscientiousness in presenting neat and accurate work is generally noticed, but teachers are less aware that girls are also conscientious in their adherence to unwritten rules of classroom organization: queueing politely in line, and waiting till the teacher sees her hand up. The boisterous, demanding boys can seem to be more attractive pupils, and teachers, often without realizing it, respond to the boys' enthusiasm and 'forget' about the quieter girls.

Creating a 'masculine' context

Unconsciously teachers may gear their teaching to the boys, setting a 'masculine' context from the start:

> Discussion at the beginning mentioned acceleration of a car: chorus of shouted answers from the boys. (AK)

> Male science teacher's jokes and jovial handling of class reveal underlying assumptions: 'can I have some muscles?' asking for help carrying pump; 'we should have a picture of Adam Ant on this washing up liquid because he's right fairy.' (BS)

'Masculine' references and examples presumably come more readily to the mind of male teachers:

> Use of football to represent the earth starts argument amongst boys about whose it is, why it was confiscated, etc. (AK)

The tendency is helped along by the fact that science textbooks, too, assume a male audience and masculine interests. This orientation of science to interests and activities usually associated with the male sex carries a hidden message for children that science is 'really' for boys. The belief is more strongly held by boys. Those in the GIST sample were significantly more likely than girls to agree that 'girls who want to be scientists are a bit peculiar' and that 'learning science is more important for boys than for girls' (see Chapter 7).

The 'masculinization' of science is forcefully underlined in the way boys succeed in turning every aspect of the learning process into a 'macho' endeavour:

> Boys like playing with electrical transformers and the group mimic an interrogation using raybox as a bright light. Even a lesson which is apparently sex neutral will be interpreted in a masculine way by the boys. (AK)

> Boys create male context from neutral equipment – magnet [as] tug of war, spring balance used as catapult. (AK)

Tools and machines in the craft room and experimental equipment in the lab are used loudly and enthusiastically by the boys: the noise they make is a physical expression of their dominance:

> The boys who were not working the machines were often employed in hammering and sawing. . . [they] often seemed to seek out noisy activities. (MR)

Even in a Home Economics lesson,

> More boys than girls had electric mixers and . . . frequently put theirs on high speed or altered the speed. The girls were more inclined to keep to a low speed. It was also clear that the boys enjoyed making a noise. (MR)

It is as if a DANGER! MEN AT WORK sign had been invisibly posted. Labs and workshops, unlike classrooms or even art rooms, can be dangerous:

> . . . potentially dangerous experiment. . . When teacher said it was dangerous boys commented 'great'. Girls were scared, panicked, squealed whenever water seemed likely to suck back. . . . Several girls seemed to give up their own experiment and join the groups of boys as onlookers after this experience. Boys were advising girls 'pull it out of the water you idiot' which seemed to emphasize their superior expertise. (AK)

> The girls shrieked as they began to use the drill. . . their reactions may have been to noise levels rather than from any risk of personal danger. This was indicated in the confident way the girls handled the machinery even though they seemed to react to the noise. (MR)

> When they have finished experiments boys play around more than girls – putting ice down each other's backs, putting ice into hot water and noting effects. Girls get on with writing up. (AK)

Boys hog resources

Once a pattern has been set, it is difficult to break. Boys are on the whole keener than the girls to mess about with machines, equipment and materials, but much less interested in recording experiments in their exercise books, or making plans and drawings before they start. Where resources are in short supply, and especially when some are in better condition than the rest, boys assert their right to first use:

> There was no communication between girls and boys, unless a boy wanted a tool which a girl was using. An example of the none-too-subtle pressure exerted by boys was observed. A boy wanted a hand-drill which a girl was using. His method was not to ask her to pass the tool when she had finished but rather to

> place himself alongside her, fold his arms and stare at the tool. The girl gave in before completing her drilling and was on the point of handing over the tool when the teacher intervened. (JC)

> There were delays for pupils waiting for use of the polisher, but while girls quietly queued, boys queued and pestered, rushing the girls to finish and once using the edge of the polisher whilst one girl was working on it.
>
> At one point a boy donned the goggles that a girl had put down for a second. . . . The teacher noticed this and reprimanded him. He gave the goggles back, assuming surprise that she had not finished. (GB)

Boys are pushier and seem to regard scientific or technical resources as rightfully theirs. Girls for their part become unwilling to enter into an undignified scrabble for equipment:

> The class had been instructed to start work on the preparation of copper sulphate from dilute sulphuric acid and copper oxide. The boys were much quicker off the mark than the girls. They had collected the apparatus together and lit their Bunsens before very much happened at the girls' end of the lab. . . .
>
> When the girls did set up their Bunsens two groups seemed to have very low gas pressure – but, in fact, the Bunsens were blocked up. The teacher got two new Bunsens from the store for the girls. At this point, the copper oxide could not be found and teacher accused David of 'hiding it away' on his bench. Another girl then complained. . . there were no safety glasses left and teacher returned with a pair for her.
>
> Finally the girls started work. Are the girls in this class slower than the boys because they have learned to avoid the rush for equipment at the beginning? It did not seem they were less enthusiastic about the work once they had started. (BS)

The most complete and dramatic example of how boys' behaviour can 'edge girls out' came in a lesson with experimental work heating carbohydrates over a flame. The teacher explained the meaning of carbohydrate and gathered the class round the front bench to tell them how the experiment should be done. He said there were not enough safety glasses for everyone, so only the person actually heating the test tube should wear goggles, and the rest should stand clear. The class then dispersed to start practical work:

> The boys rushed to grab the glasses and . . . collect the rest of the apparatus. In some groups all four boys were wearing glasses. The girls' groups had no glasses and had to negotiate with the boys, in some cases calling on the teacher to help. (BS)

All the groups except one were single-sex, and after this incident (which went unnoticed by the teacher) all the boys' groups had started working before any of the girls' groups. Boys had finished and were writing up before any of the girls. It appeared to the teacher that the boys were working more quickly and efficiently.

We know (see Chapter 7) that girls are far less likely than boys to find at home the kind of 'practical' tinkering experiences which may contribute to the development of three-dimensional skills and visuo-spatial competence. School may offer their only chance to use machines and tools or to carry out scientific experiments. Our observations suggest that during practical sessions in science and crafts girls may miss out on these opportunities. Observers noted again and again that where resources were limited, boys tended to crowd girls out and to end up with the lion's share of whatever was available.

All but a few girls then 'opt out' of the physical, practical activities. They concentrate instead on neat presentation of work and depend more on the teacher for help. Teachers, for their part, interpret girls' dependence and timidity as poorer motivation.

A study of young children in the classroom (Serbin, 1978) showed that girls are not likely to be spoken to by the teacher unless they are near her/him. Boys may be shouted at across the classroom; girls are spoken to in quieter voices, when they are closer at hand:

> Girls near teacher at front seem to get quite a lot of teacher attention, girls further away get less, for boys it doesn't make any difference. (AK)

> Girls in both workrooms positioned themselves as closely to the teacher's desk as possible.

Girls' more careful and precise way of working may lead to them avoiding practical elements in favour of the 'safer' task of writing up the experiment. But this does not imply that girls have less aptitude for science or technology:

> Boys [tried to complete the] task required of them as economically in time, effort and attention as possible. This lack of involvement with detail and the processes sometimes meant adapting a design to cover a fundamental mistake; which the girls, meticulously following the rules and thinking each step out, did not have to do. (SB)

In an observation of fourth year girls who had actually chosen to continue with science, another postgraduate observer noted:

> In control technology . . . the boys would collect the equipment required and assemble it often by trial and error; for example when making an electric circuit, a working circuit was arrived at by several guess attempts. The two girls by comparison were not so eager to construct a circuit straight away but instead chatted about how it might be constructed and what would be needed to make it work. They then constructed the circuit which worked first time.

It may be that in an all-girls' school or a girls' only group, this more orderly and logical approach would be the norm. In a mixed class of first or second years, boys' careless and joyous messing around seems to set the pattern for how science is supposed to be done. In the belief that messing around can be creative and lead to pupils solving problems or making their own discoveries, teachers may welcome it, but the implication can be that this is the only way to 'do' science or technology.

Girls 'fetch and carry'

Teachers frequently mention the difficulty of getting boys to be orderly and tidy, and the contrasting 'neatness' and 'diligence' of the girls. Girls fall into the role of servicing the untidy boys, a habitual pattern taken for granted by all concerned. At Edgehill, groups of sixth form girls studying science were regularly expected to make tea and clear up for the science staff.

Boys might be asked to carry heavy equipment or open windows – irregular rather than regular jobs. Girls are more often asked to carry messages or collect homework books, and teachers often remark that girls are more 'mature', 'sensible' or 'tidy' than boys.

> Four girls chosen (or volunteered, I didn't see) to give out

> workbooks. This accords with observations in other schools where girls fetch and carry for boys. (AK)
>
> After a practical session, one of the boys objected to washing out his concrete container, and another boy had to be told by the teacher to dampen the cloth before he wiped down the bench. A few minutes later a girl was observed washing up the whole of the front bench at which only boys had been sitting. (JW)
>
> Three boys who had left their apparatus in the sink owned up and only at the teacher's instigation cleaned up. Later the girls were asked to collect homework while some boys talked with the teacher about snooker. (BS)

Summary

School and classroom norms reinforce and underline sex divisions. In the past, this may have seemed a trivial feature of school life. Now we can see that assumptions about subjects regarded as 'masculine' can bring firm but subtle pressure on girls to 'take a back seat' in science and technology. Most girls then opt out in favour of subjects in which their presence has more traditional acceptability – English, languages, the arts and the humanities.

Physical divisions, started by boys and girls lining up separately, are carried over into the lab and workshop where children automatically form into single-sex groups. This in turn invites the teacher to treat girls and boys as separate groups with different learning needs, instead of as a homogeneous class. The use of gender divisions becomes counterproductive because it renders girls and boys a negative reference group for one another. They will not comply with the same rules or display interest in the same things. The processes by which girls are edged out of science and technology follow from this primary framework of gender division: boys succeed in getting more teacher attention, and their way of 'doing' science and crafts is stamped as the ideal or preferred mode. Girls write up, experiment cautiously, fetch and carry for the boys. They hang back from the physical hurly burly of grabbing the best equipment and leave the boys free to 'hog' available resources. The definition of science and technology as masculine is reinforced by the male-biased textbooks, teacher assumptions and boys' confident assertion of territorial rights in the lab and workshop. Girls 'lose out' in science and technology partly because they never really gain a proper foothold in the subjects.

Chapter 3

The first year

Selecting the schools

In 1978-9 when GIST began, it is probably true to say that interest in the underachievement of girls was limited to feminists in education, like ourselves, the HMIs, then preparing the investigation which led to the discussion document *Girls and Science* (1980), and one or two academic researchers. Typically, schools could respond to any query on the matter with the rather bland comment, 'Yes of course we treat all our pupils equally, irrespective of sex, race, class, etc.' The idea was floated that we might somehow identify the feminists teaching in local schools who would then form a sort of GIST cell to provide a base for project interventions. But schools are rather hierarchical institutions and we were aware that the views and activities of lowly Scale I or II teachers (which feminists were likely to be) could expect to carry very little weight with the school's senior management. The lesson was driven home when a young male teacher, his enthusiasm fired by a television programme on which one of us appeared, approached his head to ask if their school could work with GIST. When we wrote to the head to follow up this internal suggestion, we were met with a blank refusal, either because he was offended at the apparent informality of the request, or because he did not regard the project (or us) as sufficiently worthwhile or important. In another school an informal approach by a Scale II teacher meant that when GIST contacted the head (this time with the approval of the LEA) she had already heard of the project and was favourably disposed towards us. Perhaps the real difference was that she was more sympathetic to the aims of the project.

In fact the final choice of schools was determined by certain practical considerations and occurred by a process of elimination, rather than selection. Since we intended to visit each school at least once a fortnight it was important they should be quite close together and not too numerous. We had also decided to limit ourselves to coeducational comprehensives, because this is the type of school in which the majority of British children are educated, and because sex typing of subjects is more polarized in mixed than in single-sex schools (Harding, 1980; Ormerod, 1975; and see above). In a fairly small project like GIST, with the necessity for action and intervention as well as research, we would not be able to deal adequately with the complicating factor of different school types. A spread of schools between different LEAs seemed desirable, but if we were to take in the whole of Greater Manchester there would have been over one hundred schools to choose from.

Six schools would probably have been an ideal number, from the purely practical and logistical point of view, in generating intervention activities. However, for the research design it was obviously desirable to have as large a sample of children as feasible and also to establish control schools for purposes of comparison. In the event we perhaps overburdened ourselves by taking on eight action and two control schools. To cut down on expenses of time and travel and to limit the number of LEAs with whom we needed to work, we decided to concentrate on three local authorities, so reducing the possible number of schools to about forty. We were able to eliminate one LEA because it had not yet undergone comprehensive reorganization. The choice was further narrowed in two of the three authorities by asking the science adviser to recommend schools. They presumably identified schools which they felt would be responsive, but that did not mean that girls' needs were a matter of especial concern.

In our first approach to heads we were turned down only three times; one head's reaction has been described; a second school refused on the grounds that they were already involved in 'Project Technology'. In the third instance, an initial approach was made to the head of science, who was, as we later discovered, disgruntled for various reasons towards the LEA. As one of us waited in the reception hall for the meeting he was observed slipping out of a side door! We did not try again!

The effective criteria for selecting schools, then, were the practical considerations mentioned above and the presence of an initial willingness on the part of the head or head of science to accept us. In retrospect these were pretty minimal criteria; in no way can it be assumed that any school was particularly eager to launch an equal opportunities policy, or even consciously aware of girls' underachievement in science and technology.

Any schools-focused research project working from outside the school (as opposed to schools-based and working from within) will find that in the selection of schools there is really no way of avoiding the necessity to work downwards through the educational hierarchy, getting the permission and support in turn, of the LEA, the headteacher, and the heads of department. We went through this process, and were received with varying degrees of enthusiasm. For the first time we came up against a phenomenon to become all-too-familiar to us. Men in senior positions frequently related the GIST project not to their professional educational concerns, but directly to their personal experience of the working lives (employed or otherwise) of their wives or other female relations. Not surprisingly, the nature of these experiences and their associated emotional attitudes coloured these men's response to the openly feminist aims of GIST. Some headteachers and heads of science wanted to become involved; others were more cautious and said they would like to hear in more detail what was being proposed.

At this stage we stressed to potential action schools that we would not accept an immediate decision from the head, but preferred first to explain our ideas to the teachers who carried actual responsibility for teaching science and crafts in lower school. We felt that if all the teachers who would be affected had the chance to participate in the initial decision about whether or not to become involved, their commitment to the project would be greater than if GIST appeared as an additional 'chore' imposed by senior management. Meetings were arranged, generally after school, for all the science and CDT teachers. We also asked for pastoral and/or careers staff to come along, and in some cases the deputy head or head also attended.

At the meetings we provided clear information about the extent of girls' underachievement in science and technology, compared with either single-sex girls' schools or girls' achievements in other countries. We briefly indicated the theories put forward to account for the situation. We then described some of the strategies which had been suggested to counter female underachievement, for example single-sex groups, the visiting women scientists programme, the content and structure of examination assessment. We said that it would be up to the teachers to decide which strategies to implement in their school, if they agreed to take part in the project. We then left the staff to discuss our proposals among themselves and let us know over the next week or so whether they did want to become involved.

In fact none of the schools where we gave this preliminary talk turned us down. However, we were not convinced by this that most of the teachers were genuinely enthusiastic. The fact that everyone knew we could only be addressing a meeting in the school because the senior management had already given their support meant that the 'choice' of whether to go ahead, which we offered to the most junior teachers, was really rather an artificial one. Many teachers felt that they had been dragooned into acceptance, and expressed scepticism about the value of the GIST initiative.

The GIST schools

The ten schools involved in the GIST project were obviously not a random sample, but they are probably not atypical of schools in urban Britain, and could perhaps be described as a judgment sample. Only two are predominantly middle-class (New Hall, a control school, and Edgehill); some are overwhelmingly working-class; some suburban and others inner-city. Some have very few black children and some have a substantial minority. Some are large, some small; some have pleasant modern buildings and some have deteriorating facilities. Tall Trees and Hamlet, among the action schools, and New Hall, a control school, have women heads; the remainder are headed by men. Four schools were massively reorganized during the course of the project. Table 3.1 describes the schools in more detail, and the notes below fill out the picture of school circumstances and the staff whom GIST met. Readers may find it useful to refer back to the table and school notes when considering the impact of GIST in each school (see Chapters 13 and 14). Clearly that impact was likely to vary according to the existing conditions and preoccupations of the school.

Ashgrove

Ashgrove is situated on the edge of a large rehousing area and its traditional intake in the past was from council estates. In the last few years an increasing proportion of the intake has come from suburban private housing. Partly because of its planned reorganization as a sixth form college, there was rapid turnover of senior staff during the first two years, the school apparently being regarded as a training ground before promotion. This rapid advancement may have been resented by some of the 'old hands', for example the head of science who retired at the end of the academic year 1980-1. Senior management were concerned to change the former traditional and rather repressive atmosphere to a more liberal one, and to alter and improve teaching methods and discipline. The physical layout of the school was a potential encouragement to indiscipline, with untidy areas in need of redecoration, and a lift in a tower block forming a 'no man's land'.

Frequent staff changes, especially in science, made continuity difficult; one head of department stayed for only one term and met GIST only once, using the plea of too much other work to be done. For a time the science department was without a head until a new head of science took up his post in 1982. During the interregnum, there was a sympathetic female head of lower school science. The new head of department came from another GIST school, Hamlet, where he had expressed commitment to the aims of GIST but lacked the support of fellow staff. He may have found himself in a better position in this respect at Ashgrove.

The CDT department was highly traditional when the GIST intake entered the school. All five male craft teachers came from industry and saw the subject as vocational preparation, for jobs which would not be suitable for girls. A new senior teacher was for a short time in charge of curriculum development, and, as he had been a CDT specialist in his previous post, tried to make some changes in the craft department, but with little success; he soon gained a deputy headship and moved to another school. After reorganization, the new head of CDT became committed and sympathetic to the GIST project and instituted newer teaching methods and a design-based course leading to design rather than traditional exams.

The head, keen on innovation, and overseeing these rapid staff changes, was basically sympathetic to the project, but tended to leave GIST activities to the curriculum director of the day.

TABLE 3.1 *The GIST schools*

School	Ashgrove	Moss Green	Hamlet	Sutton Hill	Green Park
No. on roll	1360	929	1136	1194	1140
Age range	11–18	11–16	11–18	11–18	11–16
Social class of catchment area	Edge of large council estate; recently, more suburban intake	Multi-ethnic, inner-city area	Multi-ethnic mixed inner-city and suburban area; edge of large council estate, recently more suburban intake	Older working-class area, 1930s council housing	Inner-city: most children live in high-rise flats and maisonettes. Rehousing; traditional white working-class
School history	Early mixed comprehensive. GIST cohort last 11-year-old intake; reorganized in 1982 to become sixth form college	Purpose-built community school, college and centre; community school ethos	Comprehensive formed from secondary modern and technical high in 1967. Amalgamated in 1982 with nearby school to form 4-site, 11–16 school	Two co-educational secondary moderns amalgamated to form co-educational comprehensive	Formerly girls' and boys' secondary modern school on one site.
State of buildings	Older, custom-built	Newer, open-plan	Split site	Split site about ¾ mile apart	Custom-built comprehensive near busy city centre roads. Building in need of repair
Sex of head teacher	M	M	F	M	M
% of female teachers at scale IV or above	33	25	8	11	35
Ratio of boys: girls in the GIST intake	1.1 to 1	1.1 to 1	1.5 to 1	1.3 to 1	1 to 1
*% middle-class	25	22	(19)**	(7)**	10
% mothers described as housewives	16	5	41†	15†	6
% fathers manually employed	83	84	67	54	91
% fathers unemployed	12	22	39†	14†	18

* From children's description of father's and mother's job then categorized as fathers in professional/intermediate/white-collar occupations *or* mothers in professional/intermediate occupations (see Chapter 7)

Tall Trees	Meadowvale	Edgehill	New Hall	Burnbank
930	1359	1386	1970	690
11–16	11–18	11–18	11–18	11–16
Inner suburban; mixed owner-occupied semis and council flats	Edge of conurbation; traditional mill town serving older working-class area. Both council and owner-occupied	Suburban, semi-rural, mainly owner-occupied.	Surburban, largely owner-occupied, middle-class area	Inner-city
Former mixed secondary modern	Early (1960s) purpose-built comprehensive	Former mixed secondary school	Formerly co-educational grammar school	Formerly girls' and boys' secondary modern schools on one site
Pleasant site. Buildings in reasonable repair	Custom-built comprehensive school. Buildings badly in need of repair	Custom-built, pleasant split site about 300 yds apart. Buildings in good condition	Newer comprehensive, pleasant site	Original building, in need of repairs
F	M	M	F	M
11	18	24	29	12
0.8 to 1	1 to 1	1 to 1	0.7 to 1	0.9 to 1
41	23	49	72	19
4		13	9	9
60		53	27	85
6	5	6	3	17

** Based on father's occupation only, derived from school records
† Derived from school records

The need for GIST

Moss Green

This is a multi-ethnic community school, college and centre, split into lower and middle schools and an FE college. In 1979-81, the lower school comprised only years 1 and 2, but from September 1981, year 3 was also included for administrative purposes. The Moss Green intake is essentially working-class; some children and groups are difficult to discipline, but most established staff have a fairly relaxed attitude towards them. New staff who do not find it easy to cope tend to leave. For the GIST cohort, senior staff in the lower school were predominantly female, though at the upper end of the school most of the senior staff were men.

Laboratories in the lower school were open plan (though the school is now returning to conventional classrooms) and at some distance from the middle school science area where much of the equipment is stored. Teaching could sometimes be difficult if the class next door was particularly noisy. The heads of the lower school and of lower school science were both strongly sympathetic to GIST and accepted many of the intervention and curriculum proposals. Several women teachers in senior posts were consciously feminist in their attitudes. This was not so with the centre science consultant, an older women physicist who retired in the summer of 1981 and was replaced by a young and enthusiastic biologist determined to make his mark. Together with the new head of school, formerly curriculum director at Ashgrove, he planned and implemented the single-sex science setting experiment.

The head of CDT was also a young, go-ahead teacher, initially not very active because he was on study leave, but later more sympathetic to GIST. The main workshop areas in the lower and middle school were separated, causing some problems in science. In the lower school, woodwork, metalwork and technical drawing were taught as separate areas, but the only exams offered were AEB design 'O' level.

Hamlet

In 1979 Hamlet School was separated into a lower and an upper school, on split sites about a quarter of a mile apart, in a semi-suburban district on the edge of the inner city and approximately two miles from areas where rioting took place in the summer of 1981. Its intake was predominantly working-class and multi-ethnic, with noticeably more boys than girls (ratio of 1.5 to 1). From September 1982 it was combined with another comprehensive to form, temporarily (and until the end of the project), a four-site school.

Before reorganization, the head of science was very pleasant and helpful to GIST, although he himself only taught remedial groups; other staff did not share his commitment to the project. He left the school to go to Ashgrove in 1981-2 and was replaced by a second sympathetic man who may, however, have had difficulty in gaining support for the GIST initiative from his colleagues.

The technical crafts department had no head, and was consequently somewhat fragmented. Workshops were not well provided with basic tools, and the approach was highly traditional, with wood/metal subjects, and a craft option at the end of the first year 'circus', resulting in a predictable sex split in second year.

The headteacher voiced her sympathy with GIST but instigated no effective change. Deputies and senior teachers were largely responsible for decisions of curriculum organization which would affect the GIST cohort, and expressed only cautious sympathy in line with the head's attitude, also doing very little to change the status quo within the school. A temporary senior teacher who had formerly been head of a CDT department attempted to develop the craft curriculum beyond traditional wood and metal, but met with little success, partly due to the temporary nature of his job in the run-up to reorganization. A young maths teacher became very interested in classroom observation, and observed some of her colleagues, but with minimal support from senior staff, the venture did not develop into a full-scale review of gender interactions in the classroom. The home economics department was antagonistic to suggestions that the crafts mini-option system be altered.

Sutton Hill

Sutton Hill can be described as a traditional school, serving a traditional working-class area, and under a certain amount of pressure as an inner-city comprehensive. Well run, especially at the upper school end, the split site sometimes seemed to mean that the lower school was slightly out of touch. The attitude of the head to GIST was at first condescending, but later supportive. He did not believe the project could offer useful advice on the school's practice of equality, and placed GIST concerns on a rather lower priority compared with more pressing social issues. Fragmentation may have reduced the impact of GIST: the move to the upper school building took place at the end of the children's second year, and coincided with a reorganization in the local authority, which resulted at Sutton Hill in a 50 per cent turnover of staff.

A number of younger and probationary teachers are largely responsible for lower school science, which is taught through the school's own independent learning scheme. The new head of science after reorganization was particularly active in support of GIST, and actually joined the local teachers' group which continued the VISTA scheme.

The craft department is fairly traditional, and understaffed for technical work, with no technical drawing room. All the teachers are men who have worked in industry, and the head of department is making strenuous efforts to innovate in his subject. He agreed to help organize the visit of a group of girls to the College of Building. His own background was in the construction industry, and he believed that women were bound to be excluded from many jobs because of their relative lack of physical strength.

Green Park

Staff at Green Park are highly conscious of the relatively deprived backgrounds of children in the school. An inner-city comprehensive, with an intake drawn largely from the traditional white working class, it was formed from two secondary modern schools contained in one building. It still bears the signs of this sex division with, for example, separate, formerly single-sex wings, two assembly halls and two dining rooms. A traditional and somewhat disciplinarian atmosphere prevails between staff and children.

The head of science, a woman, was initially favourable to the project, but wavered and finally succumbed to the negative attitudes of most senior staff and several of her colleagues, who felt the GIST initiative was largely irrelevant for their pupils.

The CDT department had four well-equipped workshops, but in 1979-80 girls were not permitted to take CDT. There is no move towards a design-based curriculum, and mixed crafts were introduced for the intake of 1981 chiefly as a result of GIST pressure. The head of department has developed a PSE (personal and social education) curriculum for the first year. He expressed interest in bringing girls into the department, but his staff were on the whole negative about the idea.

The head teacher, newly appointed in May 1980, did not want to make too many changes too quickly. His support for GIST was reluctant rather than enthusiastic (and was reflected in the indifference of the deputy head). The head of the GIST year however was most helpful and was also the head of chemistry in the school.

Tall Trees

Compared with Hamlet's head, the female headteacher in this school is a much more dominant figure, credited with improving the atmosphere and discipline beyond all recognition since her appointment. She had done so largely by an emphasis on the traditional values of good manners, conventional dress and conformity to school discipline. Schools-industry links are strongly encouraged, and she vigorously supported GIST, seeing it as a means of increasing employment opportunities for girls. In some ways there was a slight mismatch between the emphasis on traditional sex divisions in minor matters of dress and behaviour, and the 'progressive' aims of GIST.

During the course of the project, three different people, all men, the second an 'acting' head, were in charge of the science department. The first expressed enthusiastic support for GIST and took part in a television programe about gender interactions in classrooms, with Tall Trees featuring as a GIST action school, and the head of department as an enlightened teacher. He later gained promotion to deputy headship of a London school in 1981. The interim acting head of department, a physicist, was reluctant to take on extra work or to engage in any kind of 'positive discrimination' for girls, but agreed to run a special electronics club, which was attended by girls as well as boys. In contrast, the head of department appointed in 1982 organized a girls-only work experience course which took place in October 1983, just too late, unfortunately, to influence option choices. He was also very active within the Association for Science Education (ASE) and at the end of the project said he would like to instigate a continuing group of GIST teachers.

The sex split in the science department was rather pronounced, with two female biologists teaching in converted domestic science/art rooms at one end of the building, and male physicists and chemists in laboratories close to the main preparation room. The male lab technician seemed to spend more time in the laboratories than at the 'biology end'. A male chemistry teacher who was very positive about encouraging girls, and the fact that the first head of department was a chemist, may have been responsible for high numbers of girls opting for chemistry.

Technical crafts are fairly traditional where curriculum content is concerned, but Tall Trees had been one of the earliest schools to implement a mixed crafts course. The head of department is proud of this record. There is a two-year crafts circus, with children opting for two out of three subjects (home economics, art or technical crafts) at the end of the second year. The crafts head of department claimed to be enthusiastic about GIST, but occasionally appeared to patronise girls, although he was not aware of it; in the last year of the project he was preparing for early retirement.

Meadowvale

This is a comprehensive school in a largely working-class area, with a democratic form of staff organization (frequent full staff meetings) and noticeably harmonious relations between teachers and pupils. The headteacher, a friend of the Edgehill head, has a similar progressive and democratic philosophy; he sometimes appeared rather condescending to GIST women, but was basically supportive of the project. It is one of the schools in which a film was made for television.

The head of science was actively supportive of GIST, especially in the first two years; he was promoted in September 1982 and became involved in additional upper school responsibilities. In the science department there were several, younger, pro-feminist teachers who readily made the connection between girls' avoidance of science and technology and sex stereotyping in the 'hidden' curriculum. Their views were not always shared by male staff, though GIST was broadly supported.

The crafts department is well equipped and the curriculum is structured on a design-based, problem-solving approach, taught commonly to all children throughout the first three years. The head of department and his staff were supportive of GIST and implemented many suggestions put forward by the GIST Liaison Officer for Crafts.

Edgehill

Of all the GIST schools, only New Hall, a control school, and Edgehill could be described as middle-class, with an estimated middle-class intake of 72 per cent and 49 per cent respectively. However, 49 per cent of Edgehill fathers were employed in manual occupations, so the class background in the two schools is rather different. Edgehill has a good local reputation, despite being 'second best' because of the neighbouring grammar school. As a 'good' comprehensive, it may be somewhat complacent about its character as an innovative school, apparent largely in the faculty structure.

The head delegates a good deal of responsibility to faculty and deputy heads, and is a conscious promoter of innovation, largely in terms of curriculum. Teaching methods are fairly formal, and the school has the good discipline characteristic of grammar schools.

The science department is divided into environmental and physical sciences. The staff are mostly men, the few women occupying lower-scale posts. These science teachers tried to play devil's advocate by advancing biological as well as socialization models as the intellectual explanation for sex differences in science take-up, and were only too happy to enter into debate on the issue. The original head of science was an older, courteous man, who took the view that girls and boys were inherently different; he confessed at one meeting that he felt fatherly towards female pupils and would not push them to participate more in class if they preferred to stay quietly in the background; yet he was broadly in sympathy with the aims of GIST. His replacement by a younger man took place smoothly and did not seem to change the character of the science department in any marked degree.

The craft faculty incorporates art and home economics as well as technical crafts, and pursues an integrated design-based syllabus. Girls were well represented in the design faculty in the fourth year, but only because most of them were doing design in textiles. The head of crafts was proud of having espoused a dynamic new CDT curriculum, but rather disinclined to make any special efforts to encourage girls to take technical subjects in fourth year. He expressed concern at the prospect of a large increase in the number of girls opting for technical crafts, and doubted if the department could cope with a large influx; his doubts may have become something of a self-fulfilling prophecy.

Table 3.1 also shows the percentage of mothers in each school said by their children to be occupied as full-time housewives. It may surprise some readers that so many women, who were, remember, the mothers of 11-year-old children, are employed outside the home, or looking for employment. The highest proportion of full-time housewives lived in the green belt suburbs, or the older, well-established council estates. Mothers of children in inner-city schools were more likely to be out at work, at least for part of their time.

Local industry

In the autumn of 1979 and the following winter we visited a number of local employers and training organizations with the purpose of establishing how many girls were currently entering non-traditional forms of employment, and what were the attitudes of the training and employing groups. We were always assured that industry 'does not discriminate' and that the real problem was the lack of female applicants. We also received a few homilies about the terrible standards of arithmetic of children today, and how much a few intelligent girls would be appreciated. We retained some scepticism about the 'unprejudiced' views of industrialists. Yet there was evidence that bias against females is considerably less than schoolteachers seem to imagine. The East Manchester Engineering Training Association had just moved into new quarters, and though they had never recruited more than two or three girl apprentices or technicians in any one year, there was a female lavatory block equal in size to the male one. We also gathered information about the Engineering Industry Training Board's positive discrimination scheme whereby employers who take on a girl technician trainee would receive a grant of £5,000 not available for taking on a boy. The visits to industry may seem to have been rather remote from the central purposes of the project, but were an extremely useful activity in two ways. We were able to carry back to the schools with us positive messages about some of the initiatives being taken to encourage girls, and to back them up with some local knowledge of training opportunities. Industrial and trade union contacts provided no useful leads in our search for VISTA women, but the Women in Manual Trades group was more helpful.

From the outset of the GIST project, it was clear that the question of girls and technology, the goal of opening up an avenue into traditional male jobs, especially in manually based occupations such as plumbing and engineering, would present major difficulties. Originally a team of graduate women, only one of us (Barbara Smail) had the smallest experience of these fields of work, and the visits to employers and training officers were undertaken not least as a way of beginning to remedy that deficiency. A day spent at the Budenberg Gauge factory taught us a great deal about what was likely to be involved. This is a small family firm, employing engineers with a wide range of skills, typical of the older style of engineering employers in the north-west. Budenbergs export their gauges all over the world and are proud of the sophistication and reliability of their product. We went into all the workshops and were immediately surprised to discover just how many women were working there. To the lay person, the work they were doing appeared to be very similar to the men's. On closer examination, it turned out that men and women worked at different 'stations' or areas in the workshops, but all were engaged in some part of the production process. There were clear hierarchical divisions, reflecting the wage differentials between men and women. An article about job segregation in the engineering industry (Wilkins, 1983) shows that women are excluded from work 'traditionally regarded as heavy' or where the 'technological content of the work is greater'. Clearly some of these divisions owe more to past practices than to real differences between the work that the men and women do. We had gone to Budenbergs to see Catherine (not her real name), a newly appointed technician apprentice, and her story dramatizes some of the difficulties experienced by young women who try to challenge these deep-seated conventions. She had attended a girls' grammar school, where no technical subjects were offered in the curriculum; in fourth year, an announcement was made that girls who wished might attend technical classes at the neighbouring boys' school, while the boys would be permitted to take home economics in Catherine's school. Catherine duly approached the head and expressed interest. At that point no arrangements were made for her, but she went ahead and told her form teacher that she had permission to go to the boys' school. She somehow found out when the classes ran, and had begun attending before the head had quite realized what was happening. It was only by effecting this cheeky *fait accompli* that Catherine ultimately succeeded in gaining the qualification in technical drawing, at which she proved to be very able, which gave her entry to the technicianship. When we met her, she was already aware that within the factory she was regarded as something of an oddity, and that she felt the necessity to perform as efficiently as possible, being very much on trial as the only female in this position. Research on women who have been successful in all-male fields indicated that a good deal of determination and a highly extroverted personality, which we might take to mean being more than a little thick-skinned, are necessary prerequisites. Catherine is a typical example, it would seem, of the kind of girl who can manage, more or less on the basis of her own personal qualities, to break through the barriers of sex segregation. It is clear that many other girls, more thin-skinned, or with less determination, fail to get so far even when they have the necessary abilities.

Teacher workshops

Our next step was to explain to schools that we needed adequate time to discuss with teachers, in some depth, the nature and likely causes of girls' scientific and technical 'underachievement', and also to prepare for chosen intervention strategies.

One of the factors in female underachievement is the differential treatment of girls and boys by their schools: the greater power enjoyed by male pupils in and out of classroom, the 'male as norm' in the curriculum, and staffing practices and structures which place women at a disadvantage. Delamont has pointed to the need for 'action research on attitude change' on the ground that only teachers committed to changing sex role relationships in schools are likely to be able to shift pupils' attitudes and then only if they are skilful in their approach (Delamont, 1980).

Teachers operate within gender expectations, not only in their personal and familial roles, but in the professional capacity also. For instance, in their interactions with pupils they may reinforce sex role stereotypes by expecting and tolerating different standards of behaviour from boys or girls (Clarricoates, 1980; Delamont, 1980). The majority of teachers believe themselves to be genuinely committed to fostering the development of all their pupils. But the question of what roles are appropriate for girls or boys or men and women is also of immediate personal interest to every individual. Sex differences may be perceived as natural and unchangeable in line with self concepts as man/woman, husband/wife, mother/father. We felt that not only attitudes, but behaviour and classroom practices of teachers needed to shift if any change in outcome was to be possible.

One of us had already taught a full-length option in an initial teacher training course, and had conducted various shorter in-service seminars or talks for teachers. On the basis of this experience, we decided that six hours would be the minimum time required to acquaint teachers with the problem, and to begin the process which we saw as continuing throughout the life of the project, of making teachers aware of the part that their own attitudes and expectations could play in perpetuating pupils' stereotyped subject choices. We intended the workshops to be the start of a broadening dialogue between the teachers and ourselves, with two-way communication in the sense that we wanted to adapt the programme to the unique context of each school. The format which emerged was three separate 'workshops' each lasting approximately two hours, and therefore a natural division into three elements of the work. These were, first, the passing on of information about girls and science and technology, second, what we called 'destereotyping' – increasing consciousness of stereotyped expectations – and third, agreeing with the teachers the intervention strategies they would be prepared to implement immediately. We wanted the school to release teachers from timetable and hold workshops in school time. The teachers would then have appreciated the importance given to the project by the senior management, and we could avoid any 'demotivating' effect that might result from asking uncommitted teachers to give up their own spare time.

We were not in a position to insist on these points, and not all schools complied. Many released only a section of all the staff who should ideally have attended the workshops, and some held them after school. A number of teachers attended only one or two of the workshops, and we were often met with slightly different groups of people each time. Almost all the schools refused to agree to workshops in the spring term and postponed them until the summer term of 1980 when more free time was available. An unanticipated consequence of these restrictions was that we had to mount twenty-four sessions (three workshops in each of the eight action schools) within the space of a very few weeks. This considerably stretched our limited resources, and gave us little chance to modify our approach as we went along.

In an ideal situation, self-selecting groups of teachers would have approached the team and expressed their willingness to work towards the general aims of GIST on their own initiative. Something like this has happened in a few schools such as Clissold Park and Haverstock in London, where feminist teachers within the schools promoted discussion and then adoption of equal opportunities policies. In contrast, the GIST initiative started from 'cold' and took more than a year to 'warm up'. We were faced at the start with largely sceptical and not entirely willing groups of teachers who darkly suspected us of being both 'airy-fairy' researchers and rampant feminists.

According to the broad plan for workshops, our first task was to persuade teachers that a problem of female underachievement did exist, that it was an educational, professional issue and not simply the 'natural' outcome of social realities. We tried to alert teachers to the negative repercussions of sex stereotyping in the classroom, and to arouse their professional interest in redressing the educational balance. Unconsciously, we ourselves were probably gearing our message to the perceptions of the men in the groups we met. A great many women teachers were fully prepared to see the issue as one of justice and fairness, but the men who were ready to go along with us often did so because the reasoning we presented seemed to make sound educational sense, that is for reasons extraneous to equality. Men were typically interested in the intricacies of research evidence or in theoretical issues such as whether multiple choice types of assessment benefit boys and disadvantage girls. In the role of 'information-givers' the teachers appeared to feel quite comfortable with us. It was what they expected a research team from the university/polytechnic to do. Quoting 'objective' research evidence also made the GIST team comfortable because it was in effect our only means of establishing an authority role, in our precarious position of outside advisers.

The very first workshop took place at Moss Green, which had offered the earliest starting date, near the end of April. It was a pretty sticky occasion, for two main reasons; first of all only four teachers came along and with three of us the GIST presence seemed overpowering. Second, we were very nervous because it was the first one, and experienced all the discomfort of a team teaching situation and some of the misunderstandings, for instance, 'When J. said girls had greater verbal skills, [craft teacher] made "yak-yak" movement with hand to other teachers (indicating females talk too much). J. didn't notice' (note by AK, from field notes). And, 'J. did notice but chose to ignore because seemed semi-aggressive. Attempted to defuse by staying behind later to talk to [craft teacher]' (JW's response, also from field notes). We never really resolved our own internal disagreement about the best way to deal with teachers who were resistant to the feminist inspiration of GIST. Was it better to confront and challenge stereotyped notions such as 'females talk too much' by, for instance, referring to research by Spender and others which show that females are *perceived* to talk more when they merely take a 50 per cent share, or to classroom research which shows that boys initiate more interactions with the teacher? A 'cathartic' model of attitude change was proposed, i.e. that 'sexist' teachers would at first feel hostile and uncomfortable when their prejudices were revealed, but would ultimately change their views because of the strength of that uncomfortable experience. This theory was never really tested, as it seemed only too clear that teachers who were made to feel uncomfortable could easily find means of avoiding us and retreating altogether from the GIST project. Instead we pragmatically adopted a flexible, opportunist policy of building on whatever professional or other interests would fit with our broad aims. We suggested that 'enlightened' teachers are naturally going to be concerned about and interested in the problem of female underachievement.

By the end of the summer term, many points of workshop organization had much improved, and we on the GIST team began to understand one another's style of working better. By then of course it was rather too late for the good effects to pay off in other schools. But when we did a special in-service workshop course at the university about a year later, the performances were much more polished and the delivery of paper handouts perfected. Ironically, several teachers from New Hall, one of the control schools, attended this course, and may have received a much better introduction to GIST than some of the teachers in the action schools.

The rest of the workshops took place in a great flurry, mostly during the summer term of 1980, the workshops in each school overlapping. Notes on Green Park describe the first workshop meeting as 'icy' and 'an unnerving experience'. A female teacher 'put her head round the door and said she hoped I wouldn't be like the other lady who'd come' (a different member of the team) because 'she put me off'. The unknown teacher wouldn't be drawn about what was off-putting and said she hadn't discussed it with others; she disappeared again, leaving the GIST workshop leader full of trepidation.

During the workshop, several craft teachers expressed objections which we were to hear again elsewhere: 'Has this school actually agreed to do anything?' 'There aren't any jobs for school leavers anyway, and employers are bound to take boys in preference to girls when there are so few apprenticeships.' One of them suggested it was really too late now to plan anything for September – although from the school which had insisted on postponing workshops until the summer months when timetables are not so heavy. None of the male teachers from Green Park turned up to the second workshop, which alerted us to the need for extra work in that school, leading eventually to John Catton's exemplary teaching exercise in the school for one term. We also realized that it would be much better if there were always at least two GIST members at each workshop, to give us time to think and provide much-needed moral support.

At Edgehill School, the staff considered themselves rather sophisticated, and were justly proud of their modern approach to science – divided into environmental and physical sciences – and to crafts, a problem-solving, integrated crafts scheme in the first three years. There was good attendance from the science department especially, which meant that eight out of the ten teachers attending were men, and only two of them could be described as initially sympathetic. The atmosphere was rather strained and seemed hostile to us at the time. The hostility appears to have been largely engendered by a piece of feminist writing (from Belotti's book, *Little Girls*, Belotti, 1975). It was used as a discussion starter for talking about sex stereotyping in schools, but was perhaps badly chosen, as it described very young children, and in an Italian context. With some inconsistency, the teachers maintained that that sort of thing never happens here, and that the examples (girls doing little 'services' for boys in the nursery) were trivial and unrelated to the girls and science problem. Without the evidence we later gathered about girls 'fetching and carrying' in labs and workshops (see Chapter 2, above), we were unable to point out the parallels in a convincing way.

Somewhat chastened by this experience, we fell back in subsequent workshops to three relatively 'cool' destereotyping exercises. These were certainly less threatening to teachers, but the structure allowed individuals to disguise or keep unvoiced their real prejudices, if any, so that we may have learned less about the covert opposition still to be overcome.

The 'cool' exercises

Between the first and second sessions, teachers were asked to 'do a bit of homework'; this consisted of analysing part of a textbook currently in use for sex bias. The choice of book was up to them, and it is natural to suppose that many will have looked for the least biased text they could find. The exercise involves counting the illustrations of males and females, and recording what they are depicted as doing, monitoring any mention of males and females in the text, and summarizing the 'message' of the book or booklet as a whole. As numerous studies have shown (Taylor, 1970; Walford, 1980), even in the most contemporary materials, males considerably outnumber females, and women and girls are shown in limited and stereotyped roles. In one science textbook, for example, the only representation of a female is the naked figure illustrating the section on reproduction!

Teachers were almost unfailingly surprised at the extent of bias to be found when they actually went looking for it. One head of science said rather smugly that he had found no bias, as there were no pictures of people at all in the science units he used. GIST commented that this in itself indicated one of the ways in which girls might be turned off the subject; although science and technology affect every aspect of our daily lives, the subjects can be taught as if they were entirely devoid of any human relevance at all. He took the point very well and the school later requested assistance from the science liaison officer in rewriting of curriculum materials.

We often found that women teachers were much more definite in their findings and more impressed by the evidence of bias than men. For them the exercise was an eye-opener; it also concretized, in a way nothing else could have done, what exactly we meant by that over-used piece of sociological jargon 'stereotyping'.

A second 'cool' exercise (adapted from an exercise by Jackie Bould, University of Leeds Careers Counselling Unit), called 'Brainstorming', asks group members to write down all the adjectives which they, or society, apply to 'women' and to 'men'. The exercise deliberately confused societal and personal values, allowing individuals to express views they knew to be at odds with the project aims. It further clarified the nature of sex role stereotyping in a very simple way, while we hoped and assumed that the franker exchange of views would encourage private consideration of teachers' own stereotypical assumptions. In some workshops, younger feminist teachers used the exercise to make their own statement about male chauvinism and in one case at least this was clearly divisive for later work in the school. We heard only indirectly of staffroom discussions which took place when we were not there, but some men may have interpreted general complaints of sexism in school in an entirely personal way. For example, a male science teacher joined a workshop group including two female teachers who were outspoken in their criticism of the way that school indirectly contributed to girls' underachievement. He seemed to feel he was being held personally to blame for the low take-up of physical science by girls in that school. When options figures (for 1981) became available later in the year, they showed an increase in the number of girl physicists, and then his attitude to GIST became noticeably more cheerful and positive.

In the 'Denis/Denise' game (adapted from an exercise published in Nickerson *et al.*, 1975), teachers were divided into two groups. Each group was given a piece of paper describing an imaginary fifth form pupil's qualities, hopes and exam results. They were asked to reach a group consensus about the pupil's future path into further education or a career, up to the age of 30. The teachers were unaware that one group had been given a sheet headed 'Denis Johnson', the other group an identical sheet headed 'Denise Johnson' with the pronouns appropriately altered. In general, the careers predicted for Denis led to higher income, higher status occupations than those predicted for Denise. The quality of 'being interested in people' seemed to be more salient in the case of Denise, predicted to be a hotel receptionist or a nurse, jobs directly of service to people. For Denis the factor of 'wishes to start earning money as soon as possible' was often interpreted as evidence of ambition, and it was frequently suggested he would be 'in commerce' as an executive or a bank manager, so involved only indirectly with the general public and not in a service role.

For the success of this exercise, everything depends on smooth organization. Denis/e fell pretty flat in the very first workshop, because there were only four teachers to be divided into two groups, but in most other cases the teachers had to admit to the existence of their stereotyped expectations. The Denis/e 'situation play' has obvious implications for the differential treatment of boys and girls at school, and gave teachers an insight into how the single stimulus of gender may structure adult responses to children's qualities and behaviour.

In one workshop, as soon as the purpose of the exercise was revealed, both groups tried to represent a rather different picture of the discussion that had taken place; they omitted to mention that the Denise group had stressed 'helping people' and that the Denis group's discussion had centred around earning money, and maintained strong resistance to the conclusions of the exercise.

We were constrained to employ a 'softly softly' approach because of the weakness of our position as a group external to the school, and our task was to use and display sufficient expertise and balance in our subject to overcome initial perceptions of the girls and science/technology issue as trival or of 'fringe' interest. Because of their perceptions of us as feminists, teachers tended to be rather sensitive to the immediate personal implications of what was being said. The pragmatic resolution of this dilemma, in which some teachers reacted strongly against the feminist perspective of GIST, was to try to gloss over the direct implications for adult social role behaviour, for example, the question of whether a husband was being unfair to his wife in expecting her to take all responsibility for child care, and constantly to shift the focus towards the way that sex role stereotypes and expectations can affect interactions with pupils, to begin to see it in fact as a professional issue. We were considerably hampered in this task by the complete absence, in most courses of teacher training which these staff would have undergone, of any serious consideration of the issue of girls' relative underachievement in mixed comprehensives.

Adoption of intervention strategies

The third element in the workshop plan was to agree with the teachers' interventions which they were willing to launch upon the GIST cohort. We made several suggestions for things teachers and schools could do: redesigning curriculum materials (to make them less biased towards male interests), standardizing marks systems (because of the likelihood that girls are more discouraged by low marks (Fennema, 1974; Levine, 1976)), discussing the achievements of women in science, inviting women scientists into the school, single-sex grouping in classes or girls' only clubs for compensatory and three-dimensional activities (for full list of proposed interventions see Appendix 2). With sceptical caution, all schools agreed only to a minimum programme of delivering GIST tests and questionnaires and accepting VISTA visitors, i.e. those activities which could interfere least with existing school practice and required the minimum effort from teachers themselves. The burden of work largely fell to GIST. Tests and questionnaires were delivered to and collected from the schools, and all the scoring, coding and data analysis carried out by members of the team (chiefly Alison Kelly and Barbara Smail).

We had been particularly keen on the idea of single-sex groups, because of the evidence that girls seem more likely to choose 'male' subjects in all-girls' schools. The research on teacher-pupil interactions also showed that boys succeed in dominating the teacher's time and attention; not a great deal of work had been done on this issue in British schools, so we hoped for the opportunity to monitor the effects of the deliberate introduction of single-sex grouping. The suggestion was usually firmly quashed in workshop discussion, on the stated ground that it ran counter to the comprehensive coeducational policy to which staff were committed, and on the unstated feelings of teachers that 'positive discrimination' for girls is bound to be unfair to boys. Timetabling difficulties were also raised. The fact that experimental single-sex grouping *was* tried in one GIST school, as well as in various other places, indicates that organizational difficulties are not insuperable (see Chapter 8). In retrospect we can see that the teachers needed first-hand evidence of the way boys' presence in a group leads to it becoming male-dominated. At the workshop stage they certainly did not accept our word that this could be so.

Schools reported that children enjoyed completing the questionnaires, and presumably teachers found them useful to occupy the occasional spare period. GIST also organized the recruitment and briefing of VISTA visitors (women employed in scientific or technical work) and arranged for them to go into schools (see Chapter 4).

Other interventions, along the lines suggested, and actually initiated by the teacher, began to happen only some months later, when the impact of the VISTA visits and constant encouragement from the team persuaded teachers of the value of other activities such as single-sex 'clubs' and the revision of worksheets and materials. On the basis of our observations and notes made after the workshops, we were able to assign teachers to one of four categories according to what we perceived as their initial attitude to GIST. A very few teachers, mostly younger women, were already committed to or converted to the notion that sex stereotyping occurs in schools or that girls are in some way disadvantaged. This PRO group was positively interested in the proposed intervention strategies, but as all schools accepted only initial testing and the programme of VISTA visits, both of which the team were to organize, their role at this point was still essentially passive. A deputy head at Tall Trees began discussions with first year pupils on sex roles, but she was exceptional both in her seniority and commitment. She became ill later in the year, and left the school.

The largest group we described as HESITANT because they expressed doubts, were sometimes 'prevaricating', but basically interested to see how the next stage of the programme would work. Another large group whom we described as RELUCTANT were typically prevaricating, and at least initially did not expect to be interested in the project. All the teachers in these three groups were 'suspending judgment' before deciding to accept the GIST proposals (see Rudduck, 1976). A fourth, fairly small group were ANTI: openly hostile, or opposed to the egalitarian aims of the project, not interested in GIST ideas, and with a mind to reject the proposed innovation.

In a chapter about resistance to educational change, one group of writers (Zaltman *et al.*, 1977) remarks: 'It is important to distinguish between resistance whose premise is that a proposed change is the wrong solution to an acknowledged problem and resistance whose premise is that the proposed change is irrelevant because there is no corresponding problem.' Teachers in GIST schools were aware of the shortfall of girls in science and technical crafts, if only because we had pointed it out to them. What they remained to be convinced of, however, was that schools needed to concern themselves about the issue or see it as an educational problem to be tackled. Some who accepted that there was a problem were not sure there is anything schools can do to remedy it. In Chapter 9 the account of our continuing contacts with teachers shows how school visits, made on various pretexts, were used as a way of raising the issue again with teachers so as to shift them towards acceptance of the programme, and of the proposed strategies for change. Interviews with teachers by an independent team show how they responded to our programme.

Part II

The VISTA intervention

Chapter 4

VISTA

The rationale for VISTA

VISTA is not a real acronym but the short title for a programme of visits to schools by women working as scientists, technicians and craftspeople in industry, scientific research and government and educational establishments. The VISTA intervention was a central feature of the GIST project as originally conceived because it appeared to combine the merits of providing girls with role models of women in 'masculine' occupations and offering first-hand experience of science and technology as interesting and socially useful endeavours.

We were already aware of the so-called 'social implications factor' in science as more important to girls than to boys. We believed that in the mixed school science acquires a more clearly male-biased image, and that girls' preferences for a science which stresses social relevance and humanitarian concerns might well not be recognized in mixed classes. VISTA was therefore intended to deal with the double problem of giving science an attractive image for girls by showing them competent women who enjoy doing it while also stressing some of the aspects of applied science which may be missing in the school science curriculum.

The original proposal for VISTA said that 'we would invite

> women scientists and teachers . . . to
> - give lessons and/or one-off lectures
> - attend and take part in the 'confidence-building' exercises where the main part of their function will be as identification models' for the female pupils . . . .

In the second proposal and the one that was finally funded, we altered slightly the wording and the intention of the VISTA programme and referred to

> Activities designed to reduce sex stereotyped views of science such as visits by women scientists and technologists, films of the work of women scientists and discussions about attitudes to science, to sex roles and to women at work.

What has been dropped is the idea of confidence-building exercises which we later came to see would not have been possible without the necessary support from teaching staff. In this it was different from an American initiative begun by Iris Weiss in which groups of women scientists visited high schools (Weiss *et al.*, 1978). Success was measured by the number of high school girls who wrote to the project asking for a pack of material about science careers.

There were reasons for using a different approach here. In the United States girls can enter science courses in college without necessarily having two or three science passes. The formal restriction on girls in UK who have not taken chemistry or physics simply does not arise in the States, where it is relatively easy for girls to make a positive choice in favour of science at a much later age. The American programme therefore approached the problem as one of career choice rather than interest in science at a time when young people were consciously casting about for advice and direction. Many high school girls were offered a novel but attractive option. In Britain of course the separation of subject choice (at 13+) and career choice (at 16+ or later) is complete. Careers advice offered too early may appear irrelevant, and yet attempts to interest girls in scientific and technical careers after the age of 13 are already belated. GIST therefore decided that the explicit task of our 'visiting women scientists' should be to 'bring science alive' for girls, show that the science they were learning in school had real life applications and incidentally operate as role models for female pupils, but not in direct relation to career choice. A British initiative which was also of interest to us was the 'Opening Windows on Engineering' scheme operated by the Chartered Engineering Institution. They worked with an older age group, fourth, fifth and sixth formers, and were trying to change the 'oily rag' image of engineers. Hardly any of the engineers visiting schools as part of OWE were women and the majority were professional engineers with several years' experience. The VISTA scheme broke new ground in two senses: first, we were specifically aiming to bring women visitors and only women visitors in to the school, and second, we also wanted to include non-graduate women working at all levels from craft apprenticeship upwards to visit our classes.

Recruiting the visiting women scientists

A total of 192 women working in science or technology wrote to us or were contacted by GIST, mostly in 1980-1. We located the women by advertising, through local industrial contacts, the EOC newspaper cuttings file and the *Register of Women in Manual Trades*; other sources were the Dean of Lucy Cavendish College, Cambridge and local institutions such as Manchester College of Building, UMIST, Stockport College and various departments in Manchester Polytechnic. In 1982-3 some of the VISTA women already working in schools and some of the GIST teachers also suggested names of women they knew, and who might be prepared to join the scheme.

Over a quarter of the women who subsequently became active VISTA visitors had first heard of GIST through the columns of the *Guardian* or the *New Scientist.* We received between thirty and forty offers of help from these two sources alone. (An advertisement feature was also placed in the *Manchester Evening News*, in an attempt to reach local craftswomen and technicians, but produced no response. Not surprisingly the majority of women who replied were graduates; we experienced considerably more difficulty in recruiting women working in non-graduate technical occupations, such as plumbing or motor mechanics.) More useful was ‘Women in Manual Trades’, a support network of feminists who had retrained on TOPS courses to become painters and decorators, plasterers or technicians. One of them, Rita Wilcox, was an ideal ‘role model’ as she had received TOPS training in Sheffield where she worked as a foundry supervisor. Rita brought product samples to schools with her – brass doorstops cast in the shape of tortoises which delighted the children – and craft teachers were rather impressed by the extremely ‘macho’ job title of foundry supervisor. However, few of the women in manual employment were able realistically to take part in the VISTA scheme since we could not recompense them for loss of earnings. The employers of technicians and graduates were much more co-operative about releasing women on full pay and in many cases even paying travelling expenses as well. It appears that very few women are ever taken on as craft apprentices in engineering and allied industries. The few who succeed in breaking into this traditional male domain are often much more able than the boys working alongside them and are rapidly moved to technician level. As a result of these constraints we felt that our initial group of women visitors was rather top heavy and did not represent as wide a spread of jobs as we would have liked.

Briefing the women

The first groups of women we briefed were typically graduates and often mature, highly articulate people, indeed on some occasions the younger apprentices seemed somewhat overwhelmed, and some lacked the confidence or experience to address a whole class; as we shall see, this led to a change of format for both briefings and school presentations of craftspeople.

The method we chose of recruiting and then briefing the women operated essentially on a self-selection system, with some women deciding at each stage that they could not, or did not want to go ahead to the point of making school visits.

First, we asked the women to complete a rather detailed and personal questionnaire. On reflection, it is surprising that nobody objected to being asked 'how much do you earn', or 'how do you react to the suggestion that it is unusual for women or girls to be interested in science?', or 'were you employed when your children were young, and if so how did this alter your career?' We were very much feeling our way, and the questionnaire shows how unsure we were about the impact the women might make, and how worried that the strategy of presenting real life role models might somehow backfire on us. Later, we abandoned the questionnaire for younger women and craftspeople, and instead arranged to meet them individually for an informal chat.

In all, 167 questionnaires were sent out, and 84 completed and returned to GIST. We assume that at the point when they started to complete the questionnaire some women realized they were unwilling or unable to participate in the scheme. The next stage was to invite the women to a briefing session at our offices in Didsbury, part of an old house on the campus of the former teacher training college, now the School of Education of Manchester Polytechnic. We sent them informative notes on the VISTA scheme with a list of school science topics and asked them to prepare a short talk on 'some interesting aspect of your work which can be loosely tied to one of the topics being taught in the school', and also to bring some samples or materials for use as illustration. They were to be prepared to explain their job to the rest of a group of seven or eight women, and then try out their job description or practical demonstration on closed circuit television 'to build up your confidence before you face a live audience'. Twenty-four women dropped out at this stage, mostly for reasons unknown, but quite possibly apprehension about 'putting on a performance' was one factor. In all we briefed sixty women in small group sessions, and had informal interviews with a number of others.

The briefing programme was the same each time. Those women who arrived early came for lunch with us to the pub, where we tried desperately to put names to faces between obtaining pâté on toast and halves of lager for everyone and shepherding them back to the offices for 1.30 p.m. There was always a great sense of haste and urgency – the women arrived between 12.30 and 1.30 p.m. and often had to leave by 3.30 or 4.00 p.m., so we had a limited time in which to find out as much as possible about their jobs and to devise a topic which bridged their interests and the content of the science or craft curriculum. In this, Barbara Smail's experience as a chemistry teacher was invaluable. First, we asked each woman to describe her job to us. This is the list of VISTA visitors expected on 19 November 1980.

Jo Somerset, printer
Janet Jones (Dr), astrophysicist
Margaret Klinowsks (Dr), demonstrator in anatomy
Rowan Mellor (Ms), transport planner
Janet Romero, telephone engineer
Elizabeth Haslam (Dr), lecturer in biochemistry
Avril Jones, Ministry of Agriculture
Christine Brewer, technical trainee

Our 'cheeky' questionnaire had obviously made some women reflect quite deeply on their careers and with the cool objectivity of scientifically and technical trained people they told us, and each other, of the prejudices and difficulties, funny, hurtful or infuriating, which they had met with because of their choice of science or technology. We then talked about the children in the schools, their image of science and of the purposes of the GIST Project and the VISTA scheme; the visitors offered their own ideas and suggestions at this stage about how girls could be encouraged to consider careers in science and technology.

We also wanted to give the women an insight into the attitudes and interests of the 12-year-olds they were going to meet, and especially to remind our high-powered visitors how young the children were, and that this was going to be something rather different from a talk to the sixth form. The women had copies of children's replies to the following stimulus (Figure 4.1):

Imagine you are a reporter going to interview a famous woman scientist!

MISS FINGALSTIEN
Do you like your job?
yes I think it is very interesting
doing all sorts of experiments like people at the lab call me
Finky.
Finky? yes on be becos my name and bad temper
You dont seem as if you have a bad temper -
get out or I'll show it to you
bye and thanks. F

The fanas scientist Audry Dickerson
nearly got blown up doing an experiment
M

I don't have much time to spend
with my family
I enjoy science
The science experiments are quite hard
The Scientist said you can never know
everything about science
everybody needs to know science F

She is famous she make lots
of people better with Interferon. It
was not For Interferon people would
die. She is tall brainy clever
saved people lift I think she should
get a lot of money. For doing
and experimests that saxseeded.
The lady hav saved many live
IS. Miss Luisa
M

Figure 4.1 Children's interview replies

(From a pilot survey in 1979-80 with top junior children, i.e. not the GIST cohort).

Interestingly, some respondents ignored the given sex of the scientist and wrote about a man, while others 'forgot' the woman was a scientist and instead interviewed a housewife. The children's comments revealed some of the stereotypes about scientists which the VISTA programme would attempt to change. A handout on 'how to talk to children' gave advice on teaching techniques – don't try to get too much in, keep it simple, divide the talk into sections, take care to explain unfamiliar technical words, and so on. We also mentioned research which found boys tend to dominate classroom situations and asked the women to try always to choose a girl to answer the first question, rephrase it if only boys put their hands up, and always choose a predominance of girls to help with experiments.

After that part of the session we all took a short walk over to the TV studio in the main college building at Didsbury and asked the women to give just three minutes of their prepared talk before the cameras. Micro teaching is not really relaxing but very few of the women were at a loss even if they found it a bit of an ordeal. We passed from one woman to another fairly quickly so that no one seemed to be outstandingly good or bad at the exercise. During playback we picked up on good points only and the women themselves often picked out their own faults, if any: 'I need something to do with my hands' or 'I talk too fast.' We tried to be as positive and encouraging as we could, because we were afraid that some women might opt out of the scheme if they felt their performance was inadequate. Very few did so, and the exercise was a valuable guide to how well the visitors would perform in the classroom.

Occasionally, a woman attended the briefing whom we felt would not present a positive image to the highly stereotyped sub-teenage population they were going to meet. Some indeed fitted the 'typical scientist' image and either dressed with cheerful disregard for the latest fashion trends or obviously found it difficult to communicate easily with people. One or two appeared to have a 'chip on their shoulder' about discriminatory treatment they had experienced because of their choice of a non-traditional career. We stressed the need to appear positive, and for the women to present themselves as 'rounded' feminine beings, i.e. mention how they combined home and family life with their jobs. As the GIST team were responsible for liaising between schools and VISTA women, it was possible to 'cool out' any women whose personality might negatively affect children's attitudes. Amongst the women who actually visited the schools, some were excellent role models while others did not get quite such an enthusiastic response from the children.

The scientific/technical content of VISTA

After the session in the studio, we returned to the GIST office to discuss on a one-to-one basis the form each woman's presentation would take. From the individual questionnaires, combined with notes made throughout the afternoon, we had begun to formulate ideas for the sort of link which could be made between a woman's work and topics covered in lower school science or CDT. Sometimes the link was easy; for example, the food technologist who used Universal Indicator and pH meters to measure levels of acidity in cake mixes was an excellent illustration of acids and alkalis, a familiar item in first year science syllabuses. With others, the planning took longer, and the problem was often solved by a flash of inspiration. For instance, it was difficult at first to see how a chemical engineer working in the preparation of nuclear fuels could discuss her work in a way that would be understood by 11- and 12-year-olds at the beginning of their science studies. She used glove boxes for remote handling of radioactive material, and in the end the notion of approaching the design of comfortable glove boxes for people to use was fitted in as an example of the problem-solving approach in CDT lessons. Actually having a go with the gloves was fun for children too, and brought home to them something of the nature of a nuclear scientist's work as well as teaching design considerations. The matching of women's sometimes complex work activities with the scientific appreciation which the children would be capable of depended crucially on the expertise of the two schools liaison officers and their knowledge of lower school curricula.

The list of volunteers sent round to schools helped teachers make the required connections, by indicating exactly how the talks could fit into existing syllabi, for instance as shown here:

LYDIA GOOD BRITISH NUCLEAR FUELS, RISLEY	Metallurgist working in design office advising on the building of enrichment plants

Has planned two talks:

(1) The work of a metallurgist, what a metallurgist does, how much society depends on metals for everyday life and how different metals are put to different uses.

(2) The work of a nuclear engineer. A brief description of nuclear power and why we need it followed by a discussion of some of the technical investigations such as the testing of nuclear fuel containers, that are carried out to ensure that nuclear power is safe* and which demonstrates that nuclear engineers are responsible people who are concerned about the environment. Some of the by-products of nuclear research such as heart pace-makers will also be mentioned.

Once the links had been decided and agreed between GIST and VISTA women, they departed with a request to go away and prepare a paragraph outlining their talk. These formed the basis for the VISTA list circulated to schools. Visits could then be arranged, usually during normal CDT and science lesson times. The first women went into schools in January 1981, generally for half a day and giving a talk to three, four or more classes. Some preferred to spend two days together visiting more than one school rather than having to travel to Manchester twice for

* Critics may suggest that an engineer from BNF is bound to present a rather rosy view of nuclear power. It would have been beyond our brief to try and balance such talks with alternative views. Schools themselves should perhaps review the contributions of visitors on controversial topics. However, the point demonstrates one of the difficulties for a team working on only one aspect of science education.

different schools. Logistically it was a time-consuming exercise, requiring tremendous efficiency and attention to detail.

The intention was that each child should see ten to twelve VISTA visitors during the life of the project (described in Smail, 1982). No attempt could be made by GIST to design a broadly balanced input to science or technical education in the first two years of secondary school. We were entirely dependent on the women who came forward to join the scheme, and the kinds of links that could be made. There is no doubt that the knowledge of applied science they brought into the schools enriched the syllabus, excited the children, and sometimes stimulated teachers to curriculum development:

> Elizabeth Haslam was very good. [Head of lower school science] said, 'The children all want to do experiments with agar plates, coughing on them to see what grows.' (GIST file notes, 1 April 1982)
>
> Part of the impetus to look at lower school work arose from the VISTA visits. The staff were surprised by the enthusiastic response of the children to the talks. They have come to the conclusion that [children are bored by] science . . . built up as a logical body of knowledge . . . [they want to] utilize the child's interest and desire to learn about science when they come in at 11. (GIST file notes, 8 October 1981)

It is possible that sometimes the central aim of VISTA – to maintain *girls'* interest in science – faded into the background as the teachers got caught up in thinking of new teaching approaches or suddenly saw the usefulness of the visits for their own teaching situation.

> [Teacher] said at the start that he probably wouldn't 'inflict' his remedial group on Kay [Monaghan]. However when he came over at break and saw her display set out he said it looked so fascinating that he would bring them in the last period. I think he still sees [VISTA] as making science more interesting, not something aimed specifically at girls. (GIST file notes, 24 February 1981)

In a conversation with GIST about the visits, a female science teacher expressed despair that girls had not realized teachers were actively trying to encourage girls and that VISTA visits were aimed to this end. But her male colleague insisted the whole point was that it should be subtle and not overt encouragement, perhaps explaining why it would not be at all obvious to the schoolgirls themselves that VISTA was deliberately girl-focused.

Dominating boys

Each VISTA visitor was accompanied by a member of the GIST team who wrote a report as soon after the visit as possible. The system allowed some early problems to be ironed out. For example, a few visitors forgot everything we had said at the briefing and continued to use difficult words or technical terms like 'concentration' or 'modification' without explanation. Another problem we had not anticipated was the way that our visitors tended to reproduce exactly the kind of mistakes we were asking teachers to avoid. They made stereotyped references to 'your dad's car parked in the drive', 'acid on your trousers when mum comes to wash them next' or 'girls who stack supermarket shelves'. Presumably they were trying to carry out our other advice about using familiar situations to build rapport with the children! Tactful briefing and coaching continued between classes, not just to overcome such minor problems, but to increase the impact and excitement of the women's presentation. For instance, all the children had heard of North West Gas, and met one of their engineers who demonstrated temperature measurement. The GIST observer noted: 'The crayons which change colour at different temperatures work well, but I think she needs to make more out of it and to memorize the colour change and temperature so that she can tell the kids when this one turns blue it has reached 140°C.'

The best teachers usually possess a certain dramatic ability, and VISTA women were quick to take up cues like this for improving their presentations. The second and third sessions were often the most successful. Visitors soon learned how much to say and what would interest the children so that some women became thoroughly experienced teacher substitutes, much in demand. In fact as their time was given voluntarily we were often afraid of exploiting their generosity too far.

We had asked teachers to fill in a VISTA assessment form (see Appendix 1), and these along with our own observations and reports drew attention to another problem that was to prove much more intractable. The visits, so elaborately set up to encourage girls into science, seemed to be dominated by the boys. Typical comments were: 'Only one girl ever spoke' and

'The only response was from the boys.' When Jackie Marshall visited Edgehill the new lady teacher had been asked to send half her class to join another group of thirty. She chose to send the boys for the first talk and the girls for the second. It was noted that not a single girl in the first (male-dominated) group even raised her hand to ask a question. But after the second talk to a large mixed group with a preponderance of girls, several pupils remained round the front bench, and five minutes before the end of break it was necessary to evict nine girls and one boy still talking to the speaker!

In another school with a male class teacher *all* the boys sat at the front of the class with all the girls behind. Not surprisingly the session was rather dominated by boys. In a different class in the same school, the children sat in single-sex groups on either side of the lab. Even in groups where the balance was approximately equal boys were more likely to shout out comments, answer questions posed to the group or volunteer for demonstrations.

> 'In the first group of the afternoon, the children arrived and lined up with boys first and girls straggling along. When they entered the room they thus sat in a sex segregated way and this seemed to discourage the girls somewhat who were all to the side of the tables and display. Rita made great efforts to involve them and directed a lot of questions to them, but there was one boy who asked a lot of questions and tended to dominate the situation.'

> 'Sometimes it was difficult to ignore a bright knowledgeable little boy who would engage in almost one to one conversation with the visitor.'

> 'On one occasion a visitor chose two girls and one boy to do the demo, but then spoiled it by asking the boy to "be a gentleman" and let the girls go first! When this was pointed out to her, she took the criticism in good part.'

Paradoxically visitors needed to develop a constant awareness of children's sex, in order to give girls a fair chance. Talking about how atoms pack to form crystals, Sarah Galbraith broke off to ask a question, but held back some over-eager boys: 'No you've answered already, let's have someone else.' This session was a success, with the teacher joining in asking questions, and several children (three girls and two boys) stayed behind to look at the pictures in the book Sarah had brought.

On the few occasions when VISTA visitors addressed girls only groups, it was noticeable how much interest and enthusiasm the girls displayed. Any negative condition – a teacher who seemed bored with the proceedings, being outnumbered by boys, apparent reference to masculine interests, even a disadvantageous seating arrangement – would result in a much more muted response. In every case it took a great deal of conscious effort, direct invitation and careful management if girls in a mixed group were to gain as much from the VISTA experience as the boys.

The next chapter evaluates the impact of GIST on teachers and children, and focuses on the question of whether the VISTA visitors were successful in presenting children with alternative role models of women in science and technology.

Chapter 5

Response to VISTA

We had originally seen VISTA as just one of the interventions schools could introduce; in the event, the series of women visitors coming into schools was the most substantial and sustained intervention in the GIST project. Other ideas, developed by us or by the teachers, were sparked off, but were more fragmentary and occasional in character. VISTA was also the only part of the GIST initiative whose success we were able to measure separately. GIST team members accompanied the visitors to schools and made notes after each visit. Teachers were asked to complete evaluation forms, which some of them did, mostly rather blandly. More objective evidence came from four questions about VISTA included in the second survey of children's attitudes, and from the independent team of evaluators whom we asked to find out what teachers thought about VISTA. It is fortunate that we went to the trouble of doing these things, as the way in which the VISTA programme was received tells us a great deal about the nature of the problems of girls' avoidance of science and technology, and suggests some of the feasible solutions.

How VISTA was received in the schools

Despite the enthusiasm visits generated, we were often disappointed by the school's arrangements for reception. Before each VISTA visit a letter was sent to the staff member concerned clearly stating time and date and requesting appropriate audio visual aids. Yet several VISTA reports remark on the lack of preparedness to receive a visitor or comply with even simple requests for equipment.

> 'Arrived to find [visitor] already in school. Some consternation since Mr X [lower school head] did not know she was coming, Mr Y [science teacher] had not told him and "neither had GIST".'

> 'This was a full morning session, during which [the visitor] saw four groups for approximately 35 minutes each. We made rather a slow start to the first talk because projector and screen had not been set up ready (despite my written request) and the socket outlet we were attempting to use was faulty.'

> 'I bought [visitor] lunch as it seemed not to occur to anyone else what the two of us might do over the lunch hour.'

> 'A bad start to the morning because [head of science] was busy in another part of the school and no one else in the science department appeared to have details of room, classes, etc. There was no screen available, despite my written request for this, consequently . . . the class . . . had to wait for ten minutes. Luckily the visitor was not put off and gave her usual polished performance.'

We had organized the visits efficiently and we put down initial lack of co-ordination and co-operation in some schools to silent resistance and indeed scepticism as to whether the women visitors would first of all really appear, and secondly really be useful. The scepticism may quite simply have been due to a disbelief that GIST would be able to find *any* women scientists. We were asked more than once how many we had on the list, and we heard indirectly of a humorous staffroom comment that the first VISTA visitor was going to look like Tamara Press (Russian athlete suspected of taking male hormone drugs)! Some teachers displayed their reservations by not turning up for the talk until the exact hour stated, leaving no time for introductions or last minute preparation.

> 'Everyone disappears for coffee until the stroke of 10.30 a.m. Prep room is locked and when they arrive they seem to work off the top of their heads!'

It was certainly noticeable that children took their cue for response from the teacher's behaviour.

> '[The rest of the class were brought by the] English teacher. She very obviously distanced herself from the talk, despite a direct invitation from Sheila Anderson at one point to come

closer, and looked a bit squeamish when the foetuses were brought out. One or two of the girls sat close to her and presumably learned from her attitude.'

The observer noted of a young male physics teacher:

'His sceptical attitude did nothing to help the session get started well and the children in this group obviously do not find science interesting and took some settling down. The questions came mainly from the boys . . . when the thermometers and thermostats were passed round . . . the girls politely examined them . . . questions to Linda or the teacher [about] how they worked were all from boys – very depressing!'

At our request, teachers usually stayed in for the visit and were responsible for countering indiscipline, if any.

'The teacher was engaged in rearranging the children's seating. . . . There was considerable noise, disturbance . . . [Visitor] was introduced extremely briefly. I had no chance to do so. The noisy atmosphere continued. . . . They are a very restless class. . . . The teacher frequently shouted "Right now 1W1" and a moment's silence would prevail before the hubbub started again. However, the kids were responsive, and very much enjoyed MK coming round to find their funny bone individually.'

On a later visit the same class proved a bit of a handful for the temporary teacher and GIST stepped in:

'Avril did the talk with the slides quite well, but some of the kids were reading a handout from assembly rather than listening. I quietly removed the handouts I could reach which did not please them.'

One VISTA talk was a 'successful' lesson for the science teacher; he marked an entire set of exercise books while the visitors worked with the children! Teachers who were supportive and interested made a considerable difference to the children's response.

'The best session of the morning. [Craft teacher] was most actively involved and enthusing, making frequent asides to me about how good was SL and how his kids had covered such and such a topic which SL had just mentioned. His group was certainly responsive.'

Visitors themselves remarked on the difference in atmosphere when a teacher stayed with the class and showed some interest.

The children's response

From our own notes recording the reaction to each visit, it seems that the interest and impact of meeting a woman scientist depended partly on the teacher's enthusiasm on the occasion. Some teachers showed little appreciation of the possibilities offered by visits, perhaps because they had had none of the trouble or labour of recruiting and inviting the visitors. Some other teachers became interested despite their initial caution. In general, however, they may have focused on the science content of the visit, ignoring the feature we felt was more important, that is, talking to children about the opportunities for *women* in science and technology.

In order to find out how much the children remembered of the visits, and what they had liked or disliked about them, we included four questions about VISTA in the second wave of attitude testing, carried out in the spring of 1983. Each mention of a visitor by name or occupation was recorded, and all except three were referred to by at least one child. Two of these three had appeared as part of a large group, and so were less memorable than women who came alone. Eight women seemed to be especially memorable, eliciting eighty or more observations. They were, in Table 5.1, nos. 4, 20, 27, 30, 32, 34, 35 and 37. Most of them were young, in their twenties and engaged in technical or craft occupations non-traditional for their sex.

The children were asked to rate visits as:

(3) 'interesting'
(2) 'OK'
(3) 'boring'

Counting only those visitors remembered by at least ten children, out of a possible forty, twenty-six were rated as 'OK' or 'interesting' by the girls and twenty-three by the boys (see Table 5.2).

Clearly the visits were enjoyed and the overall response was very positive. Only a few described the experience as 'boring'. More boys than girls (7.8 per cent to 5.4 per cent) said in response to the question, 'What was best about VISTA?', 'Nothing'. The lower ratings given by boys are partly accounted

TABLE 5.1 *VISTA visitors by job*

VISTA *women*

(1) Senior scientific officer with sea mammal research unit

(2) Chemical engineer in the nuclear industry

(3) Research fellow in solid state physics/optics

(4) Self-employed designer in wood, etc.

(5) Product development manageress in food industry

(6) Mathematician/numerical analyst in computing

(7) Electron microscopist

(8) Metallurgist

(9) Lecturer in applied biochemistry

(10) Chartered engineer in gas industry

(11) Scientific officer at Sea Mammal Research Unit

(12) Research scientist (aerosols)

(13) Scientific officer, Civil Service (pesticides, environment)

(14) Research scientist, Health and Safety Executive

(15) University demonstrator in anatomy

(16) Technical apprentice

(17) Student/probationary teacher (CDT)

(18) Oceanographer/geologist

(19) Research chemist, Polymer Technology

(20) Coach builder, motor car manufacturers

(21) Medical chartist, hospital dept. of medical illustration

(22) Project engineer, lime kilns

(23) Aerosol technologist

(24) Technical apprentice (electronic)

(25) TV engineer

(26) Electron microscopist

(27) Telephone engineer

(28) Technical apprentice

(29) Teacher (CDT)

(30) Technical apprentice (computer systems)

(31) Foundry supervisor

(32) Motor mechanic

(33) Apprentice plumbers (2)

(34) Jeweller

(35) Furniture maker

(36) Student furniture restorers

(37) Food technologist

(38) Technical apprentice (computer systems)

(39) Safety assessor, nuclear industry

(40) Student painter and decorator

Note: Not all the VISTA women who were recruited are represented here, as this is the list only of those who visited schools sufficiently often for them to be remembered by children.

TABLE 5.1 (cont.)

VISTA *men*

(1) Home economics teacher	(5) Nurse
(2) Nurse tutor	(6) Cleaner
(3) Househusband	(7) District nurse
(4) Nursery teacher	

TABLE 5.2 *Visitors remembered by GIST children and how rated*

Women visitors remembered:	37 out of possible 40
Women visitors not remembered:	3 out of possible 40
Mentioned by children:	
Fewer than 10 times	14 out of possible 40
Between 10 and 79 times	16 out of possible 40
80 or more times	8 out of possible 40
Rated as 'interesting' or 'OK' (i.e. mean-rating 2.0 or higher):	34 by girls out of possible 40 33 by boys out of possible 40

for by their reactions to male visitors (see Chapter 8 for discussion). Eleven-year-old entrants to secondary school are very different creatures from pupils in the third year. Some of the 'blanket disapproval' responses probably reflect the more negative attitude to schooling of some older pupils.

There were interesting differences in the positive responses given by boys and girls. Many enjoyed finding out about different jobs, but the visits seem to have been more of an eye-opener in this respect for the girls (see Table 5.3).

Twice as many boys as girls thought the best thing about VISTA was examples of women working in science and technology; for these pupils, at any rate, the visitors may have operated as role models. Boys liked hearing about people's jobs, but do not seem to have been so positive about the female element in VISTA.

The difference in the way boys and girls behaved during the visits is reflected in the larger proportion of boys who were glad

TABLE 5.3 *Responses to the question, 'What did you like about VISTA?'*

	Boys (%)	Girls (%)	Significant sex difference
Different jobs	27	40	***0.1% level
Women examples	10	19	***0.1% level
No lessons	17	14	* 5% level
Asking questions	21	15	—
Visual aids	10	12	—
Science content	1	2	—

to escape from lessons, and who enjoyed asking questions. Visual aids (the seal foetuses, brass tortoises, wooden toys, etc.) were mentioned by some children, but on the whole they do not seem to have been particularly conscious of the science content of the visits. Perhaps this merely means that few children had the analytical ability to separate out the science component in the whole experience.

There were also significant sex differences, some rather small, in the visitors mentioned by girls or boys as 'interesting' (see Table 5.4).

It looks as if girls preferred the women in jobs with a more stereotypically 'feminine' flavour – the jeweller and the women working in the food industry – while the boys just liked hearing about 'masculine' jobs such as plumbing and engineering. Other factors probably entered into their response, for instance, the personality of the woman concerned, and the sort of presentation she made. The pattern found here seems to confirm the importance of changing the masculine image of science by introducing recognizable 'feminine' elements, as a starter for the girls.

In the VISTA programme, the sex of the visitor was more appreciated by the girls than by the boys, and some aspects of some women's work seemed to be of particularly 'feminine' interest. The visits may have given girls a glimpse of some of the hitherto unknown attractions of science and technology. For this to lead on to a confirmed positive attitude to the subject, the starting point of initial interest would need to be built upon and followed through. Indeed, during the visits girls were sometimes seen enthusing about even the traditionally masculine aspects of

TABLE 5.4 *Differences in girls' and boys' ratings of visitors as 'interesting' (2.5 or higher)*

	Mean rating by boys	*Mean rating by girls*
Sea mammal researcher	2.5	2.5
Research fellow in solid state physics/optics	2.5	3.0
Self-employed designer in wood	—	2.5
Product development manageress in food industry	—	2.6
Lecturer in applied biochemistry	2.5	3.0
Scientific officer at Sea Mammal Research Unit	3.0	2.6
Scientific officer, Civil Service (pesticides, environment)	—	2.5
University demonstrator in anatomy	2.5	—
Coach builder, car manufacturer	—	2.5
Medical chartist	3.0	—
Technical apprentice (electronic)		2.5
TV engineer	2.5	
Electron microscopist		3.0
CDT teacher	—	2.5
Apprentice plumbers	2.5	
Jeweller	—	2.8
Student furniture restorers	—	2.5
Technical apprentice (computer systems)	3.0	—
Student painter and decorator	3.0	3.0

science and technical crafts, because of the way women presented topics in a context familiar or interesting to girls and not just to boys. But did the teachers build on the enthusiasm which had been sparked off?

Teachers' responses

Teachers interviewed by an independent team of evaluators were asked what they thought had been the 'best feature' of the GIST programme, and nearly half mentioned the VISTA visits (page numbers refer to interview summaries, published in the report on teachers' perceptions of GIST, Payne *et al.*, 1984): 'the VISTA speakers were particularly appreciated' (p. 13); 'the strongest feature of the project was actually seeing real women scientists in the flesh; this was most worthwhile' (p. 46). Unlike the children, teachers seemed more concerned with the science content of the visits:

> On good aspects of GIST he thinks the idea of speakers was excellent (although some speakers got the level wrong). This teacher said more than once that he applauded the visits because they encouraged a general interest in science, i.e. 'it's what the project is doing for science rather than for girls and science which was welcomed.' (p. 20)
>
> He does note that the visiting speakers were worthwhile as outsiders; they brought the school into contact with the outside world, especially with industry, and this contact must be good. The speakers also made staff think. (p. 43)

Some teachers complained that children were not aware of the 'feminist' message of the visits, that women can do science and technology as well as men:

> He welcomed the opportunity to get some visiting speakers into the school; in his view education does not relate sufficiently to the real world, so these speakers would help to overcome this deficiency. In fact he found that they were the best feature of GIST, though he did not believe they helped in the aim of breaking down traditional attitudes by presenting female images of masculine jobs. (p. 35)

We had suggested to the teachers that in preparing children for the visits, they should explain that 'in the past' science and technology may not have been for girls, but that nowadays, things are changing. We even stressed that because of their position as teachers of science and technology, this sort of positive encouragement would have greater value than the same expression of support from other teachers not directly involved in teaching the subjects. However, the teachers appear to have been startlingly reluctant to say anything at all which might give the children a clue as to why all the visitors from GIST were women. No doubt this well-kept secret explains why relatively few children mentioned as a feature of VISTA the fact that women were talking about their experience of jobs non-traditional for their sex.

Positive support from the teaching staff was crucial if girls were to come to believe science and technology can really be for them.

A few teachers provided the right sort of encouragement, but many more revealed their ambivalence about the aims of the project by adopting a 'wait and see' policy. Teachers' 'ambivalent' responses are more fully discussed in Chapter 12. Teachers complained that VISTA did not have a 'role model' effect, yet some seem to have ignored our suggestions that as they were the people best placed to reaffirm the 'message' that girls can go into science and technology, they should do so before and after visits.

The efficient professionalism of the visits, remarked on by some teachers, may also have given the impression that VISTA was just a service offered by the team, requiring no positive effort on the teachers' part. They rarely seemed to appreciate the planning and care which had gone into the visits, far less the generosity of women and their employers in industry devoting valuable womanpower to such a purpose. In one school the head even complained on two separate occasions of VISTA women wearing jeans instead of skirts. The second time it happened the GIST team member reminded her rather sharply that the woman had come straight from work, where, as a telephone engineer, she frequently found herself crawling under floorboards.

Presumably teachers who set up their own schemes, and some have done so after hearing about GIST, will be keener to make sure their visitors have the desired effect. In fact VISTA acted as a spur to galvanize at least some teachers into action. Several from GIST schools became members of a panel set up by Barbara Smail in 1983 for the north-west, and they continue to use some of the original visitors, as well as training new ones.

Chapter 6

Girl friendly science

The GIST experience has generated many ideas about making science more 'girl friendly' and this has possibly been the project's most important outcome. The term 'girl friendly' only began to be used by the GIST team after the GASAT Conference (Girls and Science And Technology International Conference) in Oslo in September 1983, but it neatly encapsulates, in 'new technology' style, the approach we had tried to develop.

We had a number of ideas, even in 1979, for things to do to encourage girls to study science or technology. For example a considerable body of evidence had established that girls are more interested and motivated to study science if they learn something of its useful and beneficial social applications (Ormerod, 1971, 1973). However, few sources suggested how this could be directly achieved in the context of the normal school science syllabus. Some new ideas arose from the children's responses to the initial survey questionnaires and the VISTA visits. Almost all were originated and put into practice by Barbara Smail, the Schools Liaison Officer for Science, whose sourcebook for science teachers is published by the School Curriculum Development Committee (formerly Schools Council) (Smail, 1984).

During the teacher workshops, the science textbooks and worksheets normally used in each school were examined for sex bias. There were far more pictures of boys and men than of women or girls, and the content was clearly aimed at boys. Where women did appear they were shown in the most stereotyped roles. This is the most elementary facet of the masculine image of science. If all the illustrations and all the examples in the books and worksheets children use are of boys and men, or of those aspects of life usually considered to be of particular interest to boys and men – football, cars, motorbikes, aeroplanes, war – then girls are bound to feel excluded by implication. A large amount of curriculum development work has already been devoted to science materials, and we did not recommend that a completely new science scheme be developed for girls. This would have been counterproductive both because it would imply that girls can learn only one particular kind of science while boys learn another, and of course because of the financial and resource problems it would have invited.

Science materials are often written as if the value of understanding science is already taken for granted; too few links are made with the social, industrial and human applications of science in everyday life. Girls have relatively wider social and humanitarian concerns than boys and unless the social implications of science are presented integrally with the 'body of knowledge' to be learned in the first stages of science education, they are less likely to move towards a study of science for its own sake. And in any case, boys who choose to continue studying science may do so as much because it is an expected option choice for them, with clear career-related benefits, as because of an intrinsic interest in science. A reformulation of science schemes to take more account of children's other interests could probably increase the enjoyment of science for both sexes.

Bias in textbooks, and the lack of a motivating social context, are thus two of the criticisms of the way the *content* of science ignores or bypasses girls' interests. The *process* of science teaching and learning is also discouraging to girls. For example, Galton's study of science teachers indicated that their preferred teaching styles were inadvertently antagonistic to girls' full participation in the learning process (Galton, 1981). Our own observations (see Chapter 2) showed that social interactions in labs and workshops 'edge girls out' of science.

Making science more 'friendly' for girls may mean any of four things:

(1) the materials and examples used by the teacher build on girls' as much as boys' interests;
(2) the teaching approach stresses the social and human applications of science in everyday life;
(3) girls are constantly and actively involved in first-hand practical experience which will help them to a concrete understanding of scientific processes, and the teacher's

management of the classroom ensures girls participate at least as much as boys;

(4) children know, because they have explicitly been told, that science is a subject in which girls, at least as much as boys, are expected to do well: the atmosphere of the school is supportive to girls' choice of physical sciences.

Bias in curriculum materials

Materials, examples and illustrations are currently geared to a male audience and 'masculine interests'. Several studies have reviewed science materials for sex bias (Taylor, 1970; Walford, 1980), but there were no existing guidelines for teachers on how to adapt or modify existing materials, with which they might be perfectly happy on grounds other than their appeal to girls. Barbara Smail, the Schools Liaison Officer for Science, has now produced a useful sourcebook for science teachers, drawing on the GIST experience, and offering just such guidance. As it is so comprehensive, reference is made here only to some of the more important suggestions, and those which will interest the general reader; science teachers will want to read the original in order to obtain more detailed advice.

There are three main kinds of bias:

(a) where people are illustrated or mentioned at all, they are almost always male;
(b) examples and references are to 'masculine' interests;
(c) the roles of males and females at work and at home are presented in a stereotyped way.

Most of the GIST schools used two science schemes, 'Nuffield Combined Science' and 'Science for the 70s', and these were surveyed in detail by Barbara Smail, who wished to confirm her conviction that there was a bias in textbooks. She found 'an overwhelming number of male figures except in two of the booklets, numbers 3 and 9, on reproduction and insects, both biological topics' (Smail, 1984, p. 42). The implicit assumption in many of the booklets was that the reader would be male, although the schemes are designed for use in mixed classes in the lower secondary years.

There is often the implication that only boys really become

> scientists. For example 'the scientist . . . he . . . must be a super detective . . . greater than Sherlock Holmes or Inspector Barlow' . . . . In other places, stereotypically male experience is assumed as in talking about friction-drive by reference to cars, 'most of you will have had toys like this when you were younger.' (Smail, 1984, p. 43)

She points out that some efforts have been made in the revised version of 'Science for the 70s', renamed Science 2000 in 1980, to address both sexes; for instance in discussing scientists it begins 'men and women who study science . . .'; but in the illustrations females are still outnumbered three to one, and women frequently presented in a limited range of domestic roles, while male figures do active things. Barbara Smail's sourcebook reproduces, with permission to copy, some of the alternative worksheets produced by GIST teachers with her help, and also the series of drawings of girls performing standard laboratory operations which teachers were able to use when writing their own materials.

Building on girls' science interests

Girl friendly science builds on girls' known interests, so that half the class is not automatically excluded by implication.

With the data from the questionnaires, we were able to refine more carefully the distinct interests of boys and girls at 11, and more importantly, establish where their interests overlapped. Both sexes at this age are extremely interested in the human body and how it works (see Table 6.1).

Enthusiasm for human biology compares favourably as a starting point for science teaching with either physical science topics (of less interest to girls) or nature study topics (uninteresting to boys). Some examples appear in Table 6.2.

These findings were used in our advice to VISTA women choosing topics for their talks. Margaret Klinowska, whose job was lecturing in anatomy to medical students, introduced the topic of how muscles work by telling the GIST pupils that the word itself comes from the Latin 'mus' because the ancients believed muscular ripples were like a little mouse running up and down under the skin. For most science teachers, this would be a rather unexpected way of beginning to teach the physical science topic of 'forces', but it served to demonstrate to GIST teachers

TABLE 6.1 *Topics motivating for both sexes*

	% ticking 'I'd like to know more' Girls	Boys
How our muscles work	58	59
Our eyes and how we see	65	51
How children develop	70	52

TABLE 6.2 *Demotivating topics*

		% ticking 'I'd like to know more' Girls	Boys
Demotivating for girls	Torches and batteries	12	47
	Nuclear power	25	64
	Atoms and molecules	19	50
Demotivating for boys	Different kinds of trees	34	18
	The weather	48	39
	How seeds grow into flowers	54	24

that a topic normally regarded as abstract can be approached through familiar and everyday experience.

Another example is Kay Monaghan who was asked to follow up lessons on the corrosion of metals. She chose to start by asking, 'what sorts of things can be bought as aerosols?' The indirect reference to shopping immediately associated the topic with a domestic context. This was an easy question and in fact a very 'feminine' one, as girls are probably more familiar than boys with aerosol containers. Kay brought a display of aerosol cans from a storage trial, cut open to reveal progressive rusting on the inside. Metal corrosion was presented not simply as an abstract topic in second year science, but an industrial/consumer problem which she was paid to investigate and solve. It was noticeable during all her visits that, given a familiar starting point, subtly geared to feminine experience (but not alien to boys), more girls than boys made spontaneous suggestions and comments.

On the face of it, there is no connection between technical drawing and babies, but one emerged when Wendy Meakin, chartist in the Department of Medical Illustration at Manchester Royal Infirmary, came to talk to the children. She showed them her drawings of battered babies devised to help doctors identify such cases, and incidentally got the children interested in drawing and design techniques by moving on to other aspects of her work. Both these visitors combined familiar domestic references and a social/humanitarian concern in the description of their work, offering a double incentive to girls. The simplistic use of supposedly feminine examples may not work so well. The Scientific Curiosity questionnaire presented children with a number of topics they might learn about in science, including some with a domestic flavour, and asked them, for instance, if they would like to know more about 'how a vacuum cleaner works'. Girls were even *less* interested than boys in finding out.

Devices for harnessing children's interest in human biology to the laid-down syllabus of physics concepts were developed further by Barbara Smail, and readily accepted by schools as a good solution to the problem of boys' and girls' divergent interests:

> In one school, we developed a first year booklet on 'Lungs and Air Pressure'. A pocket spirometer was used to measure each child's lung capacity. They also measured their lung pressure using a giant water manometer. This led on to a discussion of diseases of the lung and a film about the dangers of smoking . . . [such] connections have been made before in printed schemes. Our innovation was to put the application first before any theory . . . whenever relevance to home life could be spelled out, girls' interest was captured. (Smail, 1984, p. 36)

Just as girls will not necessarily be interested in *any* domestic topic, the introduction of social or human applications does not appear to be enough on its own. Jacqueline Marshall was working as a materials research fellow, and she gave a talk on 'breaking things'. Both boys and girls were fascinated by the way petrol affects the plastic once used for the construction of crash helmets – they become brittle and snap. Yet questionnaire responses showed the girls had liked the visit less than the boys, perhaps because motorbike helmets are seen as a 'boys' ' interest, or because the emphasis on testing to destruction ran counter to girls' habits of thought. In contrast, a talk on water pollution was enthusiastically remembered by both sexes. Avril Jones, of the Ministry of Agriculture and Fisheries, used slides of her fieldwork and a specially designed 'effluent quiz' where children had to guess from the colour and appearance of samples where the pollution might have begun; was it a dye from a manufacturer of frozen peas or the waste from a detergent factory? Girls asked Avril a great many questions, about oil spills or seabirds, or other pollution effects, and the GIST observer described it as 'one of the most successful sessions yet'.

Such socio-political issues as the impact of science on the environment seemed to be of especial interest to girls. It may be seen as a reflection of their initial pre-disposition to be 'people'- rather than 'thing'-oriented, or it may be evidence of greater maturity and social responsibility on the part of young teenage girls compared with their male peers. Barbara Smail exploited this interest by helping staff in one school to redraft an existing unit on science and the environment:

> The twenty work card experiments were re-organised around the themes of 'Homes', 'Air', 'Water', and 'Soil'. Additional descriptive material was added to emphasise the importance to human life of a clean environment and the part played by women like Rachel Carson in raising public awareness of the problem of pollution. These adaptations drastically altered the emphasis and the style of the science lessons the children experienced. The original unit had consisted of a string of experiments linked together by rather abstract ideas or rules. The children were supposed to do the experiments individually or in small groups, work out what was happening and why. There was a lot of competition to see who could get all the right answers and finish the unit first. The new material seemed to generate a more genuine interest among both boys and girls in the content being studied, because the experiments were set firmly in context. The teacher was able to adopt a more questioning, less omniscient style and class discussions about environmental issues arose spontaneously.

The planned development of a series of lessons in this way is probably very important, as it shows children the inter-relationship between scientific understanding and human concerns. One visitor, who was well prepared with an interesting demonstration and lots of appropriate references to the effects of dust on human beings, nevertheless found the kids unresponsive. This was perhaps because her talk was not clearly linked to science lessons then being taught, or because the topic was too remote from their experience, or the visitor never really established friendly rapport.

In an American study of science teachers who were particularly successful in encouraging girls to do science, one of the common features identified was the ability of the teacher to relate science to everyday life. As a high school student put it, 'She gives us up-to-date information and relates it to how we are living today. She does not give us old stuff from the textbook.' However, the study also showed that all the selected teachers were highly competent and experienced, with an average of 18.4 years in the classroom. They were 'good science teachers' in a more general sense, using more varied techniques and reporting fewer problems in their teaching than a national sample (Kahle, 1983). VISTA women who were quick to pick up the techniques suggested by GIST soon became pretty expert at presenting science in a 'girl friendly' way, but were bound to lack some of the competencies of good experienced teachers.

Hands on experience

A third feature of 'girl friendly' science is that it should provide visual or physical, but especially first-hand experiences which will help children understand scientific processes, with girls participating at least as much as boys.

We had advised all the women to think of some visual demonstration of their work which would appeal to kids, and some of the most enjoyable sessions owed their success to the excitement of seeing or handling physical objects, especially in 1981 when the children were aged 11 and 12. They particularly enjoyed the visual attractiveness of samples of products at various stages in their manufacture – something it is relatively easy for a visitor from industry to bring into school. For instance, as a way of illustrating her work as a metallurgist, Lydia Goodey brought in plug pins, a knife/cheese slice and samples mounted in plastic blocks and polished for looking at under the microscope.

Girls were 'entranced' by the seal foetuses brought by women working at the Sea Mammal Research Institute. They stayed behind to handle the specimens and asked 'do you swim underwater to study the seals and whales?' Sheila Anderson herself does not, but other women at the institute did, and the girls agreed with each other they would enjoy a job like that. Both sexes were thrilled to see and feel foetuses, but it was noticeable at least once that boys asked factual questions, while girls were much more sentimental, including one who asked again and again about keeping a seal as a pet.

Annette Bolton, whom we contacted through a popular magazine feature about women running their own business, brought 'animal' hooks, holders and hangers neatly made and skilfully painted in bright enamels. Her display of sample products, templates, drawings, photographs and part finished pieces was like a magnet drawing the kids' attention with its instant appeal. The teacher agreed to one girl's request that the class should make pencil holders like Annette's and when a new group arrived later in the day there were cries of 'it's great, really different' from the seated class to the newcomers. The ins and outs of running your own business also interested them, and the head of the craft department incidentally helped Annette, by giving her a contact for a possible retail outlet in the Royal Exchange Building in Manchester.

If 'science by doing' is the essence of the Nuffield approach, then its worth is confirmed by the VISTA visits where children entered into an activity suggested by the woman. They sparked off a lot of interest and excitement, and some imaginative ideas were tried out. Judith Ashurst, a safety analyst from British Nuclear Fuels, designed a glove box with the help of John Catton, the GIST Schools Liaison Officer for CDT, and kids had to try to take a match out of a match box wearing the safety gloves worn by nuclear scientists. The chief problem, as far as girls are concerned, is that on every occasion space had to be created to prevent the boys monopolizing the real-life practical experiences. Janet Romero, the VISTA visitor working as a telephone engineer, demonstrated what happens when you dial a number, but girls were almost swamped by the boys' enthusiasm to get some 'hands-on' experience. The girls tended to dial once and then let the boys, clamouring for their turn, take over again and have a second go.

The oceanographer, Barbara Lees, had provided lots of practical things to do – for instance, blowing waves and pressing on a transducer – and she made real efforts to involve girls, not always successfully. At one point, she asked a girl, 'Would you like to be a wave?' to be met by a shake of the head. The visitor persisted and got another girl instead. Afterwards the teacher said this pupil was the quietest girl in the class. All these sessions generated a large number of questions from pupils of both sexes.

There is every reason to suppose the regularity and ordinariness of the pupil response pattern seen during VISTA: boys getting their hands on exciting artefacts brought in by the visitors, and managing to hold the limelight generated by a special occasion, asking the visitor more questions and chatting afterwards. It happened so often, and was remarked on by everyone – the GIST observers, the teachers (in VISTA evaluation forms returned to GIST) and the visitors themselves – all commented on the way boys' reactions dominated the visits. It is a normal feature of classroom life usually taken entirely for granted. The adults were only aware of the imbalance because the occasion had been created by the GIST project; a heightened consciousness of sex differences had made them more alert to the reality of girls' comparative invisibility and reticence.

This third aspect of 'girl-friendliness' – the chance for girls to experience science at first hand – is regarded as important by national authorities on the girls and science problem. The American study of successful science teachers already mentioned (Kahle, 1983) points to the dramatic superiority of 'successful' teachers in getting girls to use science materials such as 'microscopes, models, balances, living plants and living animals'. What the girls enjoyed in the classes taught by these teachers was precisely the chance to get involved in experimental work. The HMI report *Girls and Science* (1980) also draws attention to the 'high value girls placed on practical work'; they refer to the close correlation between a lot of practical work and high levels of interest among girls, and record: 'Even among those girls who had dropped science it was remarkable how many commented favourably on their attitude to the laboratory work of earlier years' (p. 16).

Direct encouragement

The fourth feature of girl friendly science has more to do with teachers' attitudes and beliefs and the atmosphere created in the lab. As we saw (see page 88 above), many of the teachers who were ambivalent about the aims of GIST solved their dilemma by saying very little directly to the children, hoping the unspoken messages of encouragement would nevertheless 'get through'. But given the overwhelming pressures of the 'masculine' image of science, expressed in male-biased textbooks and approaches to science content, in the numerical dominance of male teachers and pupils in physics and chemistry in the upper school and the 'masculinizing' of the laboratory context by boys, girls need more than implicit encouragement if they are to choose to continue with science.

Existing science schemes with their stereotyped assumptions will contine to be used in school. Instead of ignoring the implicit bias, teachers can stop from time to time and draw children's attention to examples of traditionalism. The value of a science teacher doing this, as opposed to a teacher of social studies or English, is immeasurably greater because it implies to children that the teacher recognizes the historical problem of girls' underrepresentation, and that he or she will actively welcome girls into the subject.

Part of the success of all-girls' schools in producing girl scientists is due in substantial measure to the clearly stated expectation that quite a number of girls will choose physical sciences and perform well in them. A recent study of the relative value of single-sex and mixed schools considers that girls' choice of sciences in all-girls' grammar schools is the consequence of a school ethos which positively values female scientific achievement:

> Girls' grammars . . . have historically espoused principles which regard the educational needs of girls as identical with those of boys. It may be, then, that their record in science subjects was at least in part a consequence of the implementation of those principles and that the single sex environment created the conditions under which these could thrive. (Bone, 1983)

From the GIST correspondence, we have several recent examples of individual teachers who have dramatically altered the pattern of option choice in their schools. In each case they seem to have done so by reproducing the positive encouraging climate of a single-sex grammar school, and, above all, by explicitly confronting the children with the issue of whether more girls should choose science.

The approaches described in this chapter were implemented by one or more of the GIST schools, in, of course, mixed classes. The effects of the project on children's choices and attitudes (see Chapter 13) provide no evidence at all of any adverse impact on boys because of GIST intervention. If anything, the reverse is probably true. Boys learned just as much from the VISTA visits as girls, and enjoyed them almost as much (see Chapter 5). Boys' attitudes, both to science and to sex roles, were more rigid and stereotyped than girls' at the start (see Chapter 7). But boys' as well as girls' attitudes were liberalized to a greater extent in the action than in the control schools during the course of the project (see Chapter 13). Teachers who will give direct, explicit encouragement to girls in class, and who make it clear that they are aware of the existing bias against females in science, can begin to counter boys' stereotyped assumptions and attitudes about the place of girls in school science. Many of the features of physical science which girls find unprepossessing are unattractive for boys as well. The incorporation of more material on the social implications and social benefits of science, the construction of syllabi around student interest, and the inclusion of topics and examples appealing to both sexes are all innovations likely to improve the learning of science for all pupils, and not just for girls.

Part III

The GIST children

Chapter 7

The GIST children: attributes and attitudes

We have already seen (Chapter 3) that the GIST children came from homes typical of British city dwellers: 80 per cent of their fathers and 66 per cent of their mothers were employed; about two-thirds of the fathers and over one-third of the mothers were in manual occupations. One of the reasons for gathering as much information as possible about the children at an early stage was so that we could see which attributes and attitudes would turn out to be predictive of girls choosing to continue their study of science or technology. Would girls whose parents were prepared to engage in non-traditional tasks in the home also be less stereotyped about subject choice than girls from more conventional homes? Would children who endorsed sex stereotypes be less interested than others in learning about an area traditionally associated with the opposite sex from their own?

Science knowledge

The first sets of questionnaires were circulated to schools in the early weeks of the autumn term, 1980 and thus before children had experience of science at school. Most 11-year-old children have received little if any formal education in science or technology at primary school. But this does not mean they are entirely ignorant about these subjects. Through reading books and magazines, talking or working with people or even just watching television, they may have acquired an understanding of scientific processes. If boys have managed to pick up more in this way than girls, then they may start off secondary school with a definite advantage over their female peers. Much to the surprise of some teachers, there was essentially no difference between boys' and girls' scores on the GIST test of science knowledge. Two years later (in 1982) the authors of the APU study of 11-year-olds' science achievement (Schofield *et al.*, 1982) seemed to show that boys in a national sample had done markedly better than girls at that age. However, in their interpretation of these results, APU had concentrated on statistical rather than educational significance. 'The sex differences found in the APU study are not "marked", on the contrary they are tiny . . . only one is statistically significant, despite large sample sizes.' (See Smail and Kelly, 1984 for further discussion of the APU result.)

A number of writers, and a much large number of teachers, intuitively accept an intellectual difference between the sexes. Physics teachers working in GIST schools were especially prone to remark that girls 'just can't do maths' and so are unsuitable material for O- and A-level physics. However, more careful analysis of apparent sex differences in study samples frequently shows that they are much smaller than originally believed. For instance the pattern of pass rates of O-level maths candidates seems to confirm that boys have better results than girls. But when the results are controlled for the other subjects pupils enter, far more boys than girls are also taking physics or technical drawing, two clearly mathematics-related subjects. When the effects of these additional opportunities for experiencing mathematics are allowed for, the sex difference in performance also largely disappears (Sharma and Meighan, 1980). Of course it could be that children choosing physics, maths and technical drawing do so because they are good at maths. But it may equally well be the case that girls drop physics and technical drawing because of their 'masculine' image and so lose the reinforcement of learning which could be available to them if they took several maths-based courses.

In the United States the tendency for girls to drop out of advanced secondary school mathematics courses is more pressing than the girls and science problem. There, the theory that girls lack an innate mathematical or visuo-spatial ability has gained considerable popularity. However, by co-varying out the differences between sexes in numbers of space-related courses, the sex-related differences in spatial visualization were eliminated (Fennema and Sherman, 1977). As one would have expected boys did better than girls on GIST tests of spatial visualization and mechanical reasoning. Because the children were aged only 11, it was not possible to point to different mathematics or space-related courses which had been taught only to boys. Instead we had somehow to measure the pre-scientific and space-related experience boys and girls had engaged in during their primary school years, at home as much as at school.

Pre-science experiences

This is the first time that information about science-related childhood experiences has been collected from such a large sample of children, with the purpose of trying to compensate for unequal familiarity with science activities.

On what we termed the Scientific Activities scale, children were asked to indicate whether they had played with a chemistry set, helped to check the spark plugs on a car, read a book about science or planted seeds and watched them grow. There were forty-two activities mentioned altogether, which were later grouped into three types. The first was 'biological activities' such as 'going on a nature trail' or 'looking at the different parts of a flower'. Girls were more likely to have done this group of activities 'quite often'. But more boys had 'quite often' 'collected fossils', 'watched "Tomorrow's World" ' or 'read about famous scientists' (theoretical activities), and far more boys had experienced what we called 'tinkering activities', such as using a hammer and nails, making a go-kart or playing with a construction kit like Lego or Meccano.

We see these sex differences in experience as rather crucial in two ways. First of all, despite the fact that boys had more pre-scientific experiences (as defined by the Scientific Activities scale) than girls, they did not do significantly better on the overall science knowledge scales. In other words, girls did not do badly, as expected. But secondly the science knowledge test comprised biological as well as physical science items, and further analysis showed that boys *had* done *slightly* better on physical science items. This seems to be where differential experiences show their influence. Sex differences in scientific curiosity also reflected very closely the differences between boys and girls in experience of scientific activities (Table 7.1).

At the beginning of secondary school, both boys and girls expressed a strong desire to learn more, particularly about the human biological and 'spectacular' (e.g. volcanoes and earthquakes, animals in the jungle) aspects of science, but this general enthusiasm for science was tempered somewhat by boys' lesser

TABLE 7.1 *Sex differences in science curiosity and pre-science experiences*

Curiosity about science	Sex comparisons		Pre-science experience
Nature study –	Moderately more girls	Moderately more – girls	Biological activities
Human biology –	Both sexes very interested		
Spectacular science –	Both sexes very interested	Moderately more – boys	Theoretical activities
Physical science –	Moderately more boys	Considerably – more boys	Tinkering activities

interest in nature study topics (water, why some animals hibernate) and girls' lesser curiosity about physical science topics such as 'how electricity is produced' or 'the stars and planets'. It seems likely that there would be some sort of connection between things children have often done, and topics they are interested in learning more about: certainly sex differences in previous experiences appear to be strongly correlated with girls' and boys' different science interests (see Table 7.1).

We were not forced simply to reflect in retrospect on the likely effects of past experience on present interests and performance. We also hoped to compensate such sex differences. As has been said (see Chapter 1), technical crafts subjects were deliberately introduced as a focus of the GIST study because we believed that the technical and three-dimensional activities characteristic of crafts work would, in all probability, have a positive effect on performance in maths and physics of children who had taken technical crafts. Evidence from a small natural experiment occurring in one action school is consistent with this hypothesis.

Spatial abilities

Half the children in the first year took technical subjects (woodwork, metalwork, technical drawing) for twelve weeks while the remainder of the year group took home economics and needlework at the same time. In the second term, the 'circus' system would rotate children round to the subjects they had not yet taken. However, GIST was able to test the children at the beginning and the end of the twelve-week period. If experience of technical crafts makes no difference to intellectual performance, then one would expect children to do only slightly better, possibly because of maturation. If boys are inherently more capable of visuo-spatial tasks, they should improve their performance equally with that of girls in the group. In fact it was found that pupils who had taken technical crafts for twelve weeks increased their score on the GIST spatial tests significantly more than the boys and girls taking home economics. And the girls in the technical groups showed the greater improvement (though this was not statistically significant) in visualizing the top surface of a block model (Table 7.2). This was the part of the test on which they had been furthest behind the boys at the start of the technical crafts course. (For a full report see Smail, 1983b.)

TABLE 7.2 *Increase or decrease in spatial test scores for girls and boys in technical and home economics groups after twelve weeks*

Subscale of spatial test	Technical sets		Home economics test	
	Boys (12)	Girls (18)	Boys (13)	Girls (18)
(1) Reversing the letter	+1.92	+0.44	+0.00	−0.33
(2) Completing the square	+0.00	+0.72	+0.00	−0.44
(3) Choosing the top view of block model	+1.08	+1.67	+0.54	+0.94
(4) Choosing cut out shape to make a solid	+1.00	+1.00	+0.85	+0.83
(5) Combined 1 – 4	3.91	3.83	1.38	1.00

The marked improvement displayed in these girls' scores in Table 7.2 is strongly suggestive that the group of skills associated with spatial 'ability' may be acquired, at least in part, through first-hand practical experience of appropriate activities such as those offered in a craft, design and technology course.

The children's attitudes

Three questionnaires explored children's opinions of science and sex roles, and perhaps the most important finding was that boys are more traditionally minded and more stereotyped than girls about both.

Attitudes to sex roles

On the stereotype inventories children were asked to rate a list of activities as 'suitable' or 'not suitable' for young people of either sex and for themselves. So, on the Gender Stereotype Inventory they had to say whether it is suitable for girls and boys to 'look after a baby', 'lift heavy things', 'climb trees' or 'cry at sad stories', and then whether they had done these things themselves. There were thirty items, and children could rate them from 5 – 'a very good thing' – to 1 – 'a very bad thing'. This structure has the advantage that respondents can voice the opinion that both stereotypically 'masculine' or 'feminine' activities may be suitable for each sex, and avoids the criticism levelled at some other work on sex stereotypes where the construction of the scale assumed that 'masculinity' and 'femininity' are mutually exclusive (Bem, 1975).

In general, boys disapproved of 'masculine' activities for girls; they did not approve the idea of girls having adventures, climbing trees or playing football as much as girls did. Boys also gave themselves much lower marks on 'feminine' items and higher marks on 'masculine' items, whereas girls' self-ratings were more moderate in both sets of items. This may be because the pressures to adjust to sex role expectations are greater for boys. Girls who are 'tomboyish' or aspire to male jobs are perceived as aspiring towards greater status or power, in a patriarchal society. It is far less acceptable for boys to be 'cissy' or to wish to carry out 'women's work'. Affective behavioural traits, tapped by such items as 'Hug and kiss people' and 'Worry over a row with friends', were not polarized to nearly the same extent as concrete examples of behaviour like 'looking after a baby' or 'being interested in guns'. (For further discussion see Kelly and Smail, 1983).

By asking children to think about specific concrete examples related to their own experience, we may not have produced the more stereotyped responses to sex-linked adjectives such as 'nagging, pretty, stern, strong', etc., which other researchers have found in children even younger than 11 (e.g. Best *et al.*, 1977, who used stories and human figure silhouettes).

Sex differences on the Gender Stereotype Inventory were quite small, but the list of jobs on the Occupational Stereotype Inventory produced more strongly sex-typed responses. Again there were thirty items from which ten 'feminine' jobs emerged, seventeen 'masculine' and three with no clear gender stereotype. This shortage of feminine jobs reflects the truly narrow range of occupations women are expected to enter. These have been narrowed down to six main possibilities: teaching, nursing, catering, office work, retail organizations and hairdressing (see Sharma and Meighan, 1980). All except catering appeared on the GIST list, together with librarian, model, looking after children, cleaner, ballet dancer and textile worker. Teacher, social worker and newsreader were in the 'neutral' category. The tendency to accept males in a wider range of occupations – librarianship and hairdressing for example – is interesting. On the one hand it might be regarded as a good thing that occupational stereotypes are less rigid than in the past. On the other hand, it is a historical fact that as men enter formerly feminine professions, they tend to rise to the top of the hierarchy rather rapidly. This has happened in nursing, and the ILEA Report on 'Female and male teaching staff' (ILEA, 1982) shows how jobs which once offered the chance of managerial experience to women have adjusted to male entry, in such a way that women lose out, even relative to the past.

The jobs included in the occupational inventory were intended to be evenly balanced between male and female occupations, yet the children perceived the majority of jobs as male, forty-seven compared with twenty-two 'feminine' jobs (Figure 7.1). One exception was reading the news, seen as equally suitable for both sexes. Female news journalists are still outnumbered by males, so perhaps this shows how the visibility of celebrity females reading the news may seem to counterbalance the numerical dominance of men. The largest sex differences occurred when children had to indicate whether they found each of the jobs desirable *for themselves*. Not only did boys make a greater distinction than girls between behaviours and jobs suitable for one sex or the other, their self-ratings were more extremely polarized. On the masculinity and femininity scales which were derived from the inventories, boys consistently saw or described themselves as high on masculinity and low on femininity, while girls' self-ratings were more moderate. Fuller discussion of these points can be

Figure 7.1 Sex stereotyping of occupations

Source: Kelly, 1982

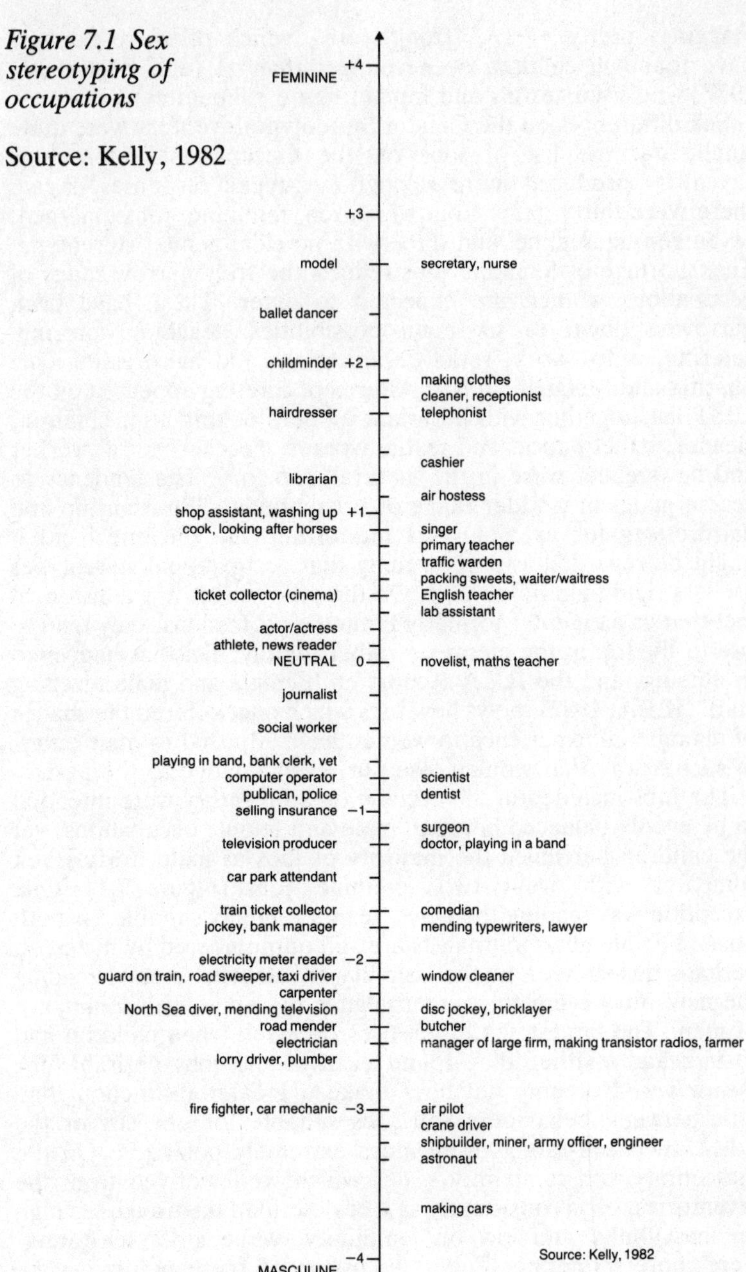
FEMININE
+4
+3
model
secretary, nurse
ballet dancer
childminder
+2
making clothes
cleaner, receptionist
hairdresser
telephonist
cashier
librarian
air hostess
shop assistant, washing up
+1
cook, looking after horses
singer
primary teacher
traffic warden
packing sweets, waiter/waitress
ticket collector (cinema)
English teacher
lab assistant
actor/actress
athlete, news reader
NEUTRAL
0
novelist, maths teacher
journalist
social worker
playing in band, bank clerk, vet
computer operator
scientist
publican, police
dentist
selling insurance
−1
surgeon
television producer
doctor, playing in a band
car park attendant
train ticket collector
comedian
jockey, bank manager
mending typewriters, lawyer
electricity meter reader
−2
guard on train, road sweeper, taxi driver
window cleaner
carpenter
North Sea diver, mending television
disc jockey, bricklayer
road mender
butcher
electrician
manager of large firm, making transistor radios, farmer
lorry driver, plumber
fire fighter, car mechanic
−3
air pilot
crane driver
shipbuilder, miner, army officer, engineer
astronaut
making cars
−4
MASCULINE
Source: Kelly, 1982

found in Kelly and Smail (1983).

These results indicate the importance of somehow dealing with boys' stereotyped attitudes, and anticipating the likely effects of their prejudices on girls' attitudes and choices.

Attitudes to science

Some of the most directly relevant material from the attitude testing emerged from the Image of Science tests. Here children had to tick a box marked 'yes I agree', 'not sure' or 'no I disagree' beside a range of statements about science and scientists. The statements were later grouped into subscales. The SCIWORLD scale assessed the extent to which children believed the effects of science in the world are beneficial: on the whole these 11-year-olds did not think science is to blame for 'killing millions of people', 'reducing our freedom', 'polluting the world' or 'making life too much of a rush'.

Girls showed more awareness of the possible social benefits of science, for instance they were likely to think scientists 'care about people' and to think money given to science was well spent. This confirmed previous research showing that girls are more interested than boys in the social implications of science.

On all four subscales, the attitudes displayed were positive, indicating that in general these 11-year-olds held a positive image of science. The largest sex difference was on the SCISEX subscale, but there were also differences between girls' and boys' image of the scientist (SCIENT) and their personal interest in learning about science (LIKESCI). Girls had a more positive image of the scientist than boys, but boys expressed a stronger personal liking for science. Girls' lower motivation was linked to their greater endorsement of such statements as 'science is a very difficult subject', 'science is only for brainy people' and 'I don't expect I'll be any good at science'.

On the SCISEX subscale, boys were more likely to see science as a male domain, and to agree with statements such as 'learning science is more important for boys than for girls' or that 'girls who want to be scientists are a bit peculiar'. In general and for both sexes it was true that those who were stereotyped on other measures would see science as masculine, which meant they had a more negative attitude to science too. A sex-neutral attitude to science seemed to fit in with a view of science as an open, beneficial and pleasurable activity (Kelly and Smail, 1983).

Home and school

Some questions on the background questionnaire invited children to say 'who usually' did a range of household tasks (see Table 7.3).

On the evidence of the children's reports, most of their homes reflected a traditional division of labour according to sex role. Mothers shopped, cooked, cleaned and washed; fathers fixed the car, did the painting, decorating and gardening and other odd jobs around the house. Some small hopes of a relaxation of roles may be gleaned from the 10 per cent of fathers who 'usually' shop for food and the 21 per cent who 'usually' cook the meals.

However, it turns out that mothers' willingness to engage in traditionally masculine tasks has more bearing on whether girls, especially, will be sex-typed and whether they will see science as a male preserve. Liberated mothers (or hard-working ones if you prefer to see it that way) produced liberated attitudes, especially in their daughters, and both sexes are less likely to see science as a male preserve if mothers participate in such activities as mending things around the home, fixing the car, gardening,

TABLE 7.3 *Percentageof children who reported that their mothers and fathers 'usually' did certain domestic tasks*

	% Mothers	% Fathers
Shopping for food	94	16
Mending things	17	91
Cooking the meals	96	21
Punishing child	64	77
Washing up	66	27
Taking out rubbish	50	41
Fixing the car	3	94
Washing the clothes	97	4
Gardening	51	74
Cleaning and dusting	89	9
Painting and decorating	52	88

Note: Children were allowed to name more than one person, so percentages frequently sum to more than 100. Siblings, the child her/himself and non-family members were also mentioned, but are not shown here. Source: Kelly and Smail, 1983 painting and decorating. This last item by the way is nicely highlighted by a recent survey by a large DIY firm which showed that when faced with a difficult home improvement job, one in eight women will do it themselves and just over three times that many would expect to share it with their husband. Ninety-four per cent of women were prepared to tackle decorating by themselves, 45 per cent tiling and some 18 per cent would tackle plastering, a job many craftsmen fight shy of (*Ideal Homes*, April 1984, reporting on surveys by Polycell and the DIY Superstore chain, Marley Payless).

Girls and boys were also asked two questions about the kind of lifestyles they would prefer in the future. On these topics, boys appeared to be less traditional than girls: nearly half of them (48 per cent) thought husbands should help with housework and childcare even if the wife was at home all day, compared with 37 per cent of the girls. (Table 7.4).

TABLE 7.4 *Responses to question, 'Should husbands share in housework/childcare?'*

	% girls answering 'yes'	% boys answering 'yes
even if wife is at home all day	37	48
only if wife goes out to work	46	32
not at all	8	11

This response could be interpreted as the girls claiming household tasks and children as their work in the same way that boys claimed science and technology as theirs on the Image of Science questionnaires. Pupils were also asked about their future spouses, and a majority of both sexes wanted a wife or husband who was about as clever as themselves, showing an encouraging wish for equality (Table 7.5). But a depressing 34 per cent of girls would look for a husband cleverer than themselves, compared with only one-sixth of boys who would seek a stupider wife! The girls seem to have internalized the stereotype of the male as dominant partner more thoroughly than the boys. Presumably they will be doomed either to disappointment or to a lifetime's pretence of being less able than they are, as there are not sufficient highly intelligent males about to provide intellectually superior husbands for all these conventionally-minded women!

TABLE 7.5 *Desired relative intelligence of a spouse for girls and for boys*

	Girls %	Boys %
cleverer	34	6
about the same	62	76
less clever	3	17

Finally the measures collected in the GIST initial survey have allowed some comparison of the relationship between sex stereotypes, socio-economic status and general ability: studies of British schoolchildren so far have not made this possible.

Social class

The interaction of class, ability and adherence or otherwise to traditional stereotypes appears to be rather different for girls and for boys. Social class was derived not only from fathers', but also from mothers' occupation. This recognizes the importance for family status of the woman's job. A child was therefore considered middle-class if either father's occupation was professional, intermediate or white-collar, or mother's occupation was professional or intermediate. All other combinations were considered working-class. Female office staff were treated as workers on a 'paper production line', not as middle-class employees. (Kelly *et al.*, 1982).

As might be expected, middle-class children did significantly better on all the cognitive tests. The only exception is the mechanical reasoning test, on which the working-class boys' score was nearer to that of the middle-class boys'. The same was not true for girls, suggesting that boys as a group benefit from informal mechanical experience, whatever their class (Smail and Kelly, 1984).

A very crude measure of IQ (which we called IQALL) was devised from the multifarious scores from tests given to pupils by their schools. Middle-class children had higher scores overall, but there was no significant sex difference. Comparison between the 'IQALL' score and GIST cognitive tests scores showed they were highly correlated, with the exception – again – of mechanical reasoning. This suggests that many of the items on the mechanical reasoning test depended upon relevant experience rather than reasoning ability. Most of the items on this test referred to experiences which are stereotypically associated with boys rather than girls, and it seems likely that different play experiences such as model building and technical or 'tinkering' activities helped the boys' performance (Smail and Kelly, 1984).

Throughout the four years of the project, we had much less direct contact with the pupils than with their teachers. It was the teachers who administered all the questionnaires – we simply drew them up, got them printed and delivered them to the appropriate staff. Teachers were given detailed instructions and also asked to complete a report form for each test. It appears that the 11-year-olds thoroughly enjoyed the attitude questionnaires, as the comment written on one form shows:

> You have finished now. Thank you for helping us.
>
> I would like to do
> more of these sheets.

Summary

In summary, the important characteristics of the GIST children, from the point of view of the project, were certain noticeable sex differences:

(1) The science knowledge girls and boys brought with them to secondary school was broadly equivalent.

(2) However, sex differences in science interests meant boys were more interested in physical science and girls in biology or nature study, while both sexes were curious to know more about human biology. The effects of sex differences in science interests were reflected in girls' and boys' scores on the physical and biological items on the science knowledge questionnaire.

(3) Boys had had far more opportunities for the kind of play experiences which might help their physical science, spatial ability and mechanical reasoning scores. Girls had more

experience of 'biological' science activities. Current science interests seemed to reflect the difference in previous experience of the two sexes.

(4) Boys displayed stronger and more rigid stereotypes about sex roles, both in relation to children and to occupations. They made greater distinctions between 'masculine' and 'feminine' activities and occupations, and were more likely to agree that science was a 'boys' subject'.

(5) There were other differences in girls' and boys' image of science, but in general and for both sexes, those with more liberal attitudes about sex roles also had more positive attitudes to science.

(6) Most of the children's homes reflected a largely traditional division of labour, and girls seemed to see the home as a 'feminine' sphere, even more than boys did.

Our hypothesis, based on the initial survey, was that the group of girls who would eventually choose to continue studying physical science, and probably technical crafts too, would be those who had most ability (as measured on the cognitive scales) and who were least stereotyped on the several attitude tests which explored stereotyping. It was a hypothesis based largely on the questionnaire returns, and not on any first-hand experience of the way these children were responding to science and craft lessons.

Part IV

Other interventions

Chapter 8

The roadshows

In June and July 1982, the team began planning the GIST input to options preparation and career education. Our strategy envisaged three kinds of activity. First, if possible, we hoped to insert some kind of pre-option and careers education, which would address the problem that girls make pre-emptive choices to avoid science and technology, before they have received sufficient careers education to understand the implications of those choices.

Option booklets had been collected from each school and returned with GIST comments on their content, sex-biased or otherwise. During that summer a third special guide for teachers was prepared called 'GIST Options and Careers'. The teachers' guide suggested some good practice ideas and has been much in demand as a publication ever since.

Second, we planned a special options evening for parents in each school with a GIST exhibition and a talk stressing to parents that their daughters should consider taking physical science and technical craft subjects. The first one was held at Tall Trees, and we were surprised by the number of eager and interested fathers who attended.

Third, we asked each school for a day or a half-day during which children in the GIST cohort would take part in a number of activities which came to be called the GIST roadshows. It was in fact the roadshows, which involved a tremendous amount of organization and preparation on the part of the Schools Liaison Officers, which formed the main part of our work in 1982-3. It is clear that subject choice, particularly in the mixed school, becomes a vehicle for the expression of youthful assertions of masculinity and femininity. The single most desirable step schools could take to increase the number of girls in science and technology would be to eliminate subject choice at 13 plus. Pupils are presently forced to make crucial decisions which may affect the rest of their lives at an age when they are bound to be swayed by the stereotyped image of the subjects. However, in 1982, we had to work with a real life school situation, with children not only making choices during the spring term of their third year at secondary school, but in many cases doing so with rather inadequate and even biased information about possible implications of their choice. In some schools such as Meadowvale, considerable thought had already gone into the design of the option system; the GIST comments on Meadowvale's options guide was: 'This booklet contains the most extensive programme of guidance/decision making we've seen. May we show it to other schools?' But in some other schools, choice of craft subject was made at the end of second year, with a show of hands at assembly, when of course only the bravest spirit would dare to make an unconventional choice. Very few did so. Third year choices were only minimally discussed, perhaps with the form tutor and the subject teacher concerned. We had no access to these private interviews in which teachers have considerable power to discourage non-traditional choice.

On reflection it is clear that the temptation was very strong for the team now to interact only or mostly with sympathetic staff, and the effort of arranging roadshows and some continuing VISTA visits in all eight schools seems to have meant that contacts with science and crafts staff were less than they had been in the previous two years. In a sense there was little more to say to those who were not already committed to the aims of the project. They all knew that we hoped a pattern of option choices might change and they should have been aware what sorts of actions might influence pupils' choices, but the framework of guided choices which applied in each school left ample space for the usual manoeuvring to go on.

Roadshow activities

The highlight of the roadshows was the meeting with men and women in non-traditional occupations. There were male nurses, a man who described himself as a househusband, a male nursery nurse, and a home economics teacher. The women we chose were all the younger VISTA visitors doing such jobs as telephone engineering or motor mechanics. We thought it was important to present role models as close in age as possible to the children who were now thirteen. The format for the day varied according to what was arranged with the schools. On some occasions a film *Jobs for the Girls* was shown, made by the Sheffield Women's Film Co-operative, about a girl who wants to be a motor mechanic; this formed the basis for a discussion with the children afterwards. An exhibition was laid on and sometimes children had to find the answers to a quiz which were all hidden in the display material. The quiz designed by the Schools Liaison Officers focused attention, not on specific qualifications needed, or other details of particular careers, but rather on the changing lifestyles and work patterns of men and women. In our discussion with teachers, they had often revealed a reluctance to embark on discussion of values of traditional and alternative lifestyles. They may have felt insecure about teaching a new subject in which they had received no training or more likely were ambivalent about the implications.

When the teachers were offered a highly structured game for the children to play they were willing to be involved in organizing it. This consisted of the two-dimensional graph and the children were required to stick labels on the graph with the names of jobs traditionally associated with men or women, having first of all discussed whether they felt the job was suitable only for men, only for women, or was somewhere along a neutral axis. Some of the children's reactions were very interesting to us, for example, in a discussion about whether an airline pilot could be a man or a woman, two little boys insisted that although women were cleverer than men they were unstable and more likely to have nervous breakdowns, and therefore unsuitable to be airline pilots. But the highlight of the roadshows was certainly the meeting with the visitors, and it was the househusband who produced the most dramatic effects. He usually arrived with his small child, aged about 2, who would inevitably, during the course of the day, get restless and need to be looked after by one of the children. The next time Zoë wanted to explore around her a teacher asked for volunteers to look after her; only girls put up their hands. When it was made clear that GIST wanted two *boys*, a whole forest of boys' hands shot up, showing they just needed the signal it was 'OK' for boys to do childcare.

It was very clear that the reactions of boys and girls to the visitors was different. Boys often protested and gave traditional arguments as to why girls and women should not do men's work, ranging from their lesser physical strength, their ignorance of things mechanical, and such clinching statements as 'my father's a builder and he wouldn't have any women on his site'.

The formula varied as we learned more about children's reactions. At first we asked the visitors to introduce themselves, say what they did and explain something of what was involved in their work. Pupils then split into groups of five or six, sometimes mixed, but more usually single-sex, to spend about ten minutes forming questions that they would like to ask of the visitor, and then return to the main group for a question time session which usually lasted for about thirty to forty minutes. This ensured that many children had the chance to ask a question.

Boys often displayed resistance to the message that was being put over. This is an example of a dialogue between Alison, who restores and makes furniture, and a third year boy.

Boy: 'What else do you make besides furniture?'

Alison: 'Well that's quite a range, tables, chairs, chests of drawers for example.'

Boy: 'Well what do you do in your spare time then?'

Alison: 'I make things in wood.'

The children were not used to interviewing people about their jobs and the boy's questions may have revealed a certain lack of understanding about the kind of life that Alison led. His probes were perhaps to find out more about her as a person, was she some kind of freak? It may even have been that he didn't really believe that Alison was a furniture restorer. This scepticism was shared in some cases by the teachers. In one school after a roadshow, a teacher said to me, in a confiding tone, 'That woman who comes as a telephone engineer, is she really an actress?' In complete contrast, more than one male teacher expressed envy at the 'lovely' job of nursery nursing, and wished they'd had a chance to do it.

The male visitors were sometimes at pains to demonstrate their masculinity. For example, Wayne, a domestic cleaner, mentioned that he liked sport and had originally intended to join the Marines when he left school, and one of the male nurses stressed that he was a happily married man with three children.

Questions to visitors

There was quite a consistent pattern to children's questioning of the visitors. Both boys and girls showed curiosity about their motives, and often asked, simply 'Why do you like doing a man's job?' or 'Why did you choose that kind of job?' The children's major doubts were about the reactions of other people; they asked:

'Do you ever get put down and called* for doing a man's job?'
'Do you think other people agree or disagree? Are you bothered what they think?'
'Did the other girls make fun of you for taking boys' subjects?'
'Did your friends call you names about your job?'
'Do you think your job puts friends off?'
'What do people say when you tell them about your job?'
'Do people mock you for what is traditionally a woman's job?'

They seemed to expect the visitors to have met with an aggressive male response to their non-traditional choice:

'Do the lads treat you the same?'
'Did you have a hard time with the men?'
'Were you given dirty or unpleasant jobs to see if you could do them?'
'Were you treated as a woman, or as one of the boys?'

A group of boys who met Stephanie, the qualified motor mechanic, immediately began to challenge her knowledge of cars and question her ability to repair them (reported in Catton, 1985). However they were soon impressed by her obvious grasp of the technicalities of car maintenance. In contrast, Andy, the househusband, was asked if women were 'more sympathetic to his situation than men are', whether he had made friends with the other mothers and if he 'went for coffee mornings with the other mums'? The anxiety about other people's comments also related to possible experiences the children had had at school:

'Was you in a class of boys and did you feel left out?'
'Did the boys try to get you out of the woodwork class?'
'Did anyone try to persuade you not to do it?'
'Did your teachers put you off your job?'

* Manchester slang, 'ridiculed'.

And several questions were asked about the visitors' choice of subject at school:

'Were you always interested in metal?' (to Lydia, metallurgist)
'Did you like cookery and needlework at school?' (to Andy, househusband)
'Did you do woodwork at school?' (to Annette, woodworker)

Many girls seemed to be worried about the difficulty of doing a 'man's' job at all: they asked Lydia if it was 'hard and interesting', whether there was 'a lot of heavy work' and whether Stephanie found it 'hard to be a mechanic'?. They also showed that they expected to meet discrimination: one girl asked, 'How many interviews did you go to before you got the job?' (In Stephanie's case, the answer was 'only one'.) Alison, the furniture maker, was asked if it was hard to get the job because she was a female, and Janet whether it was a disadvantage 'to be a woman in one of these jobs'. An interesting answer by the telephone engineer was that she had found people particularly asked for her because she did a neat and tidy job, for example by not running wires across the middle of a wall when they could be put in a more unobtrusive place. Girls wanted to know what it was like working with men, whether they got chatted up a lot, whether they were accepted.

Younger craft visitors were popular; in one session an enthusiastic craft teacher told the children to 'come and watch this' when Yvonne Richardson was bending a piece of copper pipe over her knee, and a small group of girls was 'absolutely fascinated by . . . the sheet leadwork samples which the two [female] plumbers had brought along . . . the 3D curves intrigued them – they began trying to copy the shapes in paper and realized that the material had to *stretch* to obtain the particular shape' (GIST file notes).

Sometimes boys made use of the occasion to ask women visitors career-oriented questions on their own account. However, far more questions were directed at the men, and particularly at Andy, the househusband, an extroverted nonconformist, whose 'job' was not just non-traditional, but an example of role reversal. They wanted to know if he was embarrassed telling other people what he did and whether men made fun of him on the grounds that he wasn't good enough for a 'real' job. They asked if he got bored, and did he just sit at home all day, or actually do housework. Some boys were clearly surprised on one occasion when Andy explained his experiences with nappies and how he used to use a triangular but now preferred a 'kite' method. They seemed shocked to find such knowledge in a man, and had not really considered how many times a day a 2-year-old's nappy has to be changed! The issue of male sexuality often arose, at first because Andy was in the habit of coming along wearing nail varnish. GIST file notes record that all the classes who met Andy on Thursday were intrigued by his nail varnish, and the kids agreed among themselves that he was 'queer'. Andy later left off the nail varnish, as it seemed to be so distracting, but the male nurses were also posed questions such as, 'Don't you think it's a bit poofish for a man to be a nurse?' and, 'Do people think you're queer?' More tactfully, girls asked the men questions exploring the affective sphere: did the nurse get embarrassed when asked about people's problems? Was Zoë (the 2-year-old) more affectionate towards him or his wife, since he was the one at home? The impact of the male visitors was greater, perhaps because the children were already used to meeting women in non-traditional jobs.

In many ways the visits were a new experience for the children, who were neither very used to visitors nor commonly in a position to hear adults disclosing so much personal information about themselves. Paul Barfi for instance explained that he was a single parent, cooks (he is also a home economics teacher) and looks after his children. Alison, the furniture maker, offered the observation, 'I'm really quite good at making things', and in general the visitors were prepared to reveal as much about their personal and home lives as about their experiences at work.

Response to the roadshows

The roadshows were a kind of performance put on by GIST for the schools, not necessarily with the full help or support of the teaching staff. At Green Park, discussion of non-traditional options fitted somewhat uneasily with the kids' awareness that in that school they had not even been offered the opportunity to take non-traditional crafts. The GIST report says: 'I felt we were running counter to the messages . . . from the school, by saying that girls could take technical subjects . . . . I felt we were on shaky ground and that the staff would certainly not back us up . . . .' In the same session, a female teacher said loudly at the end, 'I don't believe in all THIS!', and later that afternoon the headteacher was seen diving into his office to avoid any discussion with GIST as we were leaving.

At Moss Green, a seemingly sympathetic head of careers never actually attended any GIST roadshows, but we discovered afterwards she had run some 'alternative' sessions of her own, inviting in female typists to, as she put it, 'redress the balance'!

A more subtle form of resistance was met at Edgehill, where the rather sophisticated middle-class children appeared comparatively receptive to non-traditional ideas. One of the teachers suggested the session could be livened up by a bit of artificial opposition, and GIST agreed to let that happen the next day. It developed into an argument between GIST and a male teacher about the relative physical prowess of men and women. It looks as if the teacher was using the pretext of livening up the session to express or project some of his own reservations about non-traditional alternatives. One of the visitors who was not 'in on' the arrangement became rather angry, and the children were probably more confused than anything else by the wrangling.

The responsibility of trying to manage the roadshows as a dramatic performance which would impress the children in the right way was really a very difficult undertaking. Not only did the attitudes of the teaching staff have to be kept in mind, but the visitors did not always strike just the desired note. They did not always remember, despite careful briefing, the points we wanted them to bring out; the telephone engineer, for example had to be prodded (by a young, interested male teacher) before she admitted that it would have been useful if she had studied physics at school. One of the male nurses, invited by GIST to indicate whether chemistry was useful for nursing (a point made repeatedly in the 'GIST Options and Careers booklet) said, 'No, not really.' The despair sometimes felt at these incidents comes over rather comically in this note by one of the team about questions to a craft visitor: '[child] asked Annette if she'd ever had an accident at work. To which she was forced to recount how she lost her finger, not a very positive image' (Edgehill roadshow, 17 January 1983).

Most of what has been said so far is based on the team's notes of children's reactions during the roadshows. Questions about VISTA in the second wave of testing gave some more information. As the roadshows had just taken place when the children were complcting these questionnairs, they were probably more readily recalled than some of the earlier visits. Certainly, all the male visitors were remembered by at least some of the children.

There was a clear sex difference in response to the meetings with men in non-traditional occupations (see Table 8.1). Boys gave significantly lower ratings to the home economics teacher, nurse tutor, househusband, nurse and domestic cleaner. The nursery nurse and district nurse were slightly better received. Overall, the girls liked meeting the men more than the boys did. However, the ratings overall were positive, suggesting that the roadshows were enjoyed just as the VISTA visits were.

TABLE 8.1 *Responses of boys and girls to male roadshow visitors*

	No. of mentions	Boys' mean rating	Girls' mean rating	Significant sex difference
Home economics teacher	27	1.9	2.6	yes
Nurse tutor	19	1.4	2.6	yes
Househusband	88	1.5	2.3	yes
Nursery teacher	11	2.5	2.7	no
Nurse	44	1.8	2.6	yes
Cleaner	18	1.9	2.4	yes
District nurse	2	—	2.0	no

Below 2 = 'boring' 2.0 – 2.5 = 'OK' 2.5 or higher = 'interesting'

Boys' more negative reactions to males in non-traditional occupations can be related to their tendency to give themselves higher masculinity ratings. They also reinforce the GIST finding that boys are markedly more sex-stereotyped than girls. This confirms other research findings which indicate that the burden of sex role stereotyping weighs more heavily on boys (Golden and Hunter, 1974). They can be expected to be less flexible about adopting attitudes or engaging in activities which have a feminine image. Moreover they are less willing to consider entering stereotypically feminine occupations. The second attitude survey also asked children to say which occupation they expected to choose themselves. The choices exhibit strongly sex-typed occupational preferences, suggesting that the roadshows had only minimal effect on children's actual choices. However the attitudes to sex-differentiated jobs for men and women did shift between the two rounds of surveys, and this may have been due, at least in part, to the enjoyable and unaccustomed experiences of the roadshows (see Chapter 13).

Chapter 9

Craft, design and technology – a hard nut to crack

Traditional crafts or design-based technology?

In Chapter 3 the case of Rachel, the pioneering technician trainee, was used to highlight the dilemma of a situation in which only a tiny minority of girls succeed in breaking through the various barriers set in their way by traditional job segregation. The arguments used by school craft departments to justify doubts about girls continuing to study crafts subjects after the third year reflect this dilemma. In every school, they reiterated that even if girls managed to get qualifications in technical subjects, they would still have to confront the prejudiced attitudes of employers, and to deal with a training situation in which they would be highly visible – and risible – with the strong possibility that thereafter they would be bound to drop out. There was an element of the self-fulfilling prophecy in this argument. If only one or two girls in any one year ever did automotive engineering or technical drawing, then what the teacher said was true and they still had many further difficulties to face. The schools' argument was particularly strong in relation to the traditional crafts of woodwork and metalwork which are so closely linked to the apprenticeship entry to the craft trades.

Secondary school teachers whose subject specialism is something other than CDT continue to cling to the idea of technical studies as 'manual training'. The old distinction between work for the hands and work for the brain places technical crafts firmly in the sphere of non-academic subjects. Many would recommend it to 'remedial' boys and would not think of advising a 'bright' girl to take up technical crafts.

There have been recent attempts to change this image. The new subject of craft, design and technology has been boosted from a second-class, non-academic subject to one which at national level by those involved in CDT education, HMIs and LEA advisers is regarded as a vitally important area of the comprehensive school curriculum. We believed that the experience gained on a problem-solving design-and-make type of course would be invaluable for girls in terms of transferable skills. The discussion document 'Understanding Design Technology' (from the Assessment of Performance Unit, 1981) suggests craft, design and technology can encourage 'the skills, knowledge and values by which men and women and, therefore, boys and girls come to grips with the problem of living in, and exerting their influence on, the man made [sic] world.' An Equal Opportunities Commission Working Party on Craft, Design and Technology has a similar description: 'the problem solving nature of the activity includes the study of practical applications, methods, processes, materials, energy, control and various forms of communication' (EOC, 1983).

We felt that craft, design and technology of this type could support girls' performance in maths and physical science and help them towards greater familiarity and understanding with the world of applied science and technology. Unfortunately only three of the action schools actually offered exam courses with a design and technology base (see Table 9.1). Girls choosing technical crafts in any of the other schools would find themselves doing a course traditionally associated with manual trades, and not necessarily carrying any of the benefits of new CDT syllabi.

In 1981 the Schools Council made a grant to GIST to support the recruitment of an ex-teacher of craft, design and technology to the team, to work directly with the craft teachers. A short list of candidates did include one woman but a man was eventually appointed largely because of his longer and more senior experience, but also, it must be admitted, because it was felt that a male teacher would have more credibility with the all-male crafts staff in the schools. The first serious complicating factor arose here. Both the Schools Council and GIST were interested not simply in encouraging more girls to enter technological fields, but also in promoting curriculum development which would begin to shift the actual content of the crafts syllabus away from its narrow focus on the acquisition of traditional metal and woodwork skills to a genuinely design-based, technologically inspired curriculum. In effect the new Schools Liaison Officer

TABLE 9.1 *Technical craft provision in GIST schools*

Technical craft provision	1979-80	1982-3
Offering to boys *only*	Green Park	No school
Offering *only* traditional crafts (woodwork, metalwork, technical drawing) to both sexes	Ashgrove Hamlet Sutton Hill Tall Trees	Green Park Hamlet Sutton Hill
Offering both traditional crafts and design based O-level or CSE	Meadowvale Edgehill	Ashgrove Tall Trees Meadowvale Edgehill
Offering *only* design-based and other CDT subjects	Moss Green	No school
Considering re-introduction of traditional crafts	No school	Moss Green

was taking on two innovative tasks at once and there were only two years of the project left to go.

Circus system or integrated crafts?

Table 9.1 shows how during the four to five years of the project, schools were gradually moving towards the new syllabi. Hamlet and Sutton Hill continue to offer only the traditional crafts (wood/metalwork and technical drawing at Hamlet, wood/metalwork only at Sutton Hill). By 1982-3, both Ashgrove and Tall Trees began to offer new design-based courses in addition to the old ones; just as Meadowvale and Edgehill had done at the start, and continued to do so in 1983. Moss Green, the only school which had virtually broken with woodwork and metalwork, also offered a number of vocationally relevant options: technical drawing, control technology, graphic communication engineering and motor vehicle technology. However by 1983 they were seriously considering the re-introduction of woodwork and metalwork because of the disappointing exam results on the new courses. The changeover at Tall Trees, and more especially at Ashgrove, owed a great deal to the support and advice in adapting to the new curricula, which John Catton, as Chief

Examiner for one of the new 'O'-levels, was able to offer. The decision at Green Park to open up technical crafts to girls was almost certainly precipitated by GIST, although as we shall see (Chapter 11) the school maintained that the project had had little influence on their curriculum practice.

During the course of his first year with us, the Schools Liaison Officer chaired an EOC working party on a craft curriculum, whose report (EOC, 1983) was well received when published. It advocated a design-based curriculum and a move away from woodwork by numbers or the view of crafts as simply preparation for entry to plumbing, building, car mechanics or other traditional manual occupations. This document is still rather a call to action and change than a reflection of real changes in the curriculum of ordinary schools.

A second complicating factor was that several schools interpreted equality of opportunity in technical crafts to mean that people should experience a roundabout or circus system whereby groups would have a period of time in a range of domestic and technical craft subject areas. The design circus system poses problems:

> [It] offers all pupils a sampling or tasting process of the various areas involved, the sampling process usually operates throughout year 1 but is continued until the end of year 3 in a number of schools. The most common pattern is to invite pupils to choose a small number of material areas upon which to concentrate in year 2 or year 3. Having been given a mini-option, pupils are almost always required to opt again at the third year options for subjects studied throughout years 4 and 5. (Catton, 1985)

Organizationally, the circus may be convenient but educationally it is less than satisfactory. The reality of such a scheme is that the pupils experience a series of short and unrelated areas of study, covered in no logical sequence (because only one group could do this on a rota). The group taking 'drawing' last of all, for example, will go through precisely the same work as the group who did drawing as their first area. This makes no allowance for related learning which is likely to have taken place in one or more of the other areas. It ignores the fundamentally sound principle of learning through previous experience. Finally, both pupils and teachers face the constant frustration of a series of changeover dates with the pressure to complete work, or as is often the case, see a box full of incomplete bits and pieces of material at the end of a number of weeks' work.

Mini-options divide the sexes

A further element which has the effect of channelling girls out of craft studies is the 'mini-options' system operated by many schools. As Fig. 9.1 shows, only three of the action schools (Group 1) offered an integrated crafts scheme for the full duration of lower school years. Crafts subjects were then opted for along with other subject options before entering the fourth year. Schools of the Group 1 type are therefore offering the maximum time currently available to girls in the school system for formal curriculum experience of CDT.

A second group of schools (Group 2) required children to make a 'mini-option' at the end of Year 2. At Tall Trees and Ashgrove it would be possible for a girl either to drop CDT or to take it without necessarily abandoning the traditionally feminine subjects. However Moss Green presented a forced choice between domestic or technical crafts, repeated at the end of the third year. This kind of system marks out craft subjects as different and ensures the attrition of girls as a group from subjects characterized as masculine. Hamlet offered even more limited chances to girls developing an interest in technical studies, by presenting a forced domestic or technical craft choice at the end of first year, when both girls and boys could have had only minimal experience of subjects non-traditional for their sex. Finally, Green Park offered no choice at all, but presented a sex-segregated crafts system throughout the first three years.

Ideally, if girls are to have a genuine opportunity to develop technical expertise and interests they should enjoy a full three years of integrated crafts (textile design, design in wood and metal, home economics, etc.) and at the end of three years be able to continue with the subject without necessarily dropping 'domestic' craft interests. Only Edgehill offered this ideal possibility; a few girls normally chose textile design in the fourth year, with only the occasional brave spirit opting for technical design.

There were therefore three strands in the CDT work with schools. We hoped they would:

(1) offer an integrated craft course combining 'domestic' and

School	Year 1	Year 2	Year 3	Year 4
Group 1 Edgehill Meadowvale Sutton Hill	Integrated crafts for both sexes throughout first three years			1 from DOM. or TECH.
Group 2 Tall Trees			2 from HOME EC. CDT ART	
Ashgrove	Integrated crafts for both sexes for first two years		2 from HOME EC. N'WORK W'WORK M'WORK	
Moss Green			1 from DOM. TECH.	1 from DOM. TECH.
Group 3 Hamlet	Integrated crafts for one year only	1 from DOM. TECH.		
Group 4 Green Park	Domestic crafts for girls Technical crafts for boys			

Figure 9.1 Craft options offered at GIST schools

'technical' elements without repetition or other negative features of the circus system;

(2) move away from traditional wood and metal classes to design-based, technology-focused work;

(3) offer integrated crafts to both sexes for three years, without 'mini-options'.

Adoptions of these policies implied simultaneously *organizational* and *curricular* changes, doubling the task for the Schools Liaison Officer and the pressure on schools to innovate. Inevitably, much of John Catton's time was spent on the curricular detail of 1 + 2, with the organizational issues raised by 3 presenting a variety of problems in each school setting.

The most difficult school context of all the action schools was undoubtedly Green Park, where none of the desirable elements (1 - 3) above obtained.

Crafts at Green Park

One action school, Green Park, and one control school, Burnbank, were possibly in contravention of the Sex Discrimination Act, denying any girls the opportunity to take craft subjects in the first three years, so that they received no formal craft or technical education whatsoever. When we first discovered this, and pointed it out to a senior member of staff, he replied mildly that the Health and Safety Regulations were probably broken in some school or another every day of the year!

At Green Park, girls could in theory opt for technical craft subjects in the fourth year, but in practice it was virtually impossible for them to do so. We were told of one girl who wanted to do metalwork; she was characterized as 'butch' partly because she had also won permission to play football with the boys, and was turned down by the crafts department, apparently on the grounds that she was making some kind of protest rather than expressing a serious desire to study the subject.

The notes which follow were made after visits to the school and during the long-drawn-out negotiations, starting in 1980, which led in the end to the school agreeing to offer integrated crafts, unfortunately not to the GIST cohort, but to the year below.

Green Park

> First Workshop, 10th July 1980
>
> Discovered at the workshop that school used to have 'craft circus' but recently reverted to girls' crafts and boys' crafts. Nobody seemed sure why. Craft teacher asked what he thought about it said Domestic Science staff glad to get rid of boys. [Said] he didn't mind but I got impression he was quite glad to be rid of girls. They are allowed to take it in fourth and fifth year (but don't!). I asked if separation was legal, no one seemed to know or care.

> They did not seem keen on changing classroom atmosphere to make it more cooperative to suit girls, said, 'They've got to go into a hard competitive world no point in mollycoddling them.'
>
> VISIT REPORT Green Park
>
> GIST proposed that if the Home Economics staff would agree to mixed classes in first or second year or possibly sex integrated crafts but in single-sex groups then the aim would be to extend their new Personal and Social Development syllabus, which was being implemented by the Head of Technical Crafts, to incorporate integrated crafts; GIST would offer the services of John Catton for possibly one afternoon per week. It was then agreed we should meet all the crafts staff for a full morning to discuss in private how these proposals might be implemented.
>
> VISIT REPORT 28th April 1981
>
> Despite a lot of lip service to equality they don't feel like changing the sex divided crafts curriculum and they claim that Home Economics is the main stumbling block, but other arguments were used, e.g. the departments of Art, Technical Crafts and Home Economics are physically widely separated. One argument might have been convincing, two suggests they are not really trying.
>
> VISIT REPORT 19th June 1981
>
> There was a minority viewpoint expressed to the effect that boys should come to technical studies in boys only groups and girls should visit the department in girls only groups. I am delighted to say this was not a popular suggestion!
>
> VISIT REPORT 15th July 1981
>
> The staff have agreed to go ahead with mixed crafts for next year's first years but definitely not the second years (i.e. the GIST cohort). They may not be entirely wholehearted about this 'experiment'. [Head of Crafts Dept] said they might drop the whole thing again in 1982 'if it didn't work'.

The upshot of these discussions, drawn out during the school year 1980–1, was a kind of quid pro quo. The school would introduce technical crafts for both sexes in the first year group entering in 1981, and 'in return' John Catton would take a mixed first year group for technical crafts one afternoon per week for two terms. Teachers involved in curriculum innovation often feel that research teams are unduly remote from the realities of classroom teaching (see Chapter 11), and the offer of a member of the team to teach in the school demonstrated GIST commitment to the proposed curriculum innovation. Members of the crafts staff were invited to observe John's lesson, as a way of promoting discussion of some of the new approaches to CDT teaching. He also promised to offer an after-school craft club, in the hope of attracting some girls from the GIST cohort and giving them a taste of technical design studies. The full description of his work at Green Park and the ideas on which it was based appear in the sourcebook for craft teachers by John Catton (1985). Highlighted are some of the incidents and events he reports.

It seemed important to establish a girls' technology club at Green Park, because the GIST cohort of girls was timetabled only for domestic crafts. During a year assembly pupils were reminded that while first year girls could do technical crafts, second years did not: this was their opportunity to 'equal the boys at their own game and enjoy themselves'. Thirty-two girls signed up, but not all came to the first meeting. Eventually a regular group of fourteen to sixteen arrived in the workshop at 3.45 p.m. each Thursday.

> The sessions were mostly informal and apparently very enjoyable for all concerned, I was amazed how quickly the girls changed from being very apprehensive in a part of the school they had not used before, to being highly confident and at times even rowdy as they arrived for work. I even learned some new jokes.
>
> I attribute much of this confidence to the fact that boys were not present; if a girl didn't understand something she didn't hesitate to ask for clarification or assistance. (Catton, 1985)

However the boys were not always far away. Sometimes they gathered outside the workshop and peered through the windows to see what the girls were doing, shouting and jeering to the effect that 'girls can only make a lot of mess'. Being ignored, they drifted away, but the incident testifies to the open hostility girls must have faced from some of their male classmates. Amongst the club's activities, the 'woodpecker' project proved particularly enjoyable and satisfying to the girls (see Catton, 1985). Ten girls from the GIST cohort opted for woodwork in the fourth year, showing that even such a short experience had built up their confidence sufficiently to overcome the disadvantage of joining boys who had done technical crafts for a full three years. By September 1983, the original ten had been reduced, by processes unknown, to seven, or 8 per cent. This was the highest percentage of girls taking woodwork in any of the action or control schools.

In the last active year of the project, when the GIST cohort was preparing for option choice, Green Park agreed to a GIST presence at the parents' evening and the following notes indicate how the situation was changing for a girl who wanted to continue with crafts in fourth year:

> 'Cath Wright [not her real name] brought her Mum to see me. Cath has been a 'regular' on the woodpecker project with me in the after school club . . . she explained that she wanted to do woodwork next year. She had discussed it with [wood teacher] who had seemingly been very supportive of the idea. However, her Mum thought it rather an odd choice for a girl. Mrs Wright explained, 'it doesn't seem right for a girl. I've already told her she should have been a boy . . . .' I put the case in support of Cath's choice. After this Cath said to Mrs W., 'See, I told you it wasn't a daft idea!' Mrs W: 'Well, that's the second teacher who thought it was a good idea and I suppose they know what's best!' Cath also said that [———] and [———] also wanted to do woodwork.

On the same evening, the headteacher asked GIST for information about retraining courses for sixth form girls who 'had maybe decided they'd made the wrong choice, say had chosen Arts instead of Science'. The limited effect of the small changes described here is indicated by two further notes from that evening: '[Deputy Head] came up and asked [about GIST display] "What's in it for the boys?" ', and 'A strong and efficient team of girls serving coffee – again!'

Earlier on Thursday afternoons John taught a first year mixed group. He began the very first period by deliberately arranging the register in alternate girl/boy order. There was no immediate reaction, but at the second meeting a boy asked, 'Sir, why are the names in your book mixed up instead of boys first and then the girls?' John's response, 'Why should I list the boys first?', provoked a classroom discussion which almost developed into a battle of abuse between girls and boys. It concluded with both sides agreeing that he should have listed the names in alphabetical order, a rational proposal which John accepted.

With this class, John chose to start with a vehicle testing project. In part this was because he wanted to challenge the belief of some CDT teachers that girls are only interested in design briefs with an aesthetic element and a 'feminine' association such as jewellery making. When the project had continued for several weeks the wheeled vehicles were tested by pupils by releasing them to run down a ramp. One of the girls hung back, saying that her vehicle was 'no good' and wouldn't run. In an effort to be encouraging, John offered to test the vehicle for her, and as she had predicted, it refused to move. The ensuing mocking laughter from the boys embarrassed her considerably. Realizing his mistake, John pointed out to the group that she had known the vehicle would not work, and proceeded to draw out from her the technical explanation: the hole drilled in the wheel was rather too large so that the wheels tipped sideways on to the axle, locking on to it. His praise for her grasp of the problem boosted the girl's morale to the point where, by oiling the wheels, she managed to make the vehicle run slowly down the ramp.

The incident pinpoints an unfortunate tendency of craft teachers, faced with schoolgirls who are inhibited or reluctant in the face of boys' assumed superiority and their open scepticism, to make no attempt to build girls' confidence in working with technical equipment. Too often, teachers resolve the dilemma by simply taking over and doing the job themselves.

The patronising craftsman

John Catton was fully aware of this propensity himself, because before joining the GIST project he had asked an English teacher at his previous school to observe him teaching a mixed group of fourth year pupils. Her main observation was that he responded in a noticeably different way to girls' requests for help compared with boys'. To a boy, he would suggest that a particular process or operation was now appropriate and send him off to get the right tools. To a girl, he would offer the same advice, but then proceed actually to do a substantial part of the work with the girl watching. Not only did this frequently deprive the girls of first-hand experience, it implicitly suggested that girls are less capable than boys in technical matters, a point of view the boys are already too willing to adopt. John had not been aware of this pattern of behaviour until it was pointed out to him. For example, John observed a teacher approaching a girl sitting on a bench. Assuming she was 'stuck' at something, he asked, 'What's up, luv?' Without waiting for a reply he took the work from her hand and saying, 'I'll sort it out for you', picked up a mallet and neatly bent her copper strip around a bar in the vice, forming a smooth curve. With, as John describes it, a 'silly grin' on his face he rather patronizingly advised her to take a cloth and finish hand polishing it.

A number of craft teachers have remarked to me that girls seem to like polishing and other less technical activities because they provide a chance for a gossip. But if girls are retreating from the more skilled and technical aspects of craft work, 'helpful' teachers who take over the 'fiddling' bits are only doing them a disservice, albeit with the best intentions.

Conclusion

The direct contact between a member of the GIST team and girls at Green Park school was successful, then, in producing a small and cohesive group of girls whose confidence in their own ability was now sufficiently strong to enable them to opt for a craft subject, in the face of the school norms which excluded girls from the craft workshop. It was an extremely time-consuming and labour-intensive use of one member of the team, but the outcome dramatically demonstrates what can be achieved, even under rather difficult conditions.

However, by challenging the sex segregated ethos at Green Park in this way, GIST must have reinforced the staff's sense that the project constituted a direct criticism of their practice. This clearly had a negative effect on teachers' attitudes, judging by the response of the teachers in evaluation interviews (see Chapter 11). It may also have brought out into the open the antagonism of the boys, who may have sensed that the adults concerned were divided about the value of girls doing CDT at all. The Green Park experience illuminates all too bleakly the difficulties and prejudices which come to the surface when the sex equality issue is confronted.

There was also a weakness in the crafts work never fully overcome in the life of the project. Whereas in science a large body of research evidence offered real hope that girls in mixed schools could achieve much more in the physical sciences than they were doing, there had been relatively little investigation of the crafts curriculum. While science teachers were readily accepting of factual evidence and prepared to adjust their professional practice accordingly, craft teachers do not have the same tradition of research-led curriculum development.

Before significant numbers of girls will ‘opt in’ to craft, design and technology, a considerable refurbishing of the craft curriculum will be required. There is no reason to doubt that girls, just as much as boys, can find enjoyment and satisfaction in mastering technical skills, or in planning and following through a design brief. However, in many of the GIST schools, the content and organization of the curriculum, no less than the stereotyped assumptions of many craft teachers, prevented girls from obtaining the authentic experience of competence and delight which craft, design and technology can potentially offer.

Chapter 10

Girls only?

The policy of comprehensive education begun in the 1960s means that most British secondary schools are now mixed, because it has been assumed that the demands of equality will best be served if girls and boys are educated together. The most substantial survey of attitudes to mixed schooling published between 1969 and 1974 (Dale, 1969, 1971, 1974) noted that boys benefited in academic terms from doing their work in mixed classes. The corollary, that girls might suffer academically, if not socially, was not seriously considered at the time. As one critic has put it, 'the policy of mass coeducation entered British schools on the coattails of the campaign to abolish selective schooling. . . [but] has been harmful for girls' (Shaw, 1980).

Polarization of subject choice seems to be more extreme in mixed schools. According to Ormerod (1981), pupils in coed schools make sex-typed choices especially in maths and science and possibly as a means of asserting their sex roles at puberty. Girls appear to do better in all-girls schools (Harding, 1981; HMI, 1979), but it is difficult if not impossible to separate out the effects of selection from the effects of removing the boys. Girls' grammar schools may be particularly successful in encouraging girls to do physical sciences, only because they have always seen as desirable the kind of equality which insists that girls have identical educational opportunities at least in academic subjects (Bone, 1983). For the purposes of GIST we accepted that coeducational schools are here to stay, and so were interested in devising strategies to deal with the problem that girls may indirectly suffer from the presence of boys.

Responses on various questionnaires showed that boys were more stereotyped in their attitudes than girls, and more likely to think that girls should not really be doing science. The evidence of our own classroom observations showed that boys 'edge girls out' of science and technology, which they regard as male territory.

Girls' clubs

We first suggested single-sex science classes during the initial workshops, but the idea was not taken up until much later, and on a rather different rationale from the clubs. As reported in Chapter 3, teachers on the whole were far from keen to divide the sexes experimentally. Their objections, apart from 'timetabling difficulties', were on the stated grounds that it ran counter to a comprehensive coeducational ethos, and on a feeling, usually unstated, that positive discrimination for girls would be unfair to boys.

Children acquire skills and knowledge informally in a concrete way through spare time activities and hobbies. Girls' lesser involvement in 'tinkering' activities was highlighted by the initial survey (see Chapter 7). The finding suggested girls might be handicapped at the outset in practical laboratory work and that they would need additional time and experience of such activities if they were to 'catch up' with the boys.

Our aim in supporting girls' clubs as an intervention was to provide a space and time in which groups of girls could build up their familiarity with the workshop and its equipment and develop the confidence to step over the invisible 'gender' barrier when it came to option choice.

Teachers were particularly impressed by the data from the Scientific Activities questionnaire, when it was fed back to them by the GIST team. They appreciated the possible causal link between hobbies such as building models and girls' poorer scores on the visuo-spatial and mechanical ability tests. The lack of tinkering experience was legitimized into a cause for action.

This reveals a certain tendency for teachers to accept authoritative – because 'objective' – evidence. From first-hand observation and experience, they must have 'known' already that girls play less with mechanical toys, and that boys would do better on mechanical and spatial tests. But intuitive knowledge for many science or craft teachers is not a sufficient justification for intervention, whereas objectively measured tests and attitudes are.

A major objection to single-sex clubs was thus removed: the educational deficit of girls had been exposed. In response, several teachers offered to run special lunchtime clubs for girls.

The actual number of girls in the GIST cohort who participated directly in a single-sex club must have been very small. The exception is Moss Green school, where the largest number of single-sex activities took place. In the other schools, the longest-running club continued for two terms. The effect of clubs being abandoned for lack of support may have been more negative than positive. On the other hand, the increase in girls opting for crafts in some schools may well have been the result of even short experiences of single-sex clubs (see Chapter 9).

Many teachers still clearly felt uncomfortable about offering something to female pupils but apparently leaving out the boys. It occurred to no one but us that the proper parallel would be to compensate boys with special lessons in cookery or social skills: when we tentatively broached that idea it was laughingly dismissed. Instead they solved their dilemma in a number of other ways. The male teacher at Tall Trees, who intended to start up a special technology club, could not bring himself to say it was open only to girls: 'to . . exclude the boys . . . would seem a little unfair since we are here to serve all the pupils' (Vlemmicks, 1983). Instead he stressed that 'it could be fun', society 'needs technologists', and girls were 'welcome' to join. When the appointed hour came for the first meeting, three girls and thirty boys arrived. Over the next few weeks the boys' numbers dropped and more girls were encouraged to attend, but it is interesting to note how an intended piece of positive discrimination rapidly became watered down.

At Moss Green school, the head of lower school science solved the problem by offering two separate groups, one on biological activities for the boys, the other using Fischer-Technik materials (the Fischer-Technik company kindly donated several sets of their equipment to GIST schools), and later Lego, with girls. It may have been a mistake to plunge so immediately into the use of clearly 'masculine' toys, as the girls did not seem to like the Fischer-Technik activities; making ginger beer was much more successful.

In a third school, the head of craft reported that an open invitation to a lunchtime club attracted only four girls. He then made a new announcement, stressing that he wanted some girls in the club, and ended with equal numbers of each sex.

At Sutton Hill, an all-girls' group was entered for the Granada

TV Power Game, and came second, and at Hamlet school a craft club for girls ran for over two terms during their first year. However the project work they were given was of the 'woodwork by numbers' type which has been criticized by those advocating a problem-solving approach. The end products were displayed at the second teachers' conference in March 1982.

The likelihood of GIST girls choosing crafts was strongly determined by the organization of the crafts curriculum in each school (see Table 9.1).

Hamlet segregated the sexes at the end of the first year and three others – Ashgrove, Sutton Hill and Moss Green – asked children to choose craft 'mini-options' at the end of second year. We tried to convince schools that early options in the most traditionally sex-typed subjects were bound to lead to a clear split between boys and girls. A craft project with similar concerns to ours found that mini-options effectively foreclose non-traditional choices (Grant, 1983).

The chief barrier to girls opting for traditional 'boys' ' crafts seems to be the fear of being uncomfortably visible in a male-dominated group. This emerged in a discussion with fourth year girls at Edgehill school arranged to try and identify in advance some of the problems the GIST cohort might face. One girl said she had considered doing metalwork but decided against it because she would hate to be the only girl in the class and have the boys beat her. Another girl, who had actually opted for technical studies (one of four), said she was 'really scared the first day . . . they don't say anything, but it's the atmosphere when you walk into the room' (Visit Report, Edgehill, 10 November 1982).

Work experience course

At Tall Trees school, a new head of the science department who joined the staff part way through the project seemed keen to develop some interventions for GIST. At his previous school, an all-girls single-sex grammar, he had arranged work experience courses in engineering, and wanted to organize a similar course in a local electronics firm for the GIST cohort.

Running such a course from a mixed school presented problems under the equal opportunities legislation, as it could be considered educational provision from which boys were excluded. At this point both the headteacher and the head of science began to question whether they needed to go to all the bother of registering under Section 47 of the Act, which permits positive discrimination for either sex, if there have been traditionally limited opportunities for that sex in the past. They even wondered whether girls-only groups were really necessary. GIST strongly supported the value of girls' groups in such a context, and eventually the dilemma was resolved when the Engineering Industries Training Board (EITB), already registered under the Act, agreed to sponsor the course. By then it was unfortunately too late to run it for the GIST cohort before they made their option choices. In the end, forty girls from the third and fourth year attended the two-day courses in October 1983. (For further details, see EOC, 1984).

Trip to design workshop

Another exercise in deliberate 'positive discrimination' was carried out at Moss Green school. At the end of the second year, the GIST cohort had to opt for craft subjects (see Figure 9.1). The school was aware of our advice that mini-options are likely to reinforce the sex-typed character of crafts, but the school was undergoing reorganization at the time, and the staff did not wish to introduce further organizational changes just then. However, they did invite GIST in to speak to second years about the importance of design-based courses for girls. Possibly as a result, twenty girls opted to continue CDT for a further year, more than had ever done so before at Moss Green.

These girls were then taken on a special outing to a design workshop in the Faculty of Art and Design at Manchester Polytechnic, where there is a high proportion of women students. A lecturer in product design demonstrated a third year woman student's project, a special surgical splint and accompanying pushchair. They met women students and saw exhibits of their work in titanium, wood and glass. The day excursion is more fully reported by Toft and Catton (1983). Six months after the trip, one of the girls was interviewed by Barbara Smail, in connection with her study of a subsample of GIST girls; she said it was this visit which had inspired her to aim for a career in design herself, and determined her to opt for CDT again at the end of the third year.

Two smaller interventions at Edgehill had similar aims, but were not so directly career-oriented. Senior girls doing A-level design were invited by the Head of CDT to help him with third year classes, with the idea that they might function as 'role models' for the younger girls. By acting as teaching assistants and demonstrating the use of tools and equipment, it was hoped they would incidentally impress on third years that girls can be competent in the workshop. The 'implicit' nature of this exercise may explain why it seems to have produced minimal effects on girls' craft choice at Edgehill.

The same head of CDT was persuaded to inform the parents of pupils who had done particularly well on the GIST spatial and mechanical tests. A priori arguments suggested that performance on these tests might be relevant to achievement in CDT. After considerable discussion, it was decided letters must go to boys' parents as well, on the grounds that it would be unfair, even possibly illegal, to exclude boys. Although both sexes were included in the scheme, it was expected to have more effect for girls who might otherwise never consider taking the subject. This last example is illuminating, as it shows teachers being excessively careful not to disadvantage boys in any way, although all sorts of school provision could equally be held to be unfair, but to girls. For instance, sports facilities and expenditure are frequently much greater for boys' than for girls' sports, and girls, but not usually boys, may be expected to hand round tea or coffee and wash up after school functions.

Maths competition

In 1980, the team were grateful and touched to receive £100 donation from the friend of Valerie Myerscough, a lecturer in Applied Mathematics at Queen Mary College who had died from cancer in her early thirties. Her friend requested that the money should be used to encourage more girls to become interested in the study of mathematics. After much thought, the team decided to offer 'Valerie Myerscough Maths Awards' to second year girls in the GIST schools. Prizes of a £5 book or record token were awarded to groups of two, three or four girls for problem-solving mathematical projects. The scheme was devised and operated by Barbara Smail.

Single-sex classes

The most sustained experience of single-sex clubs or classes was enjoyed by girls at Moss Green. As well as the single-sex science clubs for girls and boys already mentioned, there were special work clinics provided by the head of lower school science, a technology club ran for a short time and a group of girls was taken on a special visit to the College of Building.

GIST was invited as a compensation for the 'no change' of options decision to come and speak to the pupils beforehand about the value, especially for girls, of taking technical options. It seems likely that the evidence of staff support for girls who wanted to continue technical studies made itself felt to the children. A relatively large group of twenty girls chose to continue with technical studies in the third year, and at the final option hurdle in the summer of 1983, there was a notable rise in the number of girls making non-traditional craft choices (see Table 13.3, page 218).

In the Tameside Authority (part of Greater Manchester), several schools have experimented with single-sex teaching. In 1979, Stuart Smith, Deputy Head of Stamford Park School, invited us in to talk about the results of his experiment with single-sex setting in maths. The scores on class tests of girls who had been in single-sex groups were higher than those of comparable girls who had spent the first two years in mixed maths groups. Smith continues to monitor the experiment, and is so far not able to show positive results with a clear statistical significance: however he and his staff feel that the experience is beneficial in many ways, and the girls certainly prefer single-sex maths groups, though they like being taught English in mixed groups (Smith, 1980).

As part of the Girls and Science Initiative in Tameside, two schools tried single-sex science teaching, and monitored the outcomes carefully. Their evaluation showed significant improvement in the performance of girls; a small increase in the number of boys' scores going below 50 per cent was not statistically significant. Despite this objective measure of modest success, teachers seemed intuitively to believe that brighter boys were being held back because of the poor discipline in all-boys' groups. Gill Rhydderch in the Progress Report of the experiment said that staff attitudes 'may be an overriding factor in determining whether the scheme continues or not, even if it can be shown objectively that girls are benefiting from it' (Rhydderch, 1982).

A year later, teachers involved in the project, and Janet Dawe, one of its leaders, were reported as saying that they felt single-sex science teaching was far from being an ideal answer, and the experiment was likely to come to an end. Among the main problems, apparently, were the indiscipline from the boys, apathy amongst the girls, negative responses from some teachers, and a fear that prolonging the scheme would lead to the 'ghettoization' of a particular, and inferior, form of 'girls' science' (*The Times Educational Supplement*, 24 February 1984).

We felt that a first and important step was for teachers to recognize and admit the justification for some kind of single-sex experience for girls, however temporary, and however limited. In the less competitive and more co-operative atmosphere of an all-girls group, the pupils would have more time to speak to the teacher and to thrash out any problems, misunderstandings or misconceptions. For a short time, they would be freed from the inhibiting presence of boys who, as one girl from Stuart Smith's school put it, 'jeer at you if you get the answer wrong, and call you a swot if you get it right' (*The Sunday Times*, 6 November 1983). It is the process of interaction between teacher and pupils and pupil and pupil which changes in a single-sex group. The different learning experience is particularly important in the male-dominated or boy-claimed subjects of maths, technology and physical sciences. This was the second major reason (in addition to the need for girls to compensate for their lesser pre-scientific and tinkering experiences) for trying to implement a single-sex grouping policy, if only as an interim measure. It would give teachers the chance to see how differently girls perform without the boys, and to guess at the lost opportunities which may go unnoticed because of mixed grouping.

In 1982–3, when the GIST cohort passed through their third year, a full-scale experiment in single-sex science teaching was mounted at Moss Green. The decision to do so was made by two men, the head of the school and the head of science. It was not purely accidental that these two were interested in trying single-sex setting. Mr A while he was at Brunel University had worked under Milton Ormerod, and was interested in his findings about girls' avoidance of physical sciences. Before becoming head at Moss Green he had held the post of deputy head in charge of the curriculum at Ashgrove and would have liked to try single-sex groups there, but as he delicately indicated, the head of department, who retired at the end of 1980, was unenthusiastic. Mr A was also joint editor of an educational journal, and he was interested in qualitative evaluation of classroom interaction. Mr B had once taught for three years in a mixed school down south, which usually divided the sexes for all teaching purposes. This experience had convinced him of the value of teaching girls and boys separately. He preferred teaching single-sex groups and believed they improved pupil behaviour. Mr A disagreed on this point, and expected possible behaviour problems, but both looked for a general improvement in attitudes to science and Mr A expected that more girls would opt for physics. (Two girls and sixty-five boys had chosen physics in 1982, so an increase was pretty well inevitable!) Both claimed they knew nothing of Stuart Smith's pilot scheme or its outcome. They said the stimulus to embark on their experiment was Margaret Crossman's talk at the GIST conference in March 1982 (Report from a teacher who had used Flanders Interaction Schedule to show greater participation by boys in science lessons: GIST Conference on Classroom Interaction). They had read some of Dale Spender's writings but found them unconvincing. They had also been motivated by the GIST findings of sex difference in science interests. In the third year, single science subjects were taught: biology, chemistry and physics. For all these classes, the year group was divided into three: one mixed group, one boys and one girls only. At the end of the year, the teachers and pupils expressed their satisfaction at the way the experiment had gone: a proof of their positive attitudes was the decision to continue single-sex grouping for the following year, 1983-4.

Significant differences showed up in girls' choice of physics in the GIST cohort at Moss Green (see Chapter 13). The second attitude survey confirmed that Moss Green was, in terms of both measures, the most successful GIST school. Figure 10.1 compares girls' scores on each of three attitude to science scales at the beginning and the end of the project with the rest of the action and the control schools. Girls at Moss Green grew considerably more sex-neutral about science, and slightly more positive in their feelings about science as a useful and desirable endeavour (see Figure 10.1.a and c, SCISEX and SCIWORLD). Boys continued to see science as a masculine domain and moved towards a more negative attitude on the SCIWORLD scale. The image of the scientist held by the boys scarcely changed, while girls' attitudes to scientists showed a considerable improvement (SCIENT). Moss Green is the only school of the ten in which girls' view of science as beneficial became more positive during the first three years (see Figure 10.1.c SCIWORLD). In all the other schools, this attitude to science became more negative, with the exception of boys at Edgehill.

At the end of this experiment the head of science believed that girls' attitudes 'have improved no end. . . they are more confident and more outgoing' (from notes taken during an interview with Mr B). Unlike staff in the Tameside schools, teachers at Moss Green were not particularly aware of discipline problems arising from the experiment. They found the boys 'if anything, less volatile'. A large group of thirty-seven boys (in

(a) SCISEX: Girls

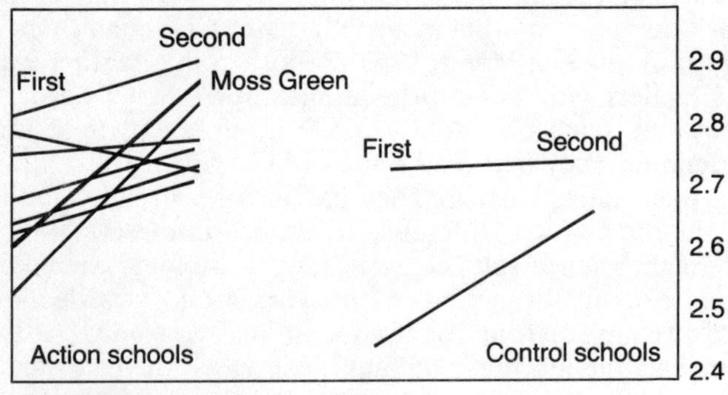

(SCISEX later changed to SCIMALE)

(b) SCIENT: Girls

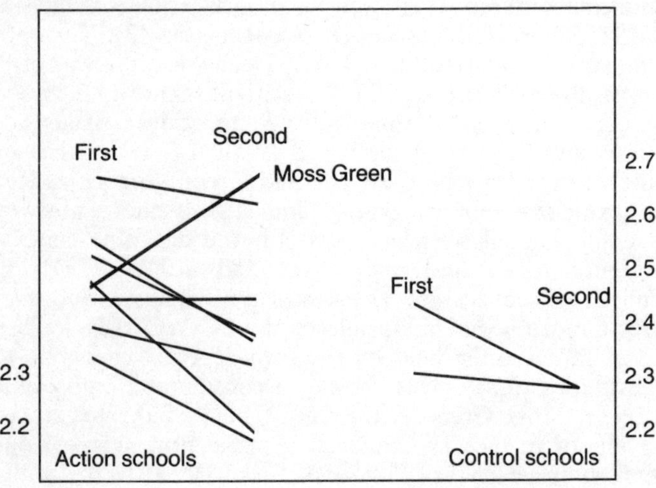

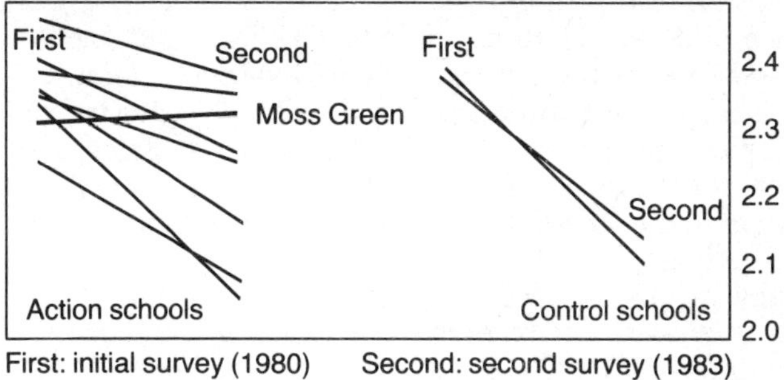

Figure 10.1 Image of science: Moss Green girls compared with girls in other schools

1983-4) was getting on extremely well, and a more awkward group was matched by an equally awkward bunch of girls. The children at Moss Green were specifically informed by their teachers that the purpose of the experiment was to encourage more girls to choose physical sciences, because the school's experience in previous years was that girls seemed to 'turn off' science in the third year. One of the positive benefits mentioned by the head of science to the children was that where sex education was concerned, topics could be discussed in mixed groups in PSE (personal and social education) but in single-sex groups in biology. Most of the teachers accept the new arrangement, even though it requires extra effort, because they feel it has proved itself in the form of improved chances of, especially, girls opting for physics.

Materials and resources to counter sex bias

Materials for science

Some supplementary materials, mainly in the form of worksheets, were produced by Barbara Smail at the request of science staff in several schools (see Chapter 6). But the image of science as a masculine subject is reinforced by the fact that women's achievements in science are largely unknown. To demonstrate to pupils that women have made important contributions to science

Other interventions

Barbara Smail produced some worksheets on women scientists suitable for use in the lower secondary school. The worksheets contain information about the women's lives and scientific work with related crosswords, quizzes and puzzles. They have now been incorporated into a booklet (Smail, 1983) illustrated by Kim Barrington, a student on the Design for Learning course at Manchester Polytechnic. The booklet and worksheets were popular in the GIST schools and have been ordered by many other schools.

Many school science laboratories display the poster series Great Scientists. The scientists featured in it are all men, with the exception of Marie Curie who is surrounded by her family. GIST suggested to the Equal Opportunities Commission that similar posters about women scientists would help to counter the masculine image of science. They agreed, and a series of six posters has now been produced. The scientific information was supplied by GIST and the graphics were done by the EOC. The posters, attractively produced, are available free of charge from the EOC.

Materials for CDT

Patterson (1980) described a tape slide presentation *Why Science?* which was developed to demonstrate to pupils, particularly girls, the range of jobs for which physical science was a useful qualification. We obtained a copy of this presentation and used it during option choice evenings and on other occasions in the GIST schools, where it was well received. However, nothing similar existed in the craft, design and technology area, so we decided to produce a similar tape-slide show called *Why CDT?*

In 1983 John Catton did so, in conjunction with photography student Susan Reynard.* The slides show the importance of CDT in a range of technical jobs and also stress the point that the interpretation of symbolic information enters into many aspects of life, from putting together self-assembly furniture to getting the best value for money when purchasing electrical equipment. Early versions were shown during option choice evenings in GIST schools. The finished product with accompanying notes will

* Susan Reynard was tragically murdered in Derbyshire later that year. *Why CDT?* contains the only published examples of her work and we would like it to be seen as a tribute to her.

be distributed through the Schools Council/Drake Distributors Ltd for use in in-service teacher training.

'Gender in our Lives' Workpack

Few materials offering information about non-traditional opportunities and lifestyles to pupils aged 12-14 actually exist. GIST prepared a pack suitable for use in personal and social education (PSE), including some published and some original discussion materials and exercises. For instance in our pilot survey of children's attitudes, a definite stereotype emerged of the female scientist as a brainy, hard-working, slightly odd woman, rather like a witch, whose experiments often went wrong. A section of 'Gender in our Lives' attempts to lead children into critical questioning of both negative and over-idealized images of women, by examining prejudices which in the past defined some women as 'witches'. The pack was piloted in three schools, and appeared to be most successful at Edgehill, where it was used in the context of an existing PSE syllabus, and taught by a group of sympathetic and interested teachers. The material needs further development and will probably be passed on to two teacher groups, one for PSE in Manchester, the other a careers education group in Sheffield.

'Fair Shares' video

A colour video was produced by third year students at the Manchester Polytechnic School of Film and Television, in consultation with GIST. It is intended for use in school-based in-service training, and illustrates some features of classroom interaction through dramatic reconstruction of incidents we had observed in laboratories and workshops. The 16-minute video, with accompanying discussion notes, will be distributed through the School Curriculum Development Committee (formerly Schools Council)/Drake Distributors Ltd.

Part V

The GIST teachers

Chapter 11

The teachers' perceptions of GIST

This chapter describes the attitudes of teachers involved in the GIST project, their increasing awareness of the issue, and of the possible sources of girls' underachievement in science and technology. Chapter 12 attempts to evaluate changes not only in teachers' attitudes but in their behaviour, especially in the classroom, and to explain why some teachers made positive independent efforts in line with the project's aims, while others adopted a wait-and-see policy, and some scarcely changed their practice at all. The degree of change in teachers' perceptions of the girls and science problem, and their consequent actions in school, depended only partly on an individual teacher's attitude. Also important was the issue of whether the atmosphere and practice of the school was supportive or otherwise to the aims of the project. The effects on teachers' attitudinal and behavioural change in the context of a particular school ethos are discussed in Chapters 12, 13 and 14.

Teachers' attitudes were studied in two ways. First, after each visit to a school we made notes on what had happened, including comments on the teachers' responses. These notes provide a record of the way in which the commitment of individuals and departments varied during the course of the project. Second, we invited a team of independent evaluators – three male sociologists from the School of Education, Manchester Polytechnic – to talk to the teachers about their impressions of GIST and to assess the way their opinions and classroom practices had altered (recorded in Payne *et al.*, 1984). (GIST schools were also included in a student survey of teachers' attitudes which did not mention the project by name but included questions about sex differences in science and technology (Kelly *et al.*, 1982) At the time of writing, analysis of this data is not complete, but references are made below to some preliminary findings.)

Following the invitation to the evaluators, several discussions were held about the nature and process of their reporting. Both teams were agreed that the GIST project, with its emphasis on sex equality, was inevitably value-laden, and that the methodology employed must at least be open to view. There was also concern to maintain the confidentiality of the interviewees without reducing the worth of the report as a reflection and summary of the impact of GIST on teachers.

The sampling technique chosen was as follows: GIST gave the evaluators a list of staff with whom we had had contact in five action schools, in the categories of 'science', 'CDT' or 'other', the 'other' category consisting mainly of senior staff – heads and deputy heads – and staff from other departments, e.g. heads of year and teachers with pastoral responsibility. The teachers in each category were further subdivided into three groups according to their estimated level of commitment to the project, and the evalutors were asked to select one teacher from each subgroup. However, as a note to the list pointed out, substantial reorganization in certain schools meant that in some subgroups no one or just one person was eligible for interview, since involved people had left. The detailed listing was necessary because our contact in most schools was only with staff teaching in lower school and we did not want the evaluators to waste time interviewing teachers with whom we had little or no relationship.

The authors, George Payne*, Ted Cuff and Dave Hustler, had a strong preference for a methodological approach offering 'detail and colour, rather than, say, statistical abstractions' (Payne *et al.*, 1984, p. 1). With some reservations the GIST team agreed to their chosen methodology. We accepted the authors' claim to objectivity in relation to feminism – '[we are] three males with no known commitment to female liberation' (ibid., p. 2) – which rested on the fact that their chosen methodology supplies the raw materials, i.e. transcripts of interviews. However, we were uneasy that their commitment to ethnomethodology implied a refusal to summarize or evaluate. Indeed for the ordinary reader, the report does not seem to reach a clear overall conclusion about GIST; the commentary needs to be studied with

* We regret to say that George Payne died of cancer shortly before the report was published. We are extremely grateful for his courage in continuing this work under the most difficult circumstances.

care to appreciate their interpretation of the findings.

Although the original agreement with the evaluation team was that they would produce transcripts of interviews with the teachers, in the event only six full transcripts were produced from thirty-four interviews. None of the teachers at Green Park school would agree to their interviews being taped and described. Thus in twenty-eight of the interviews, the only record available is the evaluators' summary, and these summaries were presented in their report. Teachers' comments in Payne *et al.* (1984) are therefore reported in two ways: direct transcripts, and summaries of what the teachers said.

The procedure for interview selection is perhaps also worth noting. Twelve teachers were interviewed in the school GIST had described as 'poor', but only seven or eight in the three schools listed as 'good' or 'medium'. Of the twelve respondents in the 'poor' school, four declined to be taped. A fifth was not on the original sample list of those who had been in contact with GIST: it was reported that he 'knew nothing about GIST. He had heard of it only yesterday. . .' (ibid., p. 37). In School B, only one member of the science staff, the head of department, remained in the school after reorganization. He was therefore the only one eligible for interview in that subgroup, but was not chosen by the evaluators. The reason given in the report is the need to protect teachers' confidentiality, but this problem of only one teacher appearing in some subgroups means that many teachers with whom the GIST team had most interaction could not be interviewed. At School B, two other teachers were chosen instead, but they had only been in the school a matter of months. The evaluators do refer to these difficulties, and readers of the report should perhaps bear in mind that the sampling technique negotiated between the two teams is in many respects unsatisfactory, with a possible bias of teacher representation, for example in School C, where six science teachers out of a possible six were interviewed.

Nevertheless, the evaluation report is, as the authors promised, rich in colour and detail. It does provide material insights into teachers' perceptions of changes at that point in time, given that a before-and-after study was never really possible. Its purpose was partly to indicate whether GIST had been a 'success'; as the evaluators say, the fact that several teachers did admit to considerable changes in attitudes and practice is a strong indication of 'success' given the general reluctance to admit to any changes at all (ibid. p. 78). But given the teachers' protestations that they really did not need to change in any case, the report requires an intelligent reader capable of appreciating the underlying implications.

The chief criticism of GIST in the report is that the team consistently viewed the teachers and schools in the context of the project and its aims, often making too little allowance for the complex web of responsibilities facing teachers at an everyday level. As outsiders, we were seen as lacking awareness of teachers' other professional concerns. This point highlights the difficulty of trying to innovate around an issue – equal opportunities – for which, at the time, no single member of staff in any school had clear responsibility. GIST could always be pushed to the back of a queue of other more pressing commitments. The evaluators suggest that this kind of innovation demands 'a more powerful and realistic model of everyday life in schools'. The report offers the best evidence which could have been collected to reflect the resistance of many teachers to the positive promotion of sex equality at school; and yet careful study of the document shows that there were many others who had consciously begun to consider new ways of encouraging girls, e.g. 'no, the one thing I've tried is modify my language . . . y'know they made me aware of that' (ibid., p. 89).

The GIST research design required a largish number of schools and schoolchildren, and a school-focused rather than school-based approach. More rapid change might result from an approach begun within schools, in which certain members of staff have clear responsibility for promoting the innovation. In our position as an external team asking for innovation in attitudes and beliefs as well as practice, we tended to be seen by teachers as curriculum developers, and/or a group offering guidance on how to change children's attitudes. It would have been counterproductive to start by asserting that teacher attitudes and school norms were also part of the problem. Nevertheless, that implied criticism was realized by most teachers, and acted on by many.

The two main sources of evidence for the teachers' response to GIST (field notes and evaluation interviews) show, first, that in spite of our 'softly, softly' approach the team were clearly perceived as feminist-inspired, albeit 'level-headed' and professional in conduct. Second, teachers' responses varied according to their age, their sex, their status and the subject they taught in the school. Third, many teachers did alter their attitudes and beliefs about the GIST problem, but were scarcely aware that they had done so (see Chapter 12).

Perceptions of GIST as feminist

Several teachers expressed the belief that by focusing on girls' underachievement, the GIST project would be neglecting the boys. The male senior teacher at Moss Green was 'worried about the effect of the project on boys in the school' and went on to remark, with unconscious circular logic, that the current shortage of physics teachers meant 'there's no point in getting more kids to do science' (from field notes). A male deputy head told us we were on 'the wrong tack: many pupils cannot do physics, we need more boys in technology, not just girls' (from field notes). A male headteacher saw underachievement as a general problem in his school 'but it affects boys as well as girls . . . why does not someone investigate why boys do not do modern languages?' (Payne *et al.*, 1984, p. 38).

The issue was highlighted by the authors of the evaluation report (all men) who chose the slightly jokey or mocking title of *GIST or PIST* for their document. They were referring to the following comment by a male science teacher: 'It has been extremely biased in that way, agh, I think the project should have been called PIST in terms that it should have been Persons' (p. 82). A teacher with a very similar attitude, who may indeed have been the same individual, took a mischievous 'enfant terrible' role from the start of his contact with GIST. He defined himself as an arch male chauvinist at an initial workshop, yet later became a strong advocate of GIST within the school, specially arranging meetings of staff to carry out interventions. On one visit he told us he had not changed his attitude towards women – he still liked to open doors for them – but felt he had changed his professional attitude about the way he should treat 'young ladies' in the classroom. In other words, he retained the right to preserve his self-image as a chivalrous and gentlemanly person, while recognizing the possibility that over-consciousness of gender in the classroom can subtly disadvantage girls.

Despite the tongue-in-cheek comment about 'Persons Into Science and Technology', the teacher who spoke to the evaluators said, 'Oh yes, obviously it's made some difference, ahh, it's no longer really farcical . . . . I . . . possibly look a little more carefully at materials . . . I think, yes, one has become aware . . .' (p.83).

The feeling of undue feminist bias was much more strongly echoed by other teachers, particularly at Green Park:

'The worst feature of GIST is in the danger of moving with "Women's Lib"; they seem to lean very heavily to the female side to the detriment of the boys, so they have to watch their balance.' (p. 50)

'It [the project] appeared to be so girl-oriented as almost to discriminate against boys.' (p. 33)

In fact the evidence on the effects of GIST suggest that boys benefited at least as much as girls from interventions such as VISTA (see Chapters 5, 8 and 13). Some teachers seemed to base their fear of feminist bias simply on the sex composition of the team; for instance, a female head of science said,

'The worst feature of GIST was the people doing it, i.e. the way they went about it. There should have been more men on the team.' (p. 33)

The only man on the team was, on the whole, better received:

'John Catton's work with third year girls was much appreciated.' (p. 46)

'Certainly . . . the project team have been hardworking and very sincere. . .' He notes that John Catton seemed very dedicated and that his work was not at the expense of the boys. (p. 53) (head of CDT)

Women's pressure groups don't help: they turn people off by their aggressiveness. This is a feature of the project team as well which, in his view, has not helped with some staff. He does say however that John Catton has been very welcome. (p. 55). (CDT teacher)

'John Catton has been helpful – he has printed stuff, got typing done and had some good ideas.' (p. 29) (head of crafts)

'He does suggest that John Catton has influenced what he does, although this is specified to refer to the visit to John Catton's [former] school.' (p. 41) (woodwork teacher)

'John Catton may have had some influence on the choice of projects.' (p. 42) (head of technical craft)

Many such comments came from craft teachers, who obviously saw more of John Catton. On the evidence both of his reports and the evaluation interviews, there was often a tendency for them to shift discussions away from the 'girls' issue and on to questions of the craft curriculum, a less controversial and per-

TABLE 11.1 *The GIST teachers*

		No. of teachers	No. of male teachers	% male
Physics	All schools	28.5	23	81
	Action schools	22	19	86
Chemistry	All schools	28.5	21	74
	Action schools	23	19	83
Biology	All schools	37.5	14	37
	Action schools	29	10	34
Technical crafts	All schools	46.5	46	98
	Action schools	36.5	46	99
All science and crafts	All schools	141	104	74
	Action schools	110.5	84	81

haps to them more rewarding topic of conversation.

As Table 11.1 shows, 80 per cent of the GIST teachers were male. On the other hand, 75% of the GIST team were female. Several teachers arranged to have informal chats with John Catton in the pub, but this never occurred with the women on the team! Our sex for at least some of the men was a fact they could never overlook, and constituted a barrier in itself. In some ways our status as an autonomous group, without a visible male 'boss', may have troubled them too. The project, directed by women, represented in a small (very small) way a picture of women in positions of some responsibility, and the reactions to us can be understood as reflecting conflict about women in assertive, non-subordinate roles: One comment, for instance, was: 'It's unfortunate that the two people from GIST he's seen most of have been women. They are very pushy, they hound you, but that's their job' (p. 30).

The head's chief criticism was 'also something of a compliment, namely that the GIST team are zealots and push their own concerns before any others in the school, for if they did not do so, they would be pushed out in the general maelstrom of school life, with its many competing activities' (p. 23). In this school the evaluators thought 'there has been positive impact and changes within both science and craft areas . . . senior staff have not been as supportive as they might' and give 'the impression of balancing interests and holding the fort, to some extent, against the demands of both team members and committed feminists on the school staff' (Payne *et al.*, 1984, p. 63).

The dilemma here is not easily resolved. A team led by a man could only have reinforced the stereotype of women as subordinate to men. A team largely composed of men would also have had real difficulty in understanding girls' classroom experiences; in pushing the feminist aims of GIST they may, as John Catton often felt happened to him, have been distracted from the sex differences issue on to basically less relevant questions of subject curriculum development. On the other hand, considerable efforts on the team's part to appear 'reasonable' were partially successful:

> the GIST project has been handled sensitively . . . he [headteacher] was particularly impressed by the fact that when the enlarged team came recently into the school, they split up in the staffroom and engaged many staff in animated conversations, whereas normally visitors tend to group together 'for protection'. (p. 41)
>
> For him the best feature of GIST is the professional way they go about a worthwhile project. The worst feature is the failure of the team to appreciate that the school has many other things to do. (p. 14).

The extra time and work involved in co-operating with GIST was an important restraint on teacher commitment, especially if not allowed for by the school. The student survey of teachers' attitudes (Kelly *et al.*, 1984b) has yet to be fully analysed, but preliminary results suggest that science teachers in the action schools were *less* likely than teachers in other schools to agree that 'it is important to find ways of encouraging girls to study physical science'. This suggests that they may be more aware than their colleagues of the work involved in implementing school-based innovations. Nisbet, in an account of the problems which inevitably accompany any innovation, describes the 'first wave of difficulty' as an increase in everyone's work load. The difficulty can be overcome, and the innovation survive, only if support services and additional time are provided to the innovating teachers (Nisbet, 1974).

Different teacher responses

Men/women

Of the eight science departments in the action schools only one was headed by a woman (Green Park). All the heads of physics and chemistry were male while six out of eight heads of biology were female. Crafts staff in the action schools were exclusively male, though Moss Green had a female CDT student on teaching practice for one term, and Edgehill had a half-time art teacher who sometimes taught CDT. It would be over-simplistic to imagine that a teacher's sex determined their attitude to the aims of GIST. All women are not feminists any more than all men are male chauvinists. However, amongst GIST teachers the most negative and traditionalist responses certainly came from craft departments.

Some female teachers of traditionally feminine subjects such as home economics, commercial studies or typing were unhappy about the possible impact of the project on their subject area, but on the whole more likely than the men to espouse the equal opportunity aims of the project. One or two female physicists seemed to have less than a full understanding of the difficulties facing girls entering a masculine area. Presumably they themselves had succeeded in physics and so not experienced insecurity about scientific study in general, or possibly they were more extroverted and androgynous in their ego identity (see Smail, 1983a).

Men have to make an imaginative and empathic leap in order to get an insight into the experience of the subordinate sex, while for women the knowledge is already available at first hand. Men teaching more 'empathic' subjects – drama, English, personal and social studies – could intuitively grasp the source of women's resentment at discrimination (see page 170 below). Without this understanding, many men appear to be strongly resistant to any suggestions of positive discrimination to redress the existing bias against girls. Even when boys considerably outnumbered girls in existing science and craft groups, male teachers were often unwilling or unable to see the point of bending the stick the other way. For instance a male teacher, asked whether he was keen to see more girls in a fourth year course where there were currently twenty-four boys and one girl, responded that he did not want to show favouritism 'to either sex'.

Characteristically, men's reasons for supporting GIST had little to do with abstract 'justice' or 'inequality', but more to do with utilitarian considerations such as improving science teaching in general, or increasing the number of pupils taking exam courses. For example, an older head of physics was worried that almost all the boys in his year had opted for physics, although he was sure many would get only CSE grade 4s. He appreciated the possible benefits of getting some more able girls. Another male subject head had told us he hoped that contact with GIST might help 'improve science teaching methods' in the department.

A male science teacher speaking to the evaluators about VISTA said that

> the idea of the speakers was excellent . . . it's encouraging a general interest in science which he applauds – i.e. it's what the project's doing for science rather than for girls in science which is welcomed. (p. 20)

Technical crafts staff in particular had a tendency to move rapidly away from the 'equality' issue towards discussion of the status and development of their subject. Of a head of crafts, Payne *et al*. report:

> When asked to name good/bad points about GIST he moves immediately into content areas – linking GIST to CDT developments automatically . . . a recurring theme throughout is the new approach to CDT.

And of a metalwork teacher:

> He is sore about what happens in upper school where the brighter boys and girls are 'streamed out' into other subject areas. (p. 31)

Age

Middle-aged and older teachers were likely to find the aims of the GIST project more problematic than younger teachers who were perhaps living out more flexible family roles in their own homes. The significance of age as a variable can be seen as related to the process of occupational socialization. Student teachers often espouse an ideology of equality and progressivism which is at odds with the within school norm of sex differentiation and inequality. However, this progressivism may be adopted largely in order to satisfy the perceived expectations of college staff (Hanson and Herrington, 1976, p. 16). When a student becomes a member of a school staff s/he reverts to the more conformist attitudes said to be characteristic of teaching as a profession (Morrison and McIntyre, 1969).

One aspect of this process of occupational socialization is the significant matter of dress. Education students frequently complain about the insistence of schools that men wear a shirt and tie and women come in dresses or skirts on teaching practice. Students' eventual willingness to comply with these norms signals a socialization into the teacher role. The issue of dress was dramatically highlighted at one of our teacher conferences where a university academic who was one of the main speakers appeared in a pair of jeans and a jumper, and gave her talk sitting on the speaker's table rather than standing behind it. Unlikely as it may seem, this attire substantially undermined the impact of what the academic had to say. One headteacher and several other teachers remarked to us afterwards that they could not seriously accept a lecture from 'somebody dressed like that'. Perhaps underlying their reaction was the feeling that as their social role required them to be 'properly dressed' it would have been courtesy for a speaker to teachers to do the same. (see page 182).

As a team of initially three women we took an entirely tactical decision to comply with these unwritten rules of dress. We often wore trousers in the office, but agreed always to wear skirts and dresses when visiting schools. Non-conformist dress on our part could only have proved a distraction. There were so many other barriers to trust which had to be overcome that this seemed a small price to pay, but can be seen as an illuminating example of the encounter between cultures (Rudduck, 1976) experienced by curriculum innovation teams. In the same way, we felt that the compliance of some of the younger staff, particularly women, with sex role stereotyped norms in the school was strategic rather than a reflection of their own beliefs. The majority, but not all, of the group who were entirely supportive of GIST aims were less conformist young teachers of this type.

Subject and status in the school

During the workshops it was noticeable to us that physical scientists as a group, while happy to discuss and analyse a table of statistics, seemed fundamentally distrustful of sociological or psychological interpretations of sex differences in behaviour and to prefer biological theories (see page 174 below). A survey of teachers' attitudes to equal opportunities carried out in 1981 found that males were more likely to be opposed to equal opportunities practices than females. However subject specialism was found to be almost as important as sex, and it was mainly teachers of 'physical sciences, maths and bench and technical subjects who were least in favour of equal opportunities' (Pratt *et al.*, 1984).

Several studies of the personality of the physical scientist picture him as not only male but intensely masculine, thing- rather than people-oriented, single-minded with a tendency to retreat from people into work on inanimate objects, with reactions to controversial issues which are often stereotyped and reveal habits of mind which tend to minimize the uneasiness created by ambiguous or conflicting ideas (Roe, 1952; McClelland, 1962).

Similar pen portraits which are less than flattering could no doubt be drawn of social scientists or artists (see Hudson, 1967, 1968); the point, however, is that in any group of teachers, not only age and sex but also subject specialism may or may not predispose individuals to accept the case that sex differences are in part a result of social conditioning, some of which occurs at school.

There is also an implication in these studies that the physical scientist will be highly conventional in his social mores. In so far as technology is related to science, teachers of craft subjects may share some of the same personality characteristics. Conventional attitudes to sex roles will include the personal conviction that sex differences are fundamental and ineradicable. These beliefs may be mirrored in the sort of social interactions, style of marriage and parenting, and style of teaching adopted by scientists and technologists.

Senior staff

Without exception four headteachers interviewed by the evaluators professed their agreement with the aims of the GIST project: but each also found a different way of saying that their support could not be taken to imply any active promotion of change within the school. Two heads insisted that their schools already provided equal opportunities, with the implication that very little, if anything remained to be done. One of these said GIST was only 'supporting the long existing school policy to give girls and boys equal access to all parts of the school curriculum'. At the same time he believed that any approach 'requiring positive action or positive discrimination would go against the existing policy of equal opportunities' (Payne *et al.*, p. 23). Another was 'pleased to be involved in a national project' and 'welcomed the interventionist nature of the project' (which he had not at first appreciated), but believed the school had already done some thinking in this area, and GIST merely served to 'focus and sharpen existing attitudes and heightened awareness'. He said staff had been kept fully informed, and was glad that 'none of the activities have disturbed the ongoing routine of the school'. (p. 47) The third head also welcomed GIST, but remarked that it was really the responsibility of the head of science as 'his own personal involvement is inevitably distant' (p. 14). The head of the fourth school began by lauding the aims of the project as 'a necessary attempt to create a fuller life for boys and girls and to reduce a wastage of personal and national talent'. He then went on to reveal that he was 'apprehensive of a possible evangelising approach' and 'fear[ed] . . . they might "go over the top with their propaganda" ', which was one of the reasons for refusing to have an in-service discussion of the issues (pp. 38-9).

The bland front presented by these men suggests that as policy implementers they were highly aware of the general desirability of at least appearing to have a commitment to female equality. At Meadowvale and Edgehill, where the management structure which had been forged was consciously democratic, the heads professed to be entirely in favour of change themselves, but unwilling to push teachers ahead any faster than they wished to go. In these schools, one wonders how authentic the commitment to female equality was. Heads appeared to be voicing broad support mainly as a peace-keeping device, and as a limitation on demands from within the school as well as from GIST for fundamental changes. Senior staff, especially deputy heads, have considerable power in relation to the option system. The evaluators remark of a deputy head, '[he] characterises his role as administrative in a minor sense. However he obviously exercises some influence on the presentation and construction of option packages' (p. 63). Individuals with responsibility for operating the option system can be seen as crucial gatekeepers in relation to the GIST innovation. A 'gatekeeper' is a person who has sufficient control over a channel of communication so as to be able to control what information flows through the channel to the rest of the social system (Zaltman *et al.*, 1977). And as Nagi (1974) says, 'When . . . controversial, gatekeeping decisions will be influenced less by organizational norms and more by the orientations of individual decision makers.'

If the change or innovation advocated is incompatible with the personal beliefs and attitudes of the gatekeeper, then he or she is likely to produce a barrier to the introduction of change in that social system.

In all the GIST schools, control of curricular options was in the hands of a male deputy head. Although he would almost certainly consult with the head and with departments, his was the ultimate responsibility for decisions about groups of subjects children should be allowed to take. It is seldom a woman who is responsible for timetabling and academic direction. Many men occupying such a position will themselves have attended a single-sex boys' school, and their own educational values may lead them to put science and maths at the top of a hierarchy of subjects and to regard CDT more highly than home economics. Their assumptions about girls' interests and abilities may well be traditional. There may be no one at a senior management level, overseeing options, who takes a female perspective on the matter or is specifically alert for girls' interests.

We found that most of the men with these responsibilities were so little interested in the aims of the project that even after GIST had been running for a year or two they were not easily able to give us the figures for option choices broken down by sex. Even in the final year of the project, the male deputy head of Tall Trees assured a member of the team that equal numbers of boys and girls had taken computer studies in 1981-2 and 1982-3. The actual figures for these two years were: boys: 17, 16; girls: 6, 7.

The heads of three schools, however, did appear to have an authentic and open commitment to female equality. At Ashgrove, the head fully supported the aims of GIST, and encouraged the new head of CDT who arrived at the school after reorganization. Ashgrove also had the highest proportion of women staff at Scale 4 and above of any school in the GIST group. We do not know whether this was due to a policy decision, or an unexpected aspect of the deliberate recruitment, even before reorganization, of suitable staff for the sixth form college Ashgrove was to become.

The head of Tall Trees frequently expressed her commitment

to the broadly feminist aims of the project (though she applied rather strict sex differential views in the matter of dress and school uniform), and drew her sometimes unwilling staff along with her. The head of Moss Green was able to count upon the existing staff ethos of commitment to curriculum innovation and sexual and racial equality which was a feature of this inner-city community school.

Teacher beliefs about sex differences

A policy of co-education in schools presupposes, at least by implication, that girls' and boys' educational abilities and needs are the same, and so stands opposed to deliberately discriminatory provisions. Teachers are, or at least are supposed to be, professionally committed to sex equality; and their initial response to GIST was broadly positive if superficial. For instance, a science teacher who spoke to the evaluation team said, 'I think it's a laudable attempt . . . to make girls . . . realise that there are other fields open to them' (Payne *et al.*, 1984, p. 82). However sex equality is still a live and controversial subject for adults: teachers operate within gender expectations not only in their professional capacity, but in their personal lives too.

Sex differences may be perceived as 'natural' and unchanging in line with self-concepts as man/woman, husband/wife, mother/father, or alternatively as subject to change. Many male teachers spontaneously spoke to us about their wishes and expectations for their own daughters or feelings about a wife's career, i.e. a personal rather than a professional response. In many cases their personal response indicated that change would be welcomed, especially for the next generation. Others were more doubtful or defensive. For instance a deputy head whose son was going to be a vet told us in a puzzled way that a lot of women were accepted on the course despite the fact that a university's pre-registration literature emphasized the need for strength in a vet's job. He was beginning to reconsider his personal assumption that all men are stronger than all women in the light of his professional belief that women should have equal access to university courses.

A number of theories of attitude change have suggested that people tend to seek out and listen to views with which they already agree (Osgood, 1955; Festinger, 1957; Rokeach, 1968), to avoid the experience of 'cognitive dissonance' involved in finding themselves unexpectedly agreeing with new views which contradict their established ones. The idea that individuals selectively expose themselves only to 'congruent' beliefs was later elaborated to show that this occurs only when some threat to personal esteem is perceived. If the issue is not 'ego-involved', the usefulness of the information will be the primary consideration in whether an individual gives his attention or not (Triandis, 1971).

Beliefs militating against change

It seems that teachers of the 'hard' and 'heavy' subjects of science and technology as a group experienced greater 'cognitive dissonance' in the face of arguments and ideas put forward by GIST. The official presumption that schools do and should treat the sexes equally perhaps explains why only a very few teachers articulated in clear terms a causal theory of girls' biological or intellectual inferiority. Nevertheless, from comments made to members of the GIST team, and to a lesser extent in the evaluation interviews, we can see that the theory of girls' 'inferior' abilities and their different 'needs' is still alive and well in many schools. For instance a male art teacher at Tall Trees told us firmly, 'there will always be differences between men and women – I think it's wrong to try and change them – after all I can't have babies.' A woodwork and metal teacher referred to 'basic differences between boys and girls'; he was 'very clear that these are genetic not cultural differences' (Payne *et al.*, p. 40), and another of his colleagues, a woodwork teacher,

> draws on his experience with his own children to argue strongly that boys and girls are different and that there's a genetic base for this. In fact he feels that GIST may be meddling a bit in this natural order of things. (ibid., p. 41)

A science teacher:

> is worried if girls do not become as involved as they should in the pastoral and family areas of life. . . [thinks] boys are different from girls basically, and schools cannot really do much about it. In fact schools should be careful not to be too quick to do things like GIST. Such notions can detract from social harmony, even erode the foundation of society.

An art and craft teacher wrote a long note to GIST, expressing doubts and fears along the same lines.

The head of Green Park also specifically referred to biological differences, remarking that 'girls have babies after all' (ibid., p. 39), and at Ashgrove, after a conversation with John Catton, an older craft teacher said very simply that 'man was made to be the hunter and woman to sit in the cave'. This underlying model of the 'biological inferiority' of the female sex has become increasingly unfashionable among sociological and psychological *cognoscenti*, and the evidence for the biological determinist position has been attacked as inadequate (e.g. Kaminski, 1982). However, for some teachers it offers a straightforward confirmation of the naturalness and inevitability of current patterns of sex differentiation. In so far as it bolsters complacency and supports the status quo, the belief in a 'genetic deficit' model of the female sex itself constitutes a powerful hindrance to change. A male science teacher said,

> 'The reasons for this [i.e. girls'] underachievement are in a sense biological, boys are different from girls basically and schools cannot really do much about it.' (Payne *et al.*, p. 43).

Several teachers who were interviewed made it clear that they did not accept a biological limitation on girls' intellectual ability, but felt nevertheless that the desired changes in behaviour would be virtually impossible to bring about. One can also be a 'cultural determinist', and hold the belief that because males and females behave differently, they are incapable of doing otherwise. A female head of lower school science said,

> 'it's a whole system of society and conditioning that y-you're only attacking it at a tiny niche and once it's over everything is going to go back again . . . . I wouldn't say it's futile . . . .'
>
> 'it's like chopping a rain forest down and you lose everything . . . it's totally against the balance of nature . . . .' (ibid., pp. 116, 117).

Teachers' attitudes which foster change

The evaluators were specifically asked to find out from teachers whether they believed schools could do anything to alter the pattern of female underachievement in science and technology. Some teachers preferred to lay all the blame at the door of other agencies – parents, the media, employers, children themselves or even just primary schools. Others were most optimistic about the school's capacity to contribute to change. Of the sixteen recorded replies to the question, 'Can schools make a difference?', thirteen were positive (Payne *et al.*, 1984). A male head of year with responsibility for teaching personal and social studies represents a belief in the potential of schools to promote positive social change:

> The causes of the underachievement problem are, in his view, located broadly in society. It's conditioning: girls and boys come to accept particular roles, girls come to accept that they are natural mothers. Certainly the home is seen as a crucial factor in this. In addition, the expectations which boys, and men, have of girls are a powerful factor: they put pressure on girls, explicitly or implicitly, and he would say that boys are generally less happy to change their views. Despite his emphasis on home factors, he does feel that schools can make a difference, certainly in the long term, and teachers can work at this now. The school can encourage resistance to home pressures. (ibid., p. 54)

A female biology teacher thought 'schools have a very difficult job on in trying to change the situation, but they have a duty to try . . .', and was described as 'an ideal subject from the point of view of the GIST aims, especially as her interest and conviction seem to have been a direct result of their intervention' (ibid., p. 16). Another teacher from the same school was aware of the complex issues involved in deciding how far it is possible for girls and boys to change:

> On the precise mix of culture/genetic contributions she wishes she had more knowledge – certainly boys put girls down in science, girls are expected to be passive, etc. She talks in a genuinely concerned, curious way about the importance of 'image' and the role of puberty changes. The emphasis throughout is on *relationships* between boys and girls, notions of self, and mutual expectations. (emphasis in original) (ibid., p. 19)

Although teachers tended not to be explicit about their theories of sex difference, it is possible to categorize three alternative positions on the nature/nurture debate, each leading by implication to distinct educational practices and outcomes.

(This analysis is based on an article written in 1974 by two American writers (Lee and Gropper, 1974) who put forward the idea that 'masculinity' and 'femininity' can be regarded as two separate 'cultures', just like belonging to a nation, or an ethnic group within a nation. It is further developed in Whyte, 1984.)

According to the GENETIC DIFFERENCES model, girls are deficient or inferior in respect of crucial intellectual abilities, because of genetically determined differences between the sexes. The theory foresees a necessary limitation on females ever being able to match male achievement, and so leads logically to separate education systems for the two sexes, geared to their genetically determined strengths.

The CULTURAL DIFFERENCES model points to sex differences in behaviour; while these 'really' exist, their source may be thought to be learned or innate. By stressing the differences rather than the similarities between the sexes, it tends to be forgotten that males' and females' 'different' behaviour may be specific to certain situations. For instance, young children will play with toys they know to be appropriate to the opposite sex, until another child enters their playspace, when they return to the conventional playthings (Serbin, 1978); white women appear to have a 'motive to avoid success' at least when they are observed by male peers; black (American) women do not (Lee and Gropper, 1974). The emphasis on notable differences between the sexes often tends to result in the dominant male culture being defined as superior or desirable; for example, females may be shown to be less achievement-oriented than males; this makes them 'inferior' if the dominant male culture values achievement over, say, interpersonal skills. The educational outcome might be to try and make girls more like boys, denying the value of the 'feminine' culture in the process. In a mixed school boys and girls will be expected to be different, and the evidence of differences will be seen as sufficient reason for sex inequality in later achievement.

The BICULTURAL model envisages compatibility between important aspects of the two cultures, because it stresses the similarities between males and females. Its basic postulate is that education currently prepares children for a traditional sexual division of labour by the production and reproduction of two distinct 'sex cultures', the 'masculine' and the 'feminine'. Nevertheless girls and boys are in reality quite capable of sharing a common range of information, interest and aspirations because sex role cultures need not be seen as mutually exclusive alternatives. Girls possess more knowledge of boys' culture than vice versa, but both sexes possess knowledge and capabilities appropriate to the two cultures and are prevented from actually making use of them only by social expectations and other barriers, overt or covert. A good example of this in practice is the fact that males are usually unwilling to engage in needlework (a singularly unpopular subject among boys at school), yet in a context where sewing ability is seen as consistent with masculinity (surgeon sewing up patient, small boy mending hole in his tent at Scout camp; see Mischel, 1975) cross-sex skills and knowledge come into play.

Educational practice on the bicultural model would stress the similarities between girls and boys as learners and regard as beneficial the blending of 'masculine' and 'feminine' interests. Schools would provide children with equal access to traditionally sex-typed educational and cultural resources. To assist in the opening up of 'bicultural' opportunities to both sexes, educators would address the 'hidden curriculum' of teacher and pupil expectations, teacher modelling and the distribution of classroom space and educational resources.

The question of the sources of sex difference is a complex one, and as the quotation above indicates, teachers who had thought most deeply about the issue fully appreciated the difficulty and complexity of the matter. The bicultural view was only partially expressed by a tiny number of teachers. Many more seemed to accept either the genetic or cultural determinist view, that the possibilities for change are naturally limited, a model which is at any rate more straightforward and easier to understand. Unless more teachers come to adopt some form of 'biculturalism', it is unlikely they will *believe* schools can promote fundamental social change, and therefore unlikely that they will be *active* in that endeavour.

Chapter 12

The teachers' response to the GIST project

The interventions in schools were mainly implemented by the teachers. The project team did not have the staff or the resources to work directly with pupils to any great extent, nor would we have wanted to, even if that had been possible. If there were to be lasting changes in the schools it was imperative that these be brought about by teachers who could continue the work after the project formally ended. Moreover we took seriously the arguments about the 'hidden curriculum' and 'teacher expectations'. If teachers indicate by their actions or even their tone of voice that they are sceptical about girls' abilities in science and technology or that they do not think it desirable for girls to continue with physics or technical crafts after the third year, pupils are bound to pick this up. Conversely, teachers who have become aware of unspoken assumptions or apparently insignificant asides which can discourage girls may be able instead to convey positive messages about girls and science and technology.

Outright hostility or opposition to the ideas put forward by GIST were rarely encountered. As a group, teachers are highly conscious of the value put upon equality of opportunity in education. A project specifically concerned with female underachievement clearly does raise doubts, even hostility in some individuals. But these negative reactions are characteristically expressed quite indirectly and often non-verbally. Notable examples come to mind; of male teachers whose body posture clearly signalled a disinclination to become involved in discussion at all; or teacher X who arrived late to a workshop meeting, bearing a piece of equipment he was mending – he apologised for his late arrival (from field notes). On another occasion teacher Y arrived late holding a class list and asked if he could 'just finish this off' while the group was talking. At a departmental meeting which GIST had been invited to attend in a craft workshop, teacher Z spent fifteen minutes roving round the room, cleaning and tidying up equipment. Meantime discussion continued with other members of the staff. When the room was obviously tidy, one of his colleagues indicated an empty chair and asked him to sit down. Instead teacher Z took a further five minutes to pack his briefcase and don his overcoat. Then he anounced he must go home now.

The non-verbal 'messages' of dissent conveyed by these teachers and the way they devised apparently legitimate distractions from discussion with GIST suggest they found it uncomfortable to hear views expressed which were in conflict with their own beliefs about sex roles. The evaluators, able to occupy a more 'neutral' role, found some teachers prepared to voice attitudes and expectations of girls and boys which were clearly 'incongruent' with the GIST proposals.

Resisters

One of the purposes of the independent evaluation was to find out more about the sources of teachers' resistance to GIST ideas. We asked the evaluation team to visit Green Park, because it was the one school where we felt the impact of GIST on children's attitudes and choices would be smallest. Although the school agreed to co-operate in the project in 1979, it was not until the time when spatial/mechanical tests were to be administered in craft lessons that we realized girls were not actually allowed to do technical crafts at all in the first three years (nor boys to do home economics). Evidently crafts had once been integrated for a short time, but the 'experiment' proved unsuccessful. In theory, children could opt for any craft at the end of the third year, but naturally pressure was brought to bear on children making a non-traditional option, for instance to ensure that they were not just 'seeking attention'.

As one of the stated aims of GIST was to change girls' attitudes to craft and technology, we had no alternative but to request the school to reconsider its sex-segregated curriculum. Discussions were long-drawn-out (see Chapter 9), and soon it became clear that practical considerations would rule out the possibility of reorganizing the curriculum to offer girls in the GIST cohort an integrated craft scheme. Ultimately, a compromise was reached: a return to mixed crafts for the year following GIST, and permission for John Catton to take a group of GIST girls for an after school club, and teach a group of first years one afternoon a week. This would both give GIST girls a 'taste' of technology and provide craft teachers with an opportunity to observe curriculum development in craft, design and technology for both sexes.

Neither GIST nor the school were entirely happy with this outcome; the teachers of craft subjects had previously succeeded in negotiating a return to the status quo, and now a group of outsiders had resurrected the whole issue. Teachers felt that 'innovations' such as mixed crafts were irrelevant for the 'kind of children we have here', a phrase used often in conversation with GIST, and which referred to the deprived background of most of the schools' pupils. Certainly, Green Park had the most working-class intake of any of the project schools, judged on the basis of both mother's and father's occupation. Their IQ levels and science knowledge, however, were not significantly lower than those of the other children.

We felt and intuited rather than heard at first hand of the teachers' opposition, at least until we read the evaluators' report, in which the extent of their hostility to the demands made by GIST came over loud and clear. The impression gained by the authors of the evaluation report, that 'the project has had a most unhappy time in this school', suffering disagreements and 'personality clashes', is in fact far from the truth. The team's experience was of polite, even friendly interaction with staff. In retrospect, it seems rather surprising that neither side proposed the school should withdraw from the project, but the nature of the relationship was such that this was never even suggested. Resentment of GIST there clearly was, however, and of two kinds: first, we were loosely associated with the unacceptable face of feminism, particularly as it appeared at the Polytechnic conference, to which most of the staff referred. Second, we were suspected of exploiting the school for our own ends.

At least one teacher claimed that there was virtually no staffroom discussion of the GIST project, yet the near-unanimity of the teachers on these two points strongly suggests that quite a lot of discussion did take place:

Anti-feminism

At the Polytechnic conference, three of the four speakers were women, and a BBC education programme (shown on video) was presented by a well-known feminist. Such a preponderance of females may have crystallized the fears of teachers who were unhappy about the feminist overtones of GIST:

> 'Militant feminism was particularly prevalent at the Polytechnic conference, where a plump and highly political female person in trousers was particularly aggravating in assuming that teachers know nothing of female struggle'. (Payne *et al.*, 1984, p. 33)

> He thought the conference at the Polytechnic was 'hysterical'. One speaker was desperate to justify the ideology of the project and overall GIST was 'scrambling for credibility'. He challenged some of the views. For example, in his experience, girls of comparable ability often do better than boys. And not all male teachers direct most questions to boys. In short, the number of sexist males in the world is overestimated and the fact of the existence of sexist women is ignored. (p. 35)

> 'Staff [were] addressed by an unkempt classical Women's Libber . . . her lecture was anecdotal and unresearched and was as sloppy as her personal appearance.' (p. 38)

> This teacher remembers with considerable annoyance the Polytechnic conference: the lectures did not seem relevant to this school and the lecturing style of one speaker was appalling. The lecturer sat cross-legged on the desk and probably did positive damage to the cause. (p. 44)

What affronted the teachers above all appears to have been the medium rather than the message: for example, the casual presentation by one woman, in fact a rather distinguished sociologist who had carried out a good deal of classroom research and written a number of books. The 'laid-back' style she adopted was both unfamiliar and infuriating, at least to the teachers from Green Park.

Perhaps in consequence, the conference as a whole was viewed with suspicion:

> He remembers attending the Polytechnic conference and feels that this had the flavour of an equal opportunities bandwagon, with women in dungarees and carrying copies of *Spare Rib*. He was suspicious about this. (p. 46)

> He went to the Polytechnic conference and this had a negative effect possibly. He remembers a woman using a child in a pram to make a point, but not an educational point. (p. 55)

Needless to say, we could not identify any feminists in dungarees, nor anyone carrying *Spare Rib*. Some students had been asked to tape-record group discussions, and their dress may have stood out as different from teachers'. The child in a pram belonged to a teacher-researcher who was on temporary maternity leave, and had come to talk about the findings of her work on classroom interaction in science lessons. A childminder was provided.

The Green Park view of the Polytechnic conference was to some degree peculiar to the school. Criticisms from other schools were mostly of a different kind. For instance, the head of Sutton Hill had been somewhat unwilling to release staff in school time, and repeated his objections to the evaluators:

> 'the mass conference activities that relied upon taking teachers out of school and getting them in dialogue with other teachers . . . but again, this affects my preference for INSET, school based in-service education for teachers . . . added to which there is the logistic problem. . . . GIST . . . tried to persuade us that if we had six months. . . warning we should be able to make provisions . . . whether in fact we thought it was a valuable activity or not was rather taken for granted.' (p. 129)

His point, of course, is a fair and important one. The conferences were held in part because they were envisaged in the original research proposal. However as the project progressed, we had hoped to have far more in-school discussion than ever proved acceptable to the schools. Only Edgehill offered the opportunity for a full-scale GIST in-service day. Sutton Hill offered half an hour at a full staff meeting, an invitation which was taken up, but was too limited in scope for the sort of extended discussion we had hoped for.

A teacher from Sutton Hill told the evaluators that she had found some of the ideas used by the GIST team (especially at the one day conference) very useful and will use them herself in subsequent years. The conference gave impetus to the series of classroom observations carried out in many of the action schools (see Teachers who changed, p. 192) and to the single-sex grouping in science experiment at Moss Green (see Chapter 8).

Anti-academic

The second source of Green Park teachers' resistance to GIST lay in a feeling that we were outsiders, who did not really understand the problems faced by the classroom teacher:

> He felt that the GIST project presented its team as producing research papers and getting doctorates rather than helping schoolchildren. He saw their basic aim, apart from self-interest, as to break traditional roles by looking for correlations between, for example, career choice and parental influence. (Payne *et al.*, 1984, p. 35)

> Teachers tend to resist outsiders making suggestions adding to their work, e.g. administering questionnaires (p. 35)

> His initial response was that it was yet another research approach of which this particular school received a lot. (p. 38)

> She remembers feeling that the questionnaire was too difficult and not appropriate for her children. This point combined with the suspicion that she and others might be used to get someone a PhD led her to a virtual opting out of the scheme. p. 44) (In fact nobody in the GIST team gained a PhD from the project.)

> 'The ladies involved have very little conception of these sort of children, of their living conditions or what it is like to work in this kind of school. They are in cloud cuckoo land. . . . Teachers at this school are fighting the environment all the time.' (p. 44) (In fact, three members of the team were qualified teachers, two with considerable experience in comprehensive schools.)

> He knows that teachers are always difficult to work with; they tend to be cynical, don't like their routines being upset. Personally it did not interfere with his routine a great deal, but some other science staff found the project a big imposition and interference and were certainly against it. (p. 46)

A few of these comments are echoed, but in much milder form, by staff from other schools, e.g.:

> 'Perhaps GIST would have been better if the research was more school-based and the GIST team had spent more time in the school.' (p. 20)

> One criticism he has is that he feels that the GIST team are too

remote from the everyday hubbub of school life. (p. 26)

His first impressions of GIST were dismay at another disturbance in the scheme of things. (p. 29)

Many of these criticisms have a familiar ring, for teachers have frequently resented the top-down, 'centre periphery' model of innovation, which assumes that schools and teachers can be regarded as passive recipients of a new approach designed elsewhere, usually by academics (see Harris, Lawn and Prescott, 1975, for a number of articles attacking this classical mode of innovation). Ironically, the barrier between academic and teacher was one which GIST had been at some pains to dismantle. Feedback of research results as soon as they became available was an inbuilt feature of the programme in every one of the GIST schools. We had been disappointed by the response thereafter; few teachers seemed to have the time or inclination to become more involved as researchers themselves. The chief reason, of course, was lack of 'quality time' (a concept for which I am indebted to Ruth Sutton, at one time a GIST teacher), that is, time away from the classroom in which to reflect upon the need for change, preferably in the context of a discussion with other members of staff in the same school. One or two meetings were held after school, to discuss curriculum development, but small numbers turned up, and the group soon petered out for lack of support.

Teachers' complaints that the GIST team could have spent more time in school had, probably, two sources. The decision to cover eight action and two control schools considerably spread the thin resources of a team consisting of initially only one full-timer, and two co-directors, each themselves occupied in teaching during term time. Teachers may also have expected to see more of the team in the belief that GIST would actually carry out all the work with pupils. It should have been clear, at least after the workshops, that this was never intended to be the case, but teachers often feel that visitors to a school can't appreciate how hard they work. A kind of 'exemplary teaching' was tried at Green Park, but proved to be extremely time-consuming, and not particularly effective in persuading teachers to devise their own interventions.

Culture of the school in opposition to GIST aims

Only at Tall Trees was it the stated wish of the head that GIST should receive full co-operation. Certain schools made it very easy for teachers to bypass requests by GIST to change their practice. At Green Park and Sutton Hill, the heads made their reservations clear to the evaluators, and no doubt to their staff also. At Meadowvale and Edgehill, the heads gave perfect freedom to staff to do as much or as little as they liked. Under these circumstances, most teachers felt under no obligation to do more than they personally wished to. Occasionally, this could be difficult for the teacher concerned, e.g.:

> It meant changes to usual arrangements and a measure of extra work. There was also a bit of 'mickey-taking'. This teacher was clearly aware of this antagonism and hostility but it did not lessen her resolve. (Payne *et al.*, 1984, p. 16)

> She was heavily involved in the organisation of a one-day GIST visit for the whole third year. In fact her involvement was perceived by some senior staff to be excessive. Here she feels that senior staff could well give more positive support to GIST. (p.27)

Both these teachers were clearly taking part in the GIST project against the background of a school climate which not only did not reward them for the extra work involved, but frowned on it as 'excessive'. For many more teachers, especially, perhaps, those at Green Park, the culture of the school, with its bias against listening to outsiders, and its even greater bias against the kind of 'positive discrimination' GIST was seen to represent, was directly opposed to their putting greater efforts, even supposing they wanted to, into forwarding GIST aims.

Ambivalent responses

Both positive and resistant responses to GIST are described in this chapter, but sometimes teachers' attitudes and behaviour appeared ambivalent, raising some questions about the underlying reasons for their reactions. First, quite a number of teachers appeared to be very supportive of the GIST aims, both in conversations with the team and in the independent evaluation interviews; however, they seemed to have stopped short of involving themselves fully in the kind of intervention which had been recommended. Second, even teachers who had responded positively to the GIST initiative frequently denied it had had any effect at all on their classroom practice.

Explicit/implicit

We were very interested in a piece of classroom work carried out by a teacher at Meadowvale, who was both head of biology and teacher in charge of personal and social education. The LEA had recently offered in-service training on the use of active tutorial work (see Baldwin, 1979, 1980 and 1981), and this teacher decided to use active tutorial work methods in single-sex groups to find out more about children's perceptions of gender interactions in the classroom.

She asked girls and boys to discuss, first in pairs, then in groups of four, and finally in groups of eight, how they thought girls and boys behaved and were treated by teachers in the science class. Groups reported back and their views were written on the blackboard. These revealed that girls were very aware of the ways in which boys 'put them down' in science. They gave their teacher a long list of about twenty points like, 'The boys steal all the best apparatus'; 'Give them a chance and they'll ruin your experiment while your back is turned'. It appeared that before this experimental lesson, none of the pupils had realized that staff were actively trying to encourage girls, or even that VISTA visits were aimed to this end. The teacher said in despair, 'You almost have to hit our girls over the head with a hammer before they get the message.' This discussion took place at a feedback meeting with science staff at Meadowvale. One of the male scientists disagreed with the explicit approach she had taken; he thought 'it should be subtle and not overt encouragement'. That this was not just an individual response, but possibly the view of many teachers involved in GIST, appears from some of the interview transcripts prepared by the evaluators. One or two specifically said that they did not think girls had understood the 'hidden message' of the VISTA visits:

> 'the VISTA visits were run well but may not have had the desired effect – her year group did not seem to have noticed that they were women'

> 'She understood the reasoning behind the use of female models

in conventionally male subjects, but the basic point did not go over, except possibly for the brighter children.'

It does not seem to have occurred to the teachers (although it was a point frequently stressed by the team) that they were in the ideal position to draw out the implications of VISTA for the children. A transcript shows the caution and ambivalence of one teacher's response:

Teacher: I don't know if they thought that oh this is a woman she is a scientist, I don't know whether it came across, that because nothing was said it was just a case of sit down and watch.'
Interviewer: Yes – was it followed up?
Teacher: No, not with the kids, no.
Interviewer: No. . . and that was intentional was it I mean or?
Teacher: Presumably, yes they were just trying to impress them subconsciously because it's never raised we are never asked to raise it, that point with the group. (p. 101)

Another teacher, who described the children as 'blissfully unaware', like someone in a 'goldfish bowl looking out at what everybody's trying to do for them', nevertheless seemed remarkably unwilling to give children more than the smallest clue of what GIST was about. She said she found things like the posters (of women scientists) very useful, because they could just be introduced as part of the hidden curriculum 'so it's just in subtle ways I think it creeps in nicely – without sort of saying YOU WILL KNOW about a woman scientist – you know which is blatantly overt you know' (p. 119).

In fact teachers had been asked to discuss the visits with children, if possible in a debriefing session in the following lesson. In this case at least, the suggestion was ignored. Perhaps the teacher's theory was that just as the 'hidden' curriculum of sex stereotyping, which had been discussed in the workshops, is an almost incidental and untaught feature of schools, so attempts to reverse stereotyping should be carefully disguised. By why on earth should information about women scientists be regarded as so potentially explosive? Why keep it all a secret from the children?

Certainly, when teachers have something they really want children to know, their behaviour is not usually so circumspect. The head of Sutton Hill remarked, 'Well I'm a teacher, my view is didactic and explicit and if want children to learn – you have to hum, har, beat them over the head with it, huh three or four times a day.' Far from doing so, some teachers seem to have felt that even suggesting to girls that they might make a non-traditional choice would be unprofessional and propagandistic. An earlier remark by the same head implies that for some, the 'dilemma' was best resolved by leaving GIST to do all the specific counter-propaganda work:

> 'during years two and three GIST seemed to have an implicit way of dealing with the children, whereas in the roadshows they have become more interventionist in their propaganda as you might say, and I think this has certainly been more effective.' (p. 129)

It could be that our slight fudging of the question of whether teachers or children were the real focus of the project allowed some teachers, whose own feelings were perhaps ambivalent, to hide behind such transparent excuses for saying nothing explicitly to the pupils. If this happened a good deal, then it is really somewhat surprising that so much did get through to the children, as seems to be the case from the evidence of their attitude change over the period of the project (see Chapter 13).

Comically, in retrospect, a teacher with pastoral responsibility at Moss Green appeared very keen to have the GIST roadshows for her third years, and indeed would have liked more visitors than, with the resources available, we could possibly have organized. Most of her requests were complied with, and the children saw quite a number of male and female visitors in non-traditional jobs, asked them questions, and engaged in the usual quizzes and games. Moss Green, in the end, received rather more 'roadshow input' than other schools. But a few weeks later, we learned that the same teacher had, on her own initiative, and as she put it, to 'bend the stick the other way', invited some typists and secretaries – all female – to come and speak to the children. As the whole purpose of the roadshows had been to redress the balance away from guiding and channelling children into traditionally sex-typed jobs, this response on the part of the teacher was somewhat frustrating to us.

Reluctance to admit to change

A second source of ambivalent response was connected not so much with what was said to pupils, but more with reaction to

GIST as an innovation directed towards teachers and their teaching styles.

In the early days of the project some teachers' initial reaction was to deny the validity of any implied criticism of the school's treatment of girls. For instance a teacher at Green Park said, 'We are already teaching in a way that is sensitive to girls' needs', a theme that was repeated again and again in the Green Park teachers' replies to the evaluators. This response is slightly different from the usual prevarication practised by teachers who were waiting to see whether GIST was something they were really going to come to grips with, for example, the craft teacher who stalled on administering GIST tests: 'Paperwork is difficult to do up there'; the teacher who asked, 'Has this school actually agreed to do anything?', or the science teacher who claimed nothing could be done about standardizing class exam marks in first year: 'No. Science *is* more difficult. I'm teaching for an exam'. Later developments showed that these sorts of excuses were typically employed as delaying tactics by teachers reluctant to commit themselves immediately.

That is rather different from the response which dominates the evaluation interviews, of claiming that nothing in the schools has changed because nothing needs to change. As the authors of the report commented, 'on balance staff seem almost grudging to concede that there have been even marginal changes in their classroom practice' (p. 73). Yet within the report itself teachers describe aspects of their own classroom practice which can be traced back to GIST:

> 'She always takes opportunities in her lessons to question sex stereotyping.' (p. 27)
>
> 'He has thought more about the use of extended writing.' (p. 20)
>
> 'textbooks are now more closely scrutinised in terms of what activities of boys and girls are contained in them.' (p. 33)
>
> 'Certainly the project has altered her *teaching*. She is more conscious of making efforts to involve girls. Her stress is on classroom management, teaching style, questioning strategies – she mentions trying to find more appropriate teaching materials.' (p. 19)

All these activities – questioning the content of sex stereotyped materials, introducing extended writing in science lessons, becoming more aware of one's classroom management – were specifically and frequently advised by GIST as things teachers could do in order to encourage girls.

The team's field notes also reveal considerable alteration in teachers' attitudes, though these were by no means uniform. Perhaps a typical reaction from a male science teacher was for an initial scepticism to change gradually into endorsement and even enthusiasm over the first couple of years of the project, as it became evident that GIST had practical ideas and could implement them efficiently (e.g. by organizing the VISTA programme, testing attitudes, producing useable curriculum materials).

Yet almost all the teachers denied that the project had impacted their teaching behaviour, or even their attitudes, in any way. The evaluators thought this may well have been a defensive reaction, as 'to admit to changes (perhaps to be aware of changes?) in one's own practices . . . might be tantamount to accepting that there were inadequacies . . . there being inequality of treatment for half . . . .

However we tried to disguise it, 'the GIST initiative was seen by teachers as involving a strong critique of teachers and schools.' It could be argued that all curriculum innovation involves a critique of teachers' previous practices, and even 'deskills' the teacher. But this is not usually felt in such a personal way. Gender roles affect us all throughout our lives. Many teachers made the link between what we were saying about girls in school and the position of females in their own families – as evidenced by the number of anecdotes we were told about wives and daughters who were either completely happy in their traditional role, or had broken into non-traditional fields with no trouble at all.

It is indeed doubtful whether the personal issues which intrude in this area could ever be properly eliminated from the attempts to change. The GIST approach allowed teachers (most of them men) to co-operate with the project without necessarily feeling that their personal mores were under examination. Yet it is apparent that those teachers who were most active in pursuit of the project's aims, and most prepared to open up discussion with pupils, had considered the personal as well as the professional implications.

Teachers who changed

One purpose in the work with teachers was to move beyond a humorous, jokey or superficial response to GIST towards serious consideration of sex differences in achievement as a professional issue.

Meadowvale's headmaster thought 'the GIST project has been successful in overcoming some initial resistance in the way of "banter" and "digs" from staff. For him the best feature of GIST is the professional way they go about a worthwhile project' (Payne *et al.*, 1984, p. 14). His perception is confirmed by a report on staffroom response, from a teacher in the same school: 'On other staff she was definite that teachers know about GIST – "having been GISTed" is a common phrase when talking about promoting girls' opportunities comes up. There is a fair amount of staffroom chat about GIST, anecdotes and discussions about materials. There is no anti-GIST feeling' (p. 19).

The deputy head at Sutton Hill also thought 'feedback from staff on the visiting speakers was good and generally he feels that the GIST team have operated sensitively, made us look at our expectation of girls (and more specifically at some obvious things like the option booklets)' (p. 30). At Edgehill an art and design teacher said that to the best of his knowledge there was no small core of opposition to GIST, not even as a joke, in his school (p. 52), a view confirmed by another colleague: 'Overall the project was well done, the questionnaires were burdensome, but needed doing. It was good that people came in, were involved, were concerned, and accepted the views of the staff. Certainly his impression is a very positive one' (p. 54).

In three out of the four schools where evaluators worked, then, staff seemed to have accepted the importance of girls' under-achievement as an educational issue for the school. Besides this 'serious' approach, a second criterion for success in the work with teachers was that not only their attitudes, but also actual aspects of their practice should have altered. The main behavioural changes we were looking for in teachers were:

(a) changing curriculum materials and approaches;
(b) becoming aware of their use of language;
(c) studying patterns of girl/boy participation in the classroom and in subject choice.

Changing curriculum content

An article written by the head of science of a GIST action school appeared in the journal *Teaching London Kids* (Thompson, 1982). It reports how the results of the initial GIST survey made staff rethink some of their approaches to the lower school science curriculum:

> As a result of these findings, we have begun to introduce elements of human biology as examples wherever possible. For instance, in work on the power of lenses, in physics, the class dissect bull's eyes to find the lens. The dissection used to be done solely by biologists. They then compare its properties to the glass ones. We also try to avoid examples which are linked to boys' interests and to substitute ones based on experience common to both sexes. For example, we used to illustrate the concept of force by asking children to pull on chest expanders. Now we use ordinary elastic and expanding luggage fasteners instead.

Thompson also notes that

> Observation of lessons by outside agencies has taught us the need for care when equipment is distributed. Boys certainly grab the best equipment if given the opportunity – and indeed if allowed they will patrol classrooms for more! Boys tend to answer first and tend to be asked first when there is a teacher-class dialogue. More structuring – handing equipment to specific children and asking named children questions – enables the girls to get a fairer deal.
>
> Several teachers have tried different policies for seating organisation in attempts to break the sex-segregated way in which children usually arrange themselves. The most successful strategy for obtaining mixed working groups has been to announce that during the lesson the class must form groups which do not contain anyone they usually sit next to or were with. If the lesson is a problem-solving one, groups can be built up gradually starting with pairs working together on the problem, then forming fours and eights. Often when prevented from forming sex-segregated friendship groups in this way, the most inventive girls and boys end up working together and producing highly original solutions.

A biology teacher believed GIST had contributed directly to her professional development:

> 'Since those early visits there has been constant contact with the project, particularly in the form of helping to prepare new materials. The project team has also provided information on tests which are not so biased towards boys on courses and conferences. This teacher is going on a computer course with two other teacchers and says she would not have gone if the GIST team had not made her aware of the possibility.' (Payne *et al.*, 1984, p. 15)

We hoped teachers would review curriculum content for male bias, and a craft teacher admitted his tendency to ignore girls' interests and teach to the boys, 'cos she is one among twenty or two among twenty, and so they just get submerged . . . because you have got nineteen boys in, say, or eighteen boys . . . you tend automatically to gear it towards their interests and as much as you would like to, the girls do get. . .' (p. 93), but at least he was coming to recognize the oversight.

Another craft teacher, talking about lower school children, who all followed the same craft curriculum anyway, said he was apprehensive about boys rejecting the making of a brooch as 'cissy'. Unfortunately and unsuspectingly he fell into a trap: 'He sells things differently to the boys at times, for example when doing enamel brooch work, boys may see it as cissy, so for them he sells it in terms of the enamelling technique they will be learning for other jobs' (p. 31). This teacher honestly thinks he is offering the same curriculum to boys and girls – both do enamelling as a technique – but by stressing to the boys and not to the girls that the important thing is acquisition of a technique, he reveals his assumption that girls are only playing at or 'tasting' technical crafts, and that the acquisition of technical expertise is not going to be so important for them, as most likely they will not continue with the subject long enough to get a qualification. If, as one might suppose, the girls picked up his inference, it may have become a self-fulfilling prophecy, as girls realized their presence in the crafts department was viewed as merely temporary.

Use of language

The head of craft at Meadowvale school accepted 'the GIST adviser's view that much can be done to help in the workshops by way of devising material and especially in improving the use of language in classroom interactions by cutting out references which demean the female role' (p. 13).

On the other hand, a physics teacher expressed more doubt. He had obviously grappled with the question of whether or not it is really important to avoid using the generic masculine, and had decided that introducing linguistic changes and 'women's topics' was too often, in his view, ludicrous or irrelevant:

> We – or I – possibly look a little more carefully at materials uhh – wording – though I still feel at times that it's a bit pedantic to call a frogman a frog person uhh y'know this is one of the things that in one of the reports the girls wrote y'know in one of my lessons, what would you call a frogman it is a frogman he always will be a frog man uhh – y'know so in some respects y'know there are still these ideologies that I think they are striving for Utopia. . .'

But he also sees the danger of characterizing 'feminine' topics in a way which further reinforces stereotyping:

> 'Over the course of a couple of years I think one's put in to one's course work uhh – possibly a few more examples of things that women come across but then you get told off because that's – well why are we talking about an iron because we've got a few ladies in the room it is y'know part of a woman to do the ironing y'know so you get hit from both ends as it were. . . . I think, yes, one has become aware, somewhat, of the activities they're trying to put forward.' (pp. 83–4)

Interactions in the classroom

In the mixed classroom, boys are perceived as more 'salient' and gain more teacher time and attention than girls (Ricks and Pyke, 1969; Spaulding, 1963). Secondary teachers are more likely to prefer teaching boys, and take longer to get to know girls' names (Davies & Meighan, 1975; Stanworth, 1981). The phenomenon of boy domination on which these research studies are based was brought home to us, and to the teachers during the VISTA visits. The class teacher and a member of the GIST team would usually be at the back of the class, watching the children respond, often with interest and excitement, to the novelty of a woman visitor from industry. We, and the teachers, soon noticed that eager little boys tended to push to the front of the demonstration desk, to ask pertinent questions and to stay behind after the session to talk to the visitors. An intervention designed to encourage girls was even more successful in turning boys on to science.

We had always hoped that teachers would begin to examine interactions in their own classrooms to look for bias, but we found they needed quite a bit of support and persuasion to do so. The conference on classroom interaction, held in March 1982, was the stimulus. Teachers were presented with a variety of research reports indicating the patterns of sex differential interaction, especially in 'masculine' subjects like maths and science. In particular, they saw a BBC programme in which Dale Spender reiterated the point which she has made elsewhere (Spender, 1978), that it is extremely difficult, if not impossible, for teachers to give girls equal time and attention. Most teachers were put on their mettle by this, and many consequently invited us to observe in their classrooms, probably motivated by a desire to disprove Spender's claims of sex bias, as much as by any purely research concerns.

The observational methods used, and the detailed results, are described elsewhere (Whyte, 1984). This account concentrates on the teachers' response to classroom observation.

The GIST teachers were surprised to find how much attention they gave to boys. Naturally, the presence of an observer under the conditions described may have led them to try harder than usual to involve the girls. Most believed they were giving far more than half their attention to the girls, and were rather disconcerted to find that they had achieved only more or less equal interaction ratios. For example, a male head of science said at the end of the observation lesson that he had *felt* as if 90 per cent of his attention was being devoted to the girls. In fact the proportions of girls' and boys' interactions with teachers were about the same. It is notoriously difficult for teachers to estimate interactions accurately while they are teaching (Garner and Bing, 1973), and it would seem that in the case of sex differential interactions, teachers' perceptions are no less unreliable.

However teachers did achieve equality of interaction in many cases, although that is no guarantee that the new pattern continued after the observer was gone. It seems likely that teachers would revert to favouring boys because their subjective monitoring pushed them in that direction. However, the evaluation interviews show that for one or two teachers, the experience of being observed was a real eyeopener, and may have had longer-lasting effects on their classroom practice:

> 'A major impact was made upon her by the observations one of the GIST team made on her classroom interaction. When the "sociological theory" was explained to her prior to the lesson she was very sceptical, but was most surprised to find that her interactions with boys and girls were recorded as 50%-50%, because she had deliberately set out to involve the girls more, aiming to give them more attention than usual. This revelation convinced her that discrimination really does take place in the classroom. . . . She feels that since the revelatory observations in her classroom practice she has become a more positive teacher, aware of the importance of making sure that girls get their fair share of the better equipment and determined to get them involved in her lessons as much as the boys.' (Payne *et al.*, 1984, p. 15)

Teachers who did not agree to be observed probably continue to believe that in their classrooms there is no sex bias, as the following comment indicates:

> 'he was not observed, nor did observed teachers discuss their experiences with him. The observations were focused on the possibility of biased interaction in relation to boys and girls. This teacher feels that if anything he is in fact biased towards the girls.' (ibid., p. 17).

It seems to have been the case that women teachers were slightly better than men in achieving balanced classroom interaction. Women were overrepresented amongst those whose classroom interaction favoured girls. Men teachers were more likely to be found favouring boys. This does not fit with the body of existing research, which suggests that it is the teacher-role, rather than the sex of the teacher, which produces a bias in favour of boys. Or more accurately, it is the characteristic teacher response to the different behaviour of girls and boys as pupils, which permits boys to dominate (French and French, 1983). The reasons for women's apparent superiority in the GIST schools could be either that they were trying harder to involve girls, because they were more motivated, as women, to do so, or alternatively, the pupils of both sexes may have reacted differently to their teachers. For example, one girl interviewed by her maths teacher some time later said she had 'guessed' what the teacher was trying to do, and so kept answering questions in order to increase the girls' score.

Some craft teachers had taken very well the point made to

them, that helping girls too much in the workshop could imply that they thought girls were not so good at the subject:

> 'the biggest thing I've done is to step back from the girls. . . if the lads came up to you I said "now look c'mon I know I can do it, you've got you've got to do it" whereas if a girl came up there was a bit of sympathy "oh well never mind" y'know. . . so now I take the same view y'know "I've got to do it, you're going to do it". . . I treat them as individuals . . . but without the not patronising . . . uhhm the old chivalry. . . hahahahahaha. . . .' (Payne *et al.*, 1984, p. 90, transcript)

Our practical aim in the observation was to help teachers become aware of the way gender impinges on classroom interaction with presumed effects on learning outcomes for girls and boys. This was apparently successful with those teachers, about thirty in all, who agreed to be observed. We had envisaged, as the next stage, that teachers would go on to observe their colleagues, and thus consolidate the insights gained; this really only happened in one school. The limiting factor, apart from a general reluctance of many teachers to be observed at all, was often the difficulty of two colleagues who were prepared to work together, finding suitable slots in the timetable when they could actually carry out the observations.

The experience of classroom observation confirmed that boys usually maintain dominance in mixed classes, perhaps especially so in 'masculine' subject areas (comparison with teaching of other subjects was undertaken, but was too limited to give clear indications of the effect of different subject styles of teaching). It showed that contrary to what some commentators, including Dale Spender, have supposed, it is not impossible to 'reduce the preferential treatment of males so that teacher time and attention are distributed equally to both sexes'. This claim is not borne out by other researchers such as Wernersson (1982) and Crossman (1981), and we were sceptical about its validity. Teachers, when they knew they were being monitored, were slightly more likely to interact with girls than with boys, and this was true of both pupil-initiated and teacher-initiated interactions. For some teachers, perhaps quite a small number, the GIST observations brought about real and lasting change in their classroom practices, as well as in their consciousness of gender as a feature of classroom interaction.

Part VI

Conclusions

Chapter 13

The effects of GIST

Evaluating the effects

Our original research design allowed for two forms of evaluating success in achieving the aims of the project. The cruder measure was of pupils' subject choices before and after the interventions. The more refined measure was of changes in pupils' attitudes to science and to sex roles at the beginning and end of the project. These results are discussed in this chapter under the headings of *'Option choices'* and *'Pupils' attitudes'* below. Later on in the final year of the project we decided on a third measure: the evaluation, by an independent team of teacher-trainers, of the teachers' response to GIST (Payne *et al.*, 1984). The effects of the project on teachers are discussed in Chapters 11 and 12.

In fact, the most important outcome of GIST may be the 'ripple' effect which has been produced not just in the GIST schools, or locally in Manchester, but in schools and amongst teachers throughout the country, and even among an interested international audience. The interest in GIST is partly explainable by the controversial nature of the issue of sex differences in school, and by our combination of 'affirmative' action combined with research. Those who wanted to see changes in schools were excited by the idea of an attempt to bring about positive change, and the built in research and evaluation element seemed an assurance that the effects of intervention could be assessed and monitored. As this 'ripple' effect was unanticipated, it has not been measured, and is indeed virtually unmeasurable. Publicity about GIST appears to have reached not only science teachers, but policy makers, educators, and parents of schoolgirls. Television and radio programmes, articles in the press, and the teachers' booklets and other publications disseminated by the team all seem to have contributed to this process. The national impact of the project may have affected so-called control schools as well as those in the action group. It is perhaps impossible to estimate how much the timing of GIST coincided with, or was itself the cause of, a rising tide of opinion in favour of more equality of opportunity in schools, and more girls being encouraged to enter the field of science and technology.

Option choices

One of the original aims of the project was to encourage more girls to choose physical science and craft subjects when these became optional in the fourth and fifth years. Figures 13.1, 13.2 and 13.3, taken from the GIST Final Report, show the proportions of girls choosing physics, chemistry and technical crafts in each of the GIST schools during the four years of the project. Option choices did not change dramatically, but the overall pattern is of small increases in the desired direction. The detail of the pattern is ambiguous. There are large differences between individual schools, and smaller differences than might have been expected, between control and action schools.

Action/control differences

For example, Figure 13.1 shows that a higher proportion of girls chose physics in the GIST cohort than in any of the previous three years at four of the action schools: Edgehill, Ashgrove, Moss Green and Tall Trees. The increases ranged from 13 per cent to 5 per cent. However, both control schools also had a markedly higher proportion of girls choosing physics in the GIST year, so the changes cannot necessarily be attributed to the GIST interventions. Physics, as the science showing the greatest underrepresentation of girls, and the most negative attitudes of school students generally, must be seen as the key to change, at least as long as physics continues to assume its present importance in the examination system.

Why should the trend of more girls taking physical science have been just as apparent in the control schools? The answer may be that neither of the control schools was in reality unaffected by the GIST project. For example, a number of

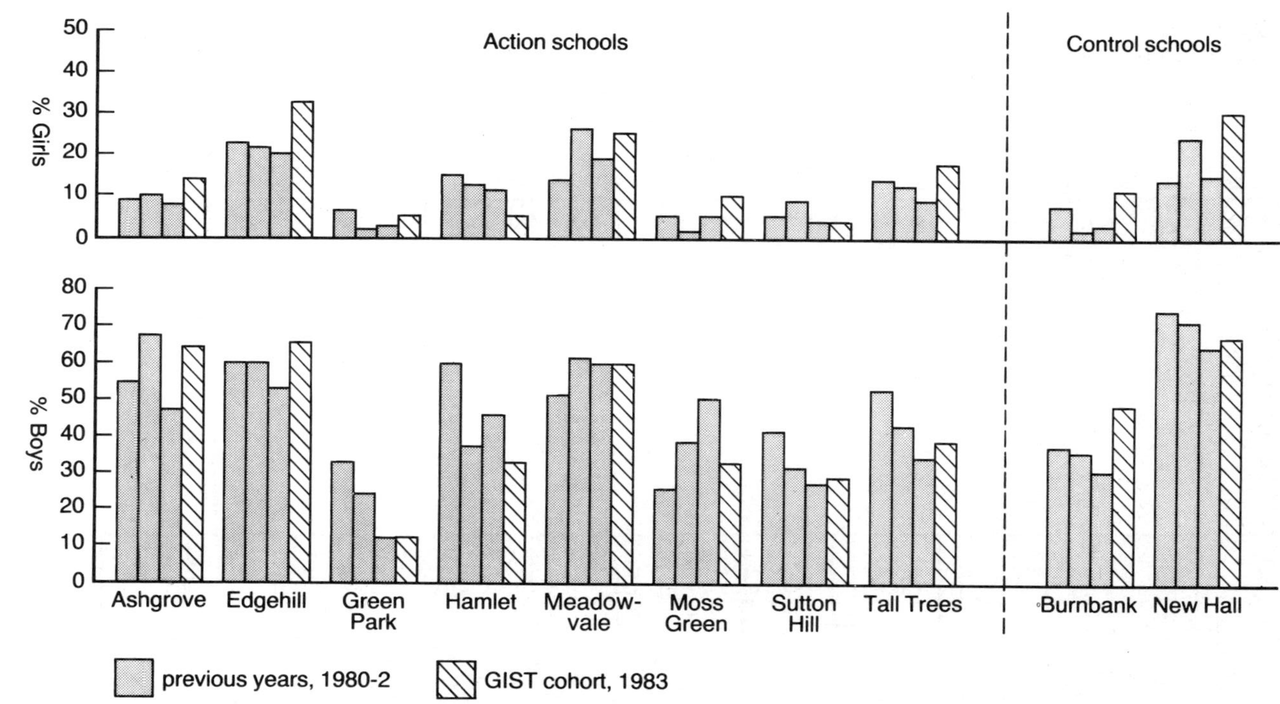

Figure 13.1 Percentage of girls and boys in the year group at GIST schools taking physics in fourth year, 1980 to 1983 Source: Kelly *et al.*, 1984a

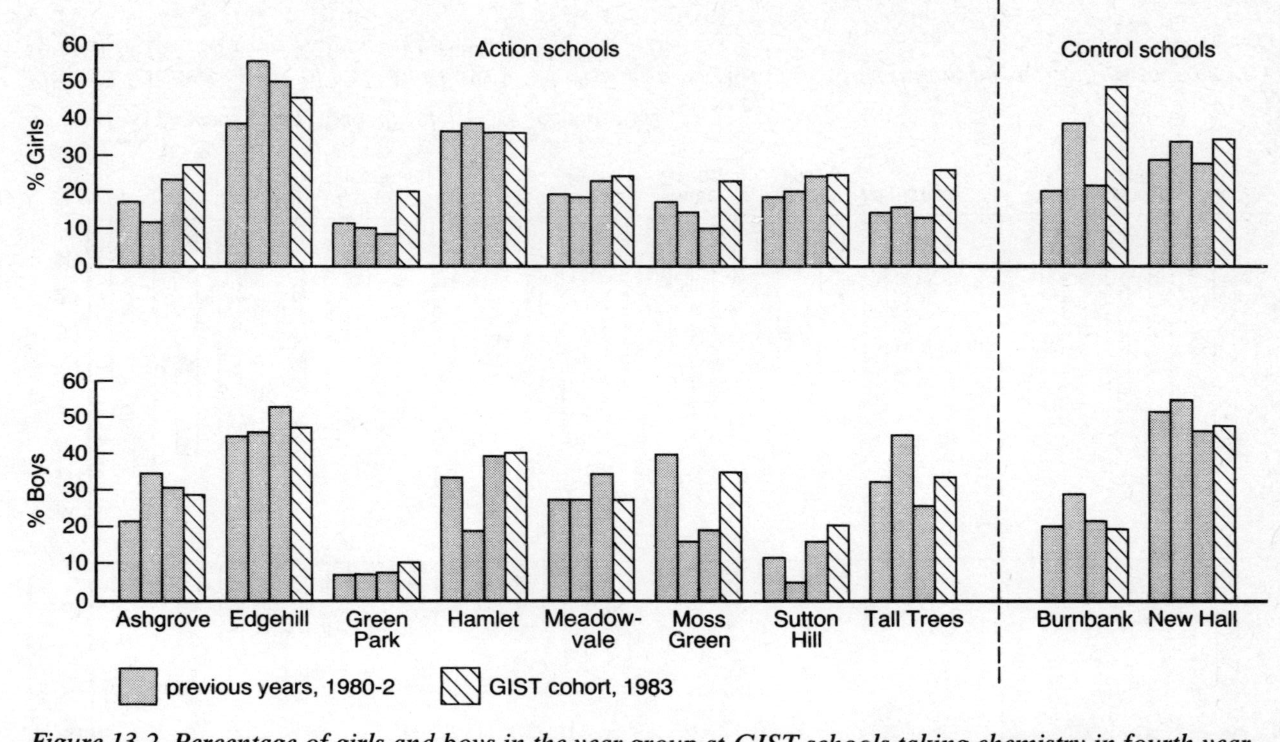

Figure 13.2 Percentage of girls and boys in the year group at GIST schools taking chemistry in fourth year, 1980 to 1983 Source: Kelly *et al.*, 1984a

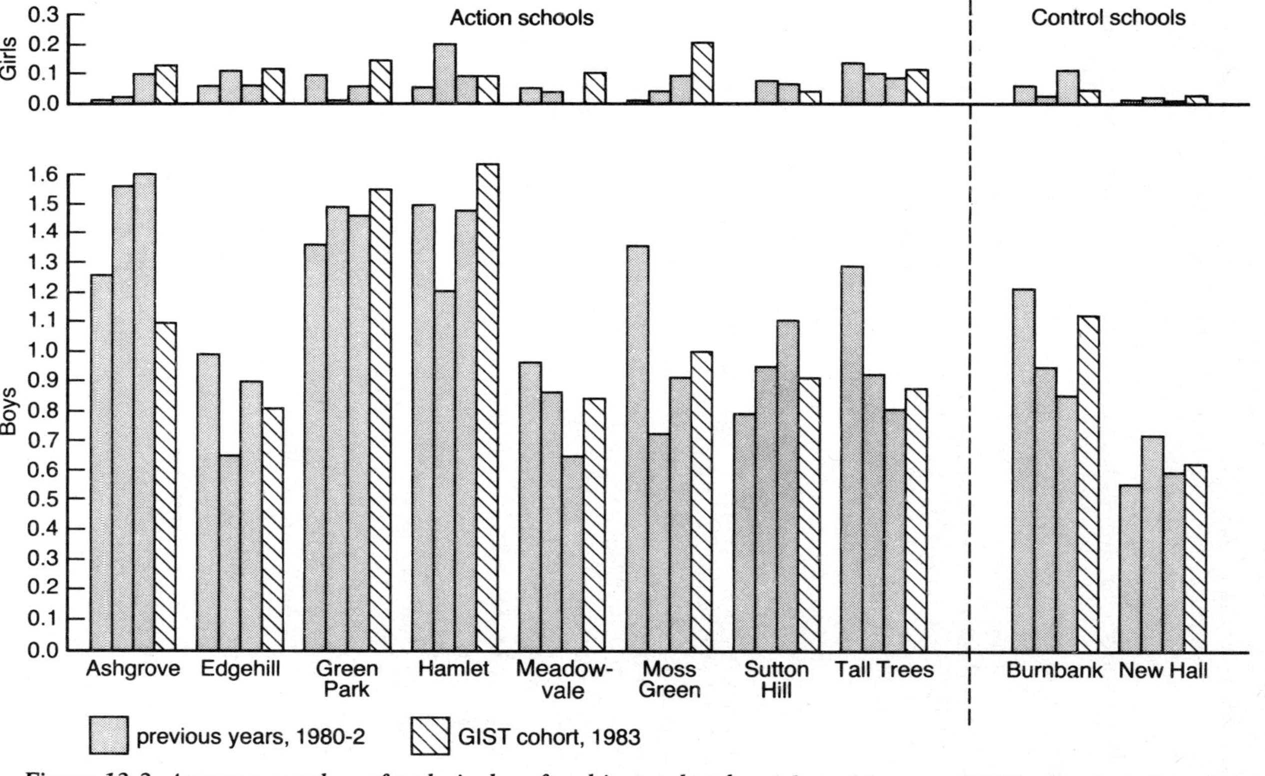

Figure 13.3 Average number of technical craft subjects taken by girls and boys at GIST schools in fourth year, 1980 to 1983 Source note: Kelly *et al.*, 1984a

science teachers from New Hall school (one of the controls) attended a series of workshops for science teachers run by GIST as a short course at the university extra mural department in the spring of 1981. All the recommendations and suggestions we had been making to 'action' teachers in fleeting conversations during visits were presented in a more coherent and relaxed fashion to a group of teachers who had volunteered to attend the course out of interest. Ironically, this may have been effective in changing teachers' practice in New Hall.

When staff at the control schools were asked why they thought the increase had come about, they strongly denied that they had changed their practice in any significant way. This is the same reaction as the one given to the GIST evaluators by action teachers. If teachers are inclined to 'forget' changes they have made, because of the implication that they were in some way at fault before, then control teachers, too, may have covered over the traces of small but significant changes in their classroom practice which occurred as a result of two or three science teachers attending the GIST course.

Alison Kelly visited the two control schools in 1984 to explore further the possible reason for changes in the control schools. (Kelly *et al.*, 1984a)

Although at first mystified about the increase in uptake of physics, the heads of science in the two control schools suggested on reflection that changes in the option system might have had some influence. At New Hall, physics was in a choice column with largely practical subjects for the GIST cohort. At this middle-class school most parents preferred their children to take academic subjects; in previous years physics had been in a column with the second languages which probably siphoned off many able girls. At Burnbank, where more boys as well as more girls chose physics in the GIST year, there was a straight choice between physics and commerce and this had not changed. But chemistry, which was previously set against history, had been set against geography for the GIST cohort and staff felt this would account for the increase in girls taking chemistry. Similar alterations in the options systems may have affected pupils' choices in the action schools.

Finally, we often had the sense that the 'control' schools felt from time to time that they were being left out of something interesting. They were much more efficient and co-operative about returning children's questionnaires than the action schools, and the head of Burnbank frequently used the opportunity of handing over questionnaire scripts to discuss the aims and ideas of GIST with members of the team. It is possible that teachers in both schools were aware of the purposes of GIST and that those who were most interested decided to encourage girls in their departments.

Physics versus chemistry

Moss Green, Tall Trees, Edgehill and Ashgrove all had more girls than ever before opting for physics. At Meadowvale, 17 per cent of girls in the year chose physics in 1980-81; a peak of 32 per cent was reached in 1981-2, dropping slightly to 29 per cent in 1982-3, when the GIST cohort were in the third year. In both control schools, 1983-4 was the peak year for girls opting for physics. The unsuccessful schools in this respect are Green Park, Sutton Hill and Hamlet (see Figure 13.1).

The pattern is slightly different for options in chemistry. Figure 13.2 shows an improvement in the GIST cohort of girls opting for chemistry in six of the action schools. The two exceptions are Edgehill, where there was a peak of 56 per cent of girls opting in 1981; even so, the 1983–4 figure is still an improvement on 1980-1. At Hamlet, there seems to have been very little change over the four years in the proportions of girls doing chemistry. The same is true of New Hall, one of the control schools, but the other, Burnbank, more than doubled the percentage of girls taking chemistry, from 21 per cent in 1979-80, to 48 per cent in 1983-4.

It is possible that there is a relationship between girls' choices for chemistry or physics, and that a shift of girls to physics affects take-up of chemistry, and vice versa. For example, at Green Park the proportion taking physics actually fell over the four-year period, but the percentage of girls doing chemistry rose. At New Hall, a drop in chemistry may be explained in part by the dramatic increase in the choice of physics. It is also conceivable that for some girls chemistry appears as the more conservative, or 'safer' choice of physical science subjects.

Boys' choices

Among boys there was much less variation in the options pattern. Only at Hamlet (where there was drop in the number of boys taking physics) and the control school Burnbank (with a striking increase) did the GIST cohort deviate from the pattern of previous years. Option choice figures were also collected for biology and show a marked increase in the proportion of boys at Moss Green and girls at Burnbank taking biology.

Fluctuating option choice patterns

Although the pattern of option changes may seem disappointing overall, the implicit comparison was a rather artificial one, i.e. between different year groups rather than the same children at different times. The explanation for certain fluctuations could lie in a whole range of factors which cannot necessarily be accounted for in precise terms. Sometimes they can be traced directly to the influence of one teacher or to policy changes within the school. In other instances the effect may be due to variations in the ability of the year group, to groups of friends deciding to do something together, or to an unusual event such as a film or visitor.

For example, Table 13.1 shows the number of children (boys and girls together) who took physics in each of the four years, 1979-83. Asterisks indicate large changes which may be due to the size of the intake in each year, the availability of staffing resources, policy differences between LEAs or the no doubt complex effect of reorganization in four of the action schools.

Only the starred change at Meadowvale arises from a deliberate policy change of which we actually know. Staff there would say that they had already, in 1980-1, come to realize the new importance of physics as a qualification, and therefore began to encourage more children to opt. It is possible that the decision

TABLE 13.1 *Pupils (girls and boys) taking physics*

	1980-1	1981-2	1982-3	1983-4
Moss Green	34	50	62	*23
Green Park	40	24	*12	13
Tall Trees	60	46	45	48
Edgehill	134	112	108	117
Meadowvale	86*	131	126	119
Sutton Hill	51	50	42	41
Hamlet	89	68	71	*39
Ashgrove	76	79	*44	74

to become involved in the GIST project, and the discussions at teacher workshops, hastened a process which had already started.

Craft choices

Figure 13.3 shows changes in the average number of technical craft subjects taken per pupil in each of the action schools during the four years of the project. In four of the action schools – Moss Green, Green Park, Meadowvale and Ashgrove – the proportion of girls choosing technical crafts reached a peak, albeit rather a low peak, in the GIST year, while this was not true of either of the control schools.

This distinct difference between action and control schools could be as a result of the GIST interventions in technology. There is less likely to have been a 'ripple' effect on teachers in the control schools, for two reasons: first, the shortfall of girls in physical sciences, i.e. academic subjects, was more readily recognized as a problem, indeed we sometimes had to remind people that we were also working on the crafts issue. Second, the resistance to encouraging more girls to take technical crafts in their fourth year was much stronger in relation to science (e.g. see Pratt *et al.*, 1984) and we certainly had no direct contact with craft teachers in either of the control schools.

Three schools had some modest success in getting girls to choose the newer CDT subjects (design and technology, craft, design and technology): 11 per cent, 8 per cent and 7 per cent respectively of girls at Moss Green, Tall Trees and Meadowvale continued with the subjects, compared with smaller percentages three years before. The increase at Moss Green is especially notable. More girls than ever before also chose technical drawing at Moss Green. This substantial increase is almost certainly due to the changes advocated by GIST. At Ashgrove, where CDT was not on offer, 8 per cent chose to take technical drawing. By 'breaking the 5 per cent barrier' these schools may have begun a small inroad into these male-dominated subjects. At Green Park, 8 per cent chose woodwork, again an effect almost certainly linked to the establishment of the GIST girls' woodwork club.

At two of the action schools (Moss Green and Tall Trees) boys took slightly more domestic crafts in the fourth year, while at three action schools (Ashgrove, Sutton Hill and Tall Trees) and one control school (Burnbank again), girls took slightly fewer. At the other control school (New Hall), girls' uptake of domestic crafts increased from an initially low level.

To summarise then: at Moss Green all the option choices altered in the direction the project intended, i.e. towards more girls and boys taking subjects traditionally associated with the opposite sex. At five other action schools there was at least one change in the desired direction and no negative changes. However, both control schools also fell into this category, so the changes cannot necessarily be attributed to the GIST interventions. At the remaining two action schools there were no overall changes in option choice except that fewer pupils of both sexes took physics at Hamlet.

Pupils' attitudes

A range of attitude, achievement and stereotyping tests was administered to the GIST cohort in their first term at secondary school. A second battery of tests was given to the same pupils in the summer term of their third year (i.e. two and a half years later). Almost all the information in this section is drawn from the GIST Final Report (Kelly *et al.*, 1984a). The work of analysis was carried out by Alison Kelly, and a number of these and earlier results are reported in several papers written by Alison Kelly and Barbara Smail (see pages 278-80).

Three of the tests – Image of Science, Science Curiosity and Occupational Stereotypes – were administered on both occasions. In summary, they show significant differences, on various subscales, between pupils' attitudes in the action and control schools. The intervention effect appears to have been greatest on the single issue of the 'masculine' image of science and technology, and associated occupations.

Three new tests were administered, questioning children about their option choices, career and lifestyle intentions and their opinions about technical craft and science lessons. The third test was primarily a service to the schools, as children were asked to rate their enjoyment of science topics and craft projects which were different in each school. The results are not reported on in this chapter, but were sent back to schools in May 1984. The options questionnaire contained some questions which had been asked in the first survey, investigating children's attitudes to school, and their self-estimates of academic competence.

Sex differences stayed much the same over the four-year period, boys continuing to display more rigid sex stereotypes than girls, for example. Class differences were minimal (but see Chapter 7). Individual children's attitudes were also remarkably stable over the period of the project, but girls' overall liking for science came to be specifically associated with their interest in physical science.

Science curiosity

Figure 13.4a (taken from Kelly *et al.*, 1984a) shows changes between the first and second survey in children's science curiosity on the four subscales. During their three years at secondary school children became *less* curious about physical science (PHYSCUR), nature study (NATSCCUR) and what we called 'spectacular' science (TVSCICUR). The exception was in human biology (HUMBICUR) which rose for both sexes, but particularly for girls.

Analysis of the data shows a small but consistent pattern of action schools having *less* negative changes than control schools, indicating that the GIST project may have had a small but positive effect on children's declining interest in science. Boys were just as much affected by GIST in this way as girls.

Image of science

Figure 13.4b compares attitude change on the Image of Science subscales in action and control schools. Again, there is a growing negativism about science: children's personal liking for science (LIKESCI), appreciation of its value (SCIWORLD) and view of scientists (SCIENT) were lower at the end of the third year than they had been at the beginning of the first year. However, on each of these subscales, the decline in the control schools was consistently greater. The difference between action and control schools was quite pronounced on SCIMALE (the extent to which science is seen as masculine). All these scales are closely related to the VISTA programme, which was specifically designed to break down the masculine stereotype of science. The women visitors endeavoured to present a view of science as personally enjoyable and socially worthwhile, and to broaden the image of scientists as cold, hard, masculine and impersonal. The scales are also possibly related to GIST interventions such as curriculum development and monitoring of classroom interactions. These

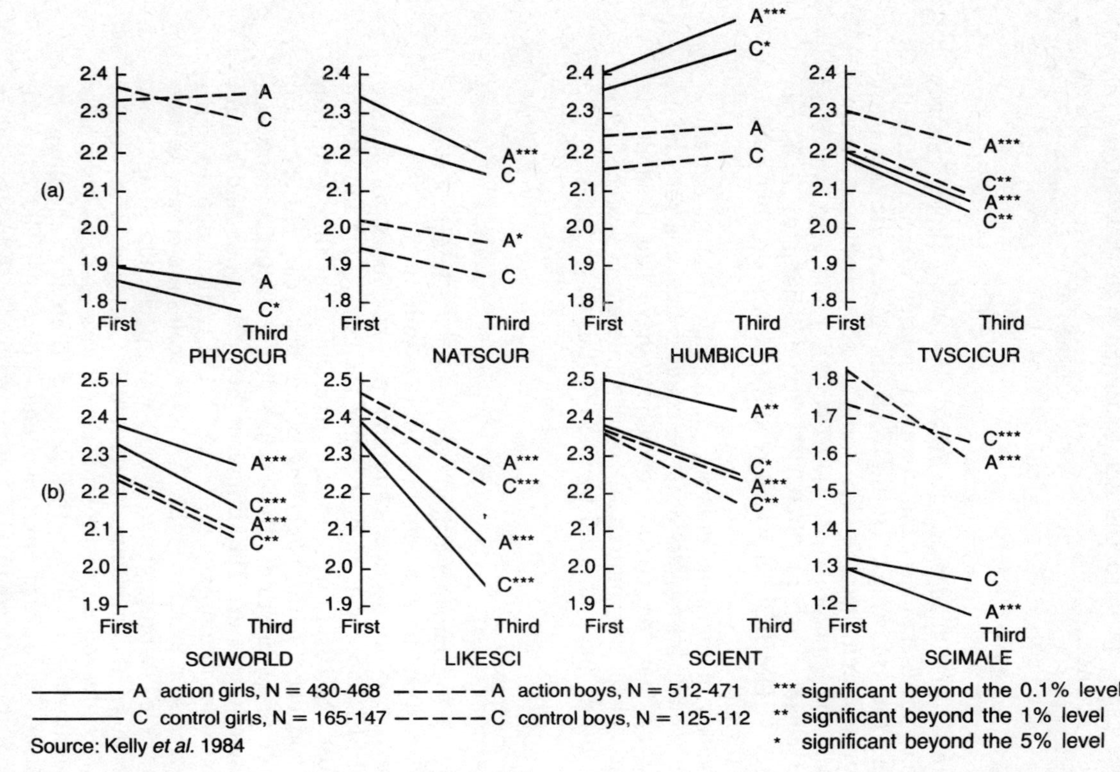

Figure 13.4 Mean attitude scores of girls and boys in action and control schools in first and third year, Image of Science subscales

results confirm (see Chapter 6) that a 'girl friendly science' will also improve the attitudes and interests of male pupils, for boys in the action schools displayed less negative attitudes than their peers in the control schools.

Sex role stereotypes

Children were asked again to rate the suitability of various jobs for men and women in general, and for themselves in particular. Figure 13.5 shows the results on three subscales: tendency to be sex-typed (SEXTYPE), inclination to consider jobs 'feminine' (FSELF) or 'masculine' (MSELF). A decrease on scores on these subscales indicates a reduction in sex typing. Both girls and boys in the action schools became much less sex-stereotyped in their views of the suitability of different jobs for women and men. Control school children also became less sex-stereotyped (presumably this is a maturation effect), but to a lesser extent than in the action schools. In addition, children became more enthusiastic about taking up jobs traditionally associated with the opposite sex, and this was most marked amongst girls in the action schools (MSELF). All these action/control differences are consistent with a causal effect of children's exposure to men and women in non-traditional jobs, during VISTA and the roadshows.

There was no second testing of science knowledge: instead a broad comparison was made between results on school tests. Obviously, as these were different in different schools, they cannot be directly compared. However, on average boys in each school did slightly better than girls on the physics tests, and girls did slightly better than boys in chemistry and biology. Analysis of the figures shows that boys' small lead over girls in physics knowledge at the age of 11 was maintained but not increased into the third year. On the other hand, girls' small initial lead in biology did increase slightly.

Sex differences in confidence were evident from a question in the second survey which asked pupils how well they usually got on in school tests. Only 27 per cent of girls, but a massive 41 per cent of boys said they expected to do 'better than average' in the future.

Children were also asked how much they liked the three science subjects, and how difficult they found them. Physics was perceived as the most difficult, and biology as the easiest, although girls were more unanimous about this than boys. Girls

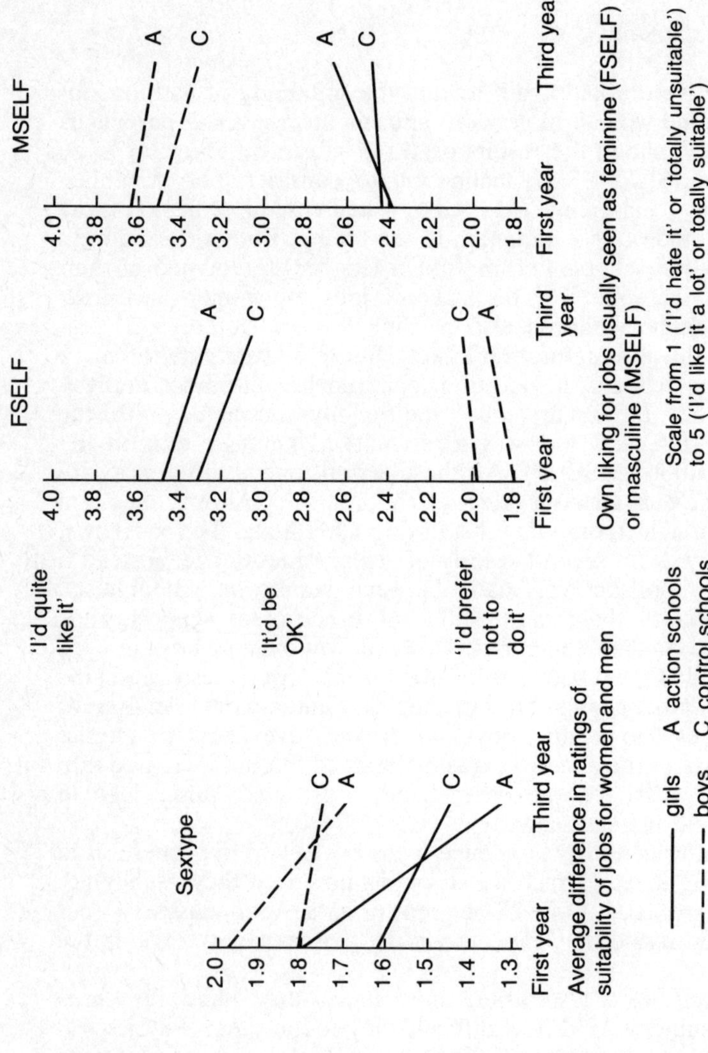

Figure 13.5 Mean scores of girls and boys in action and control schools on measures of sex stereotyping in first and third year

preferred biology and disliked physics, while the reverse was true for boys. But the correlation between difficulty and liking was different for the two sexes. Boys 'liked' physics, even though they perceived it as difficult.

Options

Pupils who opted to continue with a subject usually did so for the first time early in the spring term. Tests are generally carried out in the summer term. Not surprisingly, pupils who had chosen a subject achieved much better in it than pupils who were going to drop it. This was more marked in physics and chemistry than in biology. Girls who opted to continue with physical science performed on average slightly better than the boys. In biology there was no average achievement difference between the girls and boys who continued into the fourth year. This suggests that there is a confidence barrier for girls, and that only the more able persist with physical science.

Pupils were agreed on the three factors which weighed most in their choice of subject. All these factors had significantly high ratings:

usefulness for getting a job;
finding the subject interesting;
own performance in the subject.

The opinions of teachers and parents, the options booklet and career talks were also rated as quite important, However, the opinion of friends and older pupils, the teacher who would be taking the subject in the fourth year, and whether it was mainly girls or boys taking it were discounted as influences.

Perhaps these ratings should not be taken at face value; probably they do reflect the factors constructing pupils' decisions, but the weighting may also reflect what pupils have been told they should consider. The first three items would be frequently mentioned by the school as important considerations to be kept in mind, and teachers' and parents' opinions would also be considered legitimate to canvass. Option booklets and information given out on parents' evenings often stress these considerations. However schools also stress that one shouldn't join a group just because a friend is doing the same subject, or that teachers may change, and so liking for a particular teacher should not unduly influence one's decision. A study of occupational choice in a college of further education found students very unwilling to admit to any personal influence on their choice of vocational course at the college, though information gleaned by other means suggested they could be important (Whyte, 1972).

Career intentions

Questionnaires on option choices and careers were devised especially for the second survey, and showed up further differences between children in action and control schools. When asked about the sort of job they would like to do, girls in action schools were much more likely to mention as their expected or desired occupation a job with some scientific or technical content. This is one of the most pleasing results, as it shows unequivocally that the programme opened up new opportunities to girls, of a kind they would not have considered before. However, the occupations most frequently mentioned by boys and girls remained firmly sex-stereotyped (see Table 13.2 below).

Both boys and girls were primarily concerned with having interesting, well-paid work and pleasant companions in their jobs. But pay and promotion were more important to boys, whereas helping others, meeting people and keeping clean were more important to girls than to boys. Girls scored considerably higher than boys on a scale of person orientation, and were much more likely to mention working with children and with animals as an aspect of their ideal job.

Action school girls were also more likely to want to be employed while they had young children (in common with several of the VISTA women, or possibly as a result of discussion of

TABLE 13.2 *The five most common expected occupations for girls and boys*

	Girls % mentioning		Boys % mentioning
Hairdresser	17	Armed Forces	11
Nursery nurse, something with children	15	Engineer	11
Typist, secretary	14	Something in computers	11
Nurse	11	Electrician	10
Teacher	9	Car mechanic	10

Source: Kelly *et al.* 1984a

lifestyles during the roadshows). Compared with girls in the control group, they were also less likely to say they wanted their future husband to be cleverer than themselves.

Between school differences

The ambiguity of option choice patterns, and the large between-school differences, implied that individual school factors may be of overriding importance in determining girls' subject choices. The results of the attitude survey, however, reveal significant differences, as expected, between action and control schools. Were schools successful in option choices also successful in promoting attitude change?

Successful and unsuccessful schools

Table 13.3 schematically presents measures of comparative success and failure by individual school, using option choice and 'sex of science' increases as indicators of relative success.

Overall, Moss Green was the most successful school, with an increase in the GIST year in the proportion of girls choosing physics, chemistry and crafts, and a large increase in the sex neutrality of both girls' and boys' image of science.

Ashgrove was also successful on option choice changes, but attitude changes were consistently poor. Meadowvale was successful on the options criterion for chemistry and crafts; the peak year for girls taking physics happened in 1981, but the proportion in the GIST year was still a notable increase on the 1980 figure. Changes in children's SCIMALE scores were also large at Meadowvale.

These three schools, Moss Green, Ashgrove and Meadowvale, seem to have been the most successful in fulfilling the aims of increasing the proportions of girls opting for science and technology.

Tall Trees was more successful with science than with craft options, but girls' SCIMALE scores moved less than in some other action schools. Edgehill increased the percentage of girls taking chemistry earlier than the GIST year, but maintained the higher proportion up to 1983. The physics options were up in 1983, but craft options actually dropped. Boys and girls became considerably more liberal about the 'masculine' image of science.

TABLE 13.3 *Option choices and SCISEX scores*

a Option choices

	Increase in % of girls in year group		
	Physics	Chemistry	Crafts
Successful (i.e. GIST peak year)	Moss Green Tall Trees Edgehill Ashgrove (New Hall) (Burnbank)	Moss Green Tall Trees Sutton Hill Ashgrove Meadowvale (New Hall) (Burnbank)	Moss Green Green Park Ashgrove Meadowvale
Peak year in 1981	Meadowvale	Edgehill	Hamlet
No change or small change	Sutton Hill Green Park	Hamlet	Tall Trees
Failure (i.e. decrease in GIST year)	Hamlet	—	Edgehill Sutton Hill (New Hall) (Burnbank)

b SCISEX scores

		Increase in liberality		
		Increase in boys' score (points)	Increase in girls' score (points)	Girls' score increased to:
Very successful	Edgehill	22	10	2.9
	Moss Green	34	25	2.85
	Meadowvale	35	30	2.82
Small change	Ashgrove	20	8	2.7
	Hamlet	20	8	2.75
	Tall Trees	20	1	2.73
	(New Hall)	11	1	2.74)
	(Burnbank)	24	8	2.63)
	Sutton Hill	8	10	2.73
Failure	Green Park	–1	–8	2.71

(Originally, the scale measuring the extent to which children stereotyped science as masculine was called SCISEX, on which *higher* scores denote that science is seen as more sex neutral. On Figure 13.4, however, reporting the second attitude survey, the scores have been reconstructed to give a SCIMALE score, i.e. the degree to which science is seen as masculine. A *decrease* in this indicates a tendency to see science as more sex neutral.)

These five schools, Moss Green, Meadowvale, Ashgrove, Tall Trees and Edgehill, were successful in achieving some of the GIST aims.

At Green Park, GIST was the peak year for girls choosing chemistry and crafts, but the proportion taking physics dropped. However the number of children of both sexes taking physics was very small in each of the four years. Attitudes at Green Park became less rather than more liberal, against the trend of all the other schools.

The remaining two schools, Hamlet and Sutton Hill, must be regarded as comparative failures. Although SCIMALE attitudes improved in both schools, option choices were consistently unresponsive to intervention. The schools can therefore be grouped as follows:

Successful:	Moss Green, Meadowvale
Quite successful:	Edgehill, Ashgrove, Tall Trees
Poor:	Green Park, Hamlet, Sutton Hill

A number of factors both external and internal may have produced differences in outcome between schools; social class of intake, for instance, and the effects of reorganization (in one local authority) may have been important. Internal factors of possible significance include the curricular arrangements within departments, the option system, teacher attitudes and interventions, the presence or absence of women staff in senior positions in departments or within the school, the attitudes of senior management, and a school 'ethos' sympathetic or otherwise to GIST.

External factors

Social class

A study of curriculum options carried out in 1981 in a national sample of schools found that, on average, 16 per cent of girls in

TABLE 13.4 *Comparison of middle-class intake and girls choosing physics in GIST schools*

	% girls choosing physics, 1979	% middle-class intake	% girls choosing physics, 1983
Edgehill	27	49	38
New Hall	16	72	37
Tall Trees	16	41	20
Meadowvale	17	23	29
Hamlet	18	19	6
Moss Green	6	22	11
Green Park	7	10	4
Sutton Hill	5	7	4
Ashgrove	9	25	16
Burnbank	9	19	12

mixed schools choose to continue with physics. If we take this as a 'benchmark' for the GIST schools, then at the start of the project in 1979, only four of the action schools and one control school had average or above average proportions of girls choosing physics in the fourth year. Three of these also had a relatively high middle-class intake. Smithers & Collings (1982) have shown that middle-class girls of high ability tend to made science choices whether they go to single-sex or coeducational schools; the factor of social class has almost certainly helped some schools in increasing the percentage of girls doing physics, as we can see from the baseline of the first five schools in Table 13.4. At the *least* middle-class schools, Green Park, Sutton Hill, Moss Green, Ashgrove and Burnbank, the proportions of girls taking physics were well below those of the national sample, ranging between 5 per cent and 9 per cent. All these schools were located in working-class areas. One conclusion which could be drawn is that daughters of middle-class parents may receive more encouragement to take physics in the present climate of anxiety about job and career prospects for young people. This would be consistent with the results from the more middle-class schools. Yet Moss Green and Ashgrove were among the more successful schools, judged by the increase in taking girls taking physics between 1979 and 1983, and at Green Park, a higher proportion of girls chose chemistry than in any of the previous three years.

Social class can therefore only be one amongst other factors, in view of the equally good results at schools with a working-class intake.

Reorganization

In the school year 1981-2, four schools (Ashgrove, Moss Green, Hamlet and Sutton Hill) were involved in local authority reorganization of secondary schools, and all the teachers had to apply for new posts. This was expected to be very disruptive for the GIST project, because of the break in continuity of our relationships with staff. However the effects appear not to have been the same in every school. At Hamlet, the merger with another local comprehensive meant that the school was considerably enlarged, and the problems of coping with a school now on four sites must have overshadowed the concern for GIST. In fact the school asked that any further interventions in the next year should be addressed to the new year group who had joined the GIST cohort. This could not be done, and the net effect was undoubtedly to reduce the impact of the project. At Sutton Hill the reorganization meant massive staff changes, and although some of the new staff became interested in GIST – for example the head of the third year was closely involved in planning and back-up for the roadshows – it appears from the evaluation report that she was perceived by senior management to be too concerned with GIST. As the heads remained in three of the reorganized schools, their attitudes to the project may have had a crucial influence in guiding teachers to decide how much time they should give to GIST. If this is so, then it may explain why the reorganization at Moss Green and Ashgrove does not appear to have negatively affected non-traditional option choices. At Ashgrove, the head was explicitly trying to change the school from a rather traditional 11-16 comprehensive to become a more liberal and dynamic sixth form college, a change consistent with the 'progressivism' of GIST. At Moss Green, the new head, formerly deputy head in charge of curriculum at another GIST school, instituted an experiment in single-sex grouping to study the effects on girls' up-take of science, thereby signalling to the rest of the staff his approval of GIST aims.

Meadowvale and Edgehill had a more stable situation during the life of the project, although the promotion of the head of science to take on the additional post of head of the upper school reduced the time he had available for GIST. Both these schools were relatively successful. At Tall Trees, there were two heads of science, both of whom made a point of involving themselves in the GIST programme, not least because they knew that the headteacher supported the project. The staff changeover did not appear to have negative effects for option choice.

Internal factors

What features of internal organization did schools in each group have in common? In Chapter 3, each school is considered separately, with a description of what seemed to us the most striking or relevant features of its internal organization. This section discusses which of those features seem to explain the pattern of results in each school.

In the 'poor' group, Hamlet, Green Park, and Sutton Hill had low proportions of children from middle-class homes. Very small proportions of girls also took physics at Burnbank, the control school in a working-class area. The low uptake in science subjects, particularly physics, of children in all four schools could be related to the skewed social class intake, but the social class composition may also have depressed school and teacher expectations. In such schools, it may be less likely that girls will choose to do physics. However, this is not the whole story. Individual teachers, option systems and school ethos also have some effect. Edgehill has a less affluent population than New Hall, but a higher proportion of girls choosing physics, largely because of a faculty structure which requires most pupils to take either physics or chemistry. Meadowvale has a mixed catchment area but a strong and effective science department with a tradition of encouraging girls.

Figure 13.6 makes some further comparisons between schools, on two issues: the proportion of women staff in positions of authority (defined as Scale 4 and above), and the extent of explicit discussion of sex roles or girls-only activities carried out as part of the GIST programme, and which would have been clearly visible to the children.

Sutton Hill and Hamlet are the only action schools where no known positive action for girls took place. They are also at the bottom of the 'league table' for women in authority positions. The head of Sutton Hill was notably disinclined to favour any measure of positive discrimination, and the head of Hamlet,

	% women at scale 4 or above		Explicit discussion of sex roles (see notes below)	Moss Green[1] Meadowvale[2] Green Park[3]
Women in positions of authority	35 Green Park 33 Ashgrove (29 New Hall)* 25 Moss Green 24 Edgehill			(Tall Trees)[4] Ashgrove?[5] Edgehill[6]$_5$
Few women in positions of authority	18 Meadowvale (12 Burnbank) 11 Tall Trees* 11 Sutton Hill 8 Hamlet		No explicit discussion of sex roles	Sutton Hill Hamlet (action schools only)

Notes

1 Single-sex science clubs, day trips, single-sex science setting.
2 Active tutorial work in science. 'Gender in our lives' used.
3 Single-sex woodwork club.
4 Work experience for girls only, but did not take place until October 1983.
5 'Gender in our lives' used.
6 Letters to parents of girls and boys showing highly on GIST spatial and mechanical tests.

* Headteacher female.

Figure 13.6 Women in authority and discussion of sex roles at GIST schools

though she voiced her support of GIST and actually attended a GIST parents' evening, did not seem to have given any clear lead within the school on measures to support GIST, for example by altering the crafts mini-option system.

Hamlet and Sutton Hill also seem to have suffered from reorganization (see above), and the craft department at Hamlet, in particular, was weakly organized and did not offer a curriculum attractive to any but the most vocationally oriented boys. Senior staff in both schools offered little or no positive support to the project, and did not expect teachers to be very active interventionists. Sutton Hill also had a rather traditional atmosphere, at odds with the 'progressive' aims of GIST.

These two schools seem to have had the poorest conditions, then, for encouragement of girls.

At Green Park, girls were offered the chance to attend a single-sex woodwork club, and some of those who did so opted for woodwork in the fourth year. However it was against a background of traditional sex segregation, and in a school where staff attitudes appear from the evaluation report to have been distinctly disenchanted. Negative attitudes and their occasional open opposition to GIST (see Chapter 8) must have been obvious to the children, and their increasing 'sexism' about science probably reflects their teachers' views. Nevertheless, Green Park had the highest proportion of women in senior positions, and the only female head of science, herself a biologist. Green Park really has to be seen as a rather special case, because although the teachers presented a very negative view to the evaluators, the actual outcomes from GIST were unexpectedly positive.

Successful schools

Ashgrove had the second highest percentage of women in senior positions (33 per cent), although they tended to have pastoral or curriculum rather than science or craft responsibilities. The percentage at Moss Green (25 per cent) appears lower, but in fact the head and deputy head of the lower school, the head of year and the head of lower school science at Moss Green were all women, and, in the atmosphere of the school, consciously feminist. A new physics teacher who joined the staff after reorganization was also a woman, and took a considerable interest in GIST. At Meadowvale there was again a lower percentage of women in authority in the school overall (18 per cent), but the head of biology and PSE was a sympathetic woman, and there were several women on the science staff with strong feminist leanings, some with pastoral responsibilities.

In three of the most successful schools, then, children would be aware of women in positions of authority in the lower school, some of whom, in the light of their own views about women's role, could be expected to present strong and positive role models.

At Moss Green especially, but also at Meadowvale, children were directly told by their teachers that there was a problem about girls and science and technology and that the school wished to encourage girls. In no other school can we be sure that staff made this so clear. This visibility of teachers' concern seems likely to have been an important factor at Moss Green and Meadowvale, but there is not much evidence that it occurred at Ashgrove.

One feature these two schools had in common, however, was a willingness to innovate not just with the content and organization of the curriculum (as at Edgehill) but with teaching methods and processes – the single-sex setting experiment at Moss Green fitted easily into a community school committed to finding new approaches to the education of inner-city children. Classrooms were open plan, and the school in 1983 made a successful bid to become a pilot for the local authority's Alternative Curriculum Strategies project. It is frequently featured in the educational press for other innovatory approaches.

At Meadowvale, the science department fundamentally reviewed its lower school science curriculum and teaching methods (see Thompson, 1982), and GIST children were given 'active tutorial work' lessons on the topic of girls in science.

Not surprisingly, the more 'progressive' schools were readier to accept and adapt to an innovation concerned with bringing about equal opportunities.

Middling schools

The schools where success was more uneven shared some aspects of what appear to have been the preconditions for success. Ashgrove was a much more traditional school at the outset of the project, but its reorganization as a sixth form college was preceded by thoroughgoing departmental reviews of teaching methods, and an influx of new staff for the proposed college. There was therefore an atmosphere of positively directed change, in contrast with Hamlet and Sutton Hill, where reorganization appeared to have more negative effects, at least for the GIST cohort of girls.

Edgehill seemed likely to be a successful school; it had the highest middle-class intake of the action schools, and the most advanced provision, with integrated crafts throughout the school, and a division of science into 'physical' and 'environmental' rather than the traditional biology, physics and chemistry. A good deal of classroom observation took place there, and the school had a relatively high proportion of women in senior positions (24 per cent). 'Gender in Our Lives' was taught by a sympathetic group of staff, and in this school attitudes to sex roles changed considerably, with Edgehill girls scoring highest on 'liberality' of any in the GIST group. Indeed Edgehill was successful in increasing the proportion of girls taking physics and chemistry, but it is disappointing that the craft options did not change. The head of crafts was rather ambivalent, and frequently remarked that this department would not be able to cope with a large influx of girls into technical crafts if that should occur; in retrospect, this seems to have been a self-fulfilling prophecy. A comparison of initial and later choices shows that an initial twelve was whittled down by September 1983 to three or four. Certainly, crafts was the only stumbling block to placing Edgehill, as it would otherwise have appeared, at the top of a league table of 'successful' schools.

Tall Trees was also expected to be more successful than it turned out to be in persuading girls to take crafts. The female head of the school was very supportive of GIST, and the head of science initiated a girls-only work experience scheme. More girls chose physics and chemistry, but the craft choices showed little change. Boys, but not girls, altered their view of the masculinity of science. This may reflect the strong emphasis in the school on conformity to traditional values, and the sex differential rules about uniform. The fact that 'positive discrimination' took place too late to affect option choices may have diminished the potential for greater success.

Teacher attitudes

It is clear from the analysis of teachers' perceptions of, and response to, GIST, that there was a great deal of variation in the way teachers felt about the project, and in the consequent action they took, or in some cases did not take. In certain schools, the option results suggest that the presence of a teacher sympathetic to GIST, especially if s/he was in a key position, could have positive effects. For example, the head of science who moved from Hamlet to Ashgrove may have found it easier to promote GIST in a new department, and in the context of a school where the GIST 'stem' (last intake at 11 years) was explicitly seen as forming the backbone of the future sixth form college. The school may have seen their option choices as particularly important for that reason, and encouraged non-traditional choices.

Green Park was the only school in which teachers seem to have been of one mind about the project. Although the female head of science was initially in favour, she later became more negative about the project in the school, but presumably that did not stop her from encouraging girls to take her own subject, chemistry.

In all the other schools, individuals varied; for a positive effect to occur, one of two conditions seems to have been necessary: first, if the ethos of the school broadly supported social change, it was easier for teachers to work with the project; this was the case at Moss Green, Ashgrove, Meadowvale and Edgehill, all quite successful schools. Second, within a department, change was more likely if a group of teachers worked together to promote the aims of the project, as happened in the Meadowvale science department. The least successful schools – Hamlet, Sutton Hill and Green Park – were also the most 'traditional' and 'conservative', and none of them could boast a small cohesive group of pro-GIST teachers. This may be why even hard-working and sympathetic heads of science in all three schools, with minimal support from their colleagues, did not achieve any notable change in the pattern of girls' option choices.

Chapter 14

Implications

Implications for teachers

Teachers at the outset of the project have been described as 'cold' in their attitude in the sense that we had to start from 'cold' and could make no assumptions about any prior perception of the problem, or warmth of commitment to solving it. Against this background, their interviews with the evaluation team show how much was achieved in alerting them to GIST as a professional issue, and provoking them to think, often deeply and carefully, about possible solutions. They themselves seemed unaware how much their views and attitudes had changed, but our own field notes, the evaluation report and the student survey of teachers' attitudes all point to subtle but important differences between the GIST teachers and others.

Reasons for the teachers' initial unwillingness to take on board the GIST issue as being of serious professional concern are encapsulated in the following statement, chosen instead of a verbatim quote from a GIST teacher because they were usually too polite to express their doubts so clearly to us. It was made by a deputy head to Joan Borley, who investigated the impact (disappointing, as it turned out) of the distribution to schools of an EOC pamphlet called 'Do you provide equal educational opportunities?':

> 'I think that employers would not choose girls because of marriage, pregnancy, and the biological differences between men and women. For long term training programmes I think that employers would probably take boys, and so would I if I were running a company. I wouldn't want to waste money on

toilet conversions. I wouldn't want to create additional problems. One woman with twenty-five men. She has to be worth the hassle. Will she distract them? Can they use bad language? And, of course, girls lack motivation.' (Borley, 1982, p. 86)

Underlying this statement is a traditional view of sex roles. It assumes that biological sex differences are of crucial importance, that 'lack of motivation' is an inherently female characteristic, that there is no good reason for changing the status quo, and that provision of equal opportunities may be a nuisance to men.

If we take the statement apart, there seem to be five elements, which in combination constitute a virtually impenetrable barrier to girls in science and technology, especially if held by someone in a position to influence the pattern of girls' choices.

(1) a belief in biological determinism;
(2) a belief in 'cultural' determinism;
(3) denial that a problem exists;
(4) traditional views about sex roles;
(5) apprehension that boys will suffer from positive discrimination for girls.

(1) *Belief in biological determinism*
In discussion with teachers in the GIST workshops we were sometimes bluntly told that girls just can't do maths, that the abstractions of physics were beyond them, or that technical crafts require a physical strength girls do not possess. On examination there is really very little hard evidence for the biological theory, compared with the strong impression it appears to have made on the minds of science teachers. The GIST cognitive tests, and the suggestive link (Smail, 1983) between intellectual performance and relevant earlier experiences, went a long way to undermining teachers' biologically determinist views.

Unfortunately most educational research is not so directly fed back to the schools in a way that makes it possible for teachers to adjust their views and practice accordingly. Few teachers have the time or expertise to compare different research findings, and training courses offer little critical analysis of sex difference.

(1) *Belief in 'cultural determinism'*
Teachers seemed to accept girls' lesser interest in physical science and technology as a fact of life, and a self-explanatory reason for their absence from these spheres. The most superficial survey of

science materials revealed to them why the subject has acquired such a masculine image. The GIST tests showed that in view of girls' greater concern about the social and human applications of science, the lack of human interest or information about everyday uses of science stopped girls from seeing the real fascination and potential of the subject. Attitude tests showed that girls are very interested in some aspects of science and that these predispositions can be built on. VISTA visits convinced the teachers that science can be presented in a way that is much more interesting and accessible to the adolescent pupil. They were also able to see that without the reservoir of informal knowledge boys have picked up outside school, girls start off at a disadvantage in the unfamiliar male environment of the lab or workshop. Girls have fewer chances for three-dimensional, practical and 'tinkering' activities, depriving them of some of the concrete experiences which can feed into an understanding of mathematical and scientific processes.

(3) *Denial of the problem*
Teachers need to be convinced of existing bias before they will consider positive discrimination for girls. The GIST observations showed how, in many practically based lessons, boys monopolize available resources and gain more than their fair share of teacher time and attention. However the GIST teachers showed that the pattern of male domination in the classroom can be broken, by teachers motivated to change. Single-sex groups and clubs showed just how much girls are repressed and inhibited by the presence of boys (see below, Implications of single-sex grouping).

(4) *Traditional views about sex roles*
Like the deputy head quoted earlier, teachers tend to think of pupils' future family life as something which will only be in the hands of wives and mothers. The choices made by girls at school too often reflect a mistaken view of the life patterns they are likely to experience in the future. The average woman already spends only about seven years out of the labour market, and girls at school today can expect to be employed, full-time or part-time, for twenty-five years after their children have started school. Teachers as well as pupils need to be better informed about the future pattern of girls' lives, and the opportunities for non-traditional employment for both sexes. The roadshows stimulated discussion amongst teachers, and, together with VISTA, made significant changes in children's attitudes and beliefs about the

sexual division of labour. Fatherhood and the acquisition of social and life skills are even more important for boys, who may not have received the same amount of socialization in sensitivity to others' needs as girls. Children need to be prepared for a future in which lifestyles and sex role expectations are changing. Courses in humanities, personal and social, moral and health education can contribute to building more flexible and independent adults of both sexes.

(5) *Fears about the effects on boys*
Contrary to teachers' fears, the boys did not suffer from their involvement in a programme designed to improve opportunities for girls. The changes in their attitudes to science indicate that the VISTA intervention and changes in curriculum materials helped their understanding and appreciation of science, too. There is even some indication that they got more out of the VISTA activities than girls, asking questions of the visitors, and making use of the careers information they provided. Although the gap between the sexes remained, boys continuing to be more stereotyped, boys in action schools did become more liberal than their peers in the control schools, showing that efforts to alter their attitudes about sex roles were not in vain. However, the boys' more negative response to male visitors signals a problem area. It may be easier for them to accept women's right to 'aspire' to men's jobs than to believe that men who choose feminine occupations do not necessarily suffer a loss in status.

Girl friendly teachers

The teacher who can engage the active participation of girls is by definition a good teacher, and failure to engage them is in that respect a professional failure. It would not be surprising then if probationary teachers and teachers in training should find it even more difficult than experienced teachers not to let the mixed classroom become dominated by boys' interests, activities and interjections. Some of the worst examples of boys being allowed full scope to shout out answers, to ignore the hands up rule, and generally by their greater robustness to dominate, featured in classrooms managed by probationers. It would seem that the ideal atmosphere for a mixed class in which girls will feel comfortable about talking publicly, and participating fully in practical activities, is one in which the teacher has achieved an extremely firm management of the classroom. But the emphasis is on being firm without being authoritarian. This is a difficult and narrow line. Good science teaching and good craft teaching take a great deal of organization and a teacher who is going to be aware of children's progress has to have eyes everywhere. Very often, male teachers in these subjects adopt what can only be called a macho style of teaching, where rapid questioning and the demand for a lot of answers, not all of them necessarily right, benefits boys, who are much more willing to risk shouting out something which may prove to be wrong; but it is counter-productive for girls. The trouble seems to be not that these male teachers are somehow less socially skilled than female teachers, but that they carry in their heads a stereotype of the girl pupil, even the 'clever' girl, as someone who gets on quietly with her work. Girls seem to be more invisible to teachers, who perhaps have less of a sense than with the boys of what their futures are going to be. It takes a change of consciousness before teachers can see the need to create comfortable space for girls, to plan lessons and examples which include their interests and concerns, and to let girls know explicitly that they are doing well. The professional concern is that girls should gain sufficient confidence in male-dominated fields, eventually to catch the fascination of the subjects and to wish to pursue their studies in them.

The impact on teachers

The approach developed by the team was to minimize the threatening nature of the project by deliberately playing down the personal aspects of sex stereotyping in order to concentrate on professional concerns of equality of opportunity within school for all pupils. It would be much easier to do this in the more neutral context of regular in-service training than it was for a group of three women and one man working under an umbrella title which clearly raised the issues of feminism. The approach we adopted allowed teachers (most of whom were men) to co-operate with the project without having to re-examine their personal lives. Yet it is apparent that those teachers who were most active in pursuit of the project's aims, and most prepared to open up discussion with pupils, had considered the personal as well as the professional implications. Others resisted examining their own prejudices and motivations and by and large remained accepting of the project rather than committed to it. If this much can be achieved in the GIST context, then the prognosis for 'official' intervention to equalize opportunities between the sexes must be good.

Paradoxically, there may have been as many or more teachers outside the GIST schools who made use of our services in providing suggestions and support. Those teachers who were sufficiently interested to take the time to write to us may already have made some of the crucial personal-professional links. Future programmes of teacher education should perhaps leave space for such personal reflection, and expect it strongly to affect attitudes and outcomes, while focusing more directly on the professional implications of sex stereotyping.

Practical implications for schools

Sex differentiation in subject choice is not merely an outcome of individual decisions, attitudes or interests. It is also socially constructed and arises from the everyday assumptions which occur in every department of a school and in the 'hidden' as well as the overt curriculum. Two recent studies of subject choice and pupils' career intentions found that most pupils had no changes made in their initial set of choices (Ball, 1984; Ryrie *et al.*, 1979). This neat and convenient matching of pupil choice with the school's existing timetable arrangements seems to be a result of the internalization by pupils of the school's expectations for them. Teachers may not be aware of the unofficial grapevine by which children come to believe that some subjects are reserved for one sex only. We visited one school (not in the GIST group) to give a careers talk and were told that girls had perfect freedom to choose technical crafts in the fourth year. In discussion with pupils afterwards, we found they firmly believed that it was forbidden for girls to do technical crafts and very difficult for boys to choose cookery. In most of the GIST schools, subject choice appeared to be overdetermined this way, as columns of subjects are set against one another, producing predictable results. Only at Meadowvale were pupils allowed simply to list on a piece of paper all the subjects they would *like* to take. The computer did the rest.

The option system is in most schools a battleground in the sense that subject departments are often covertly competing for the 'best' pupils; indeed some heads of science saw the prospect of increasing exam passes in their subjects if more girls were attracted to the idea of taking two sciences. The actual construction of option packages is frequently in the hands of male senior staff, who consciously or unconsciously use their power as 'gatekeepers' to channel girls and boys into routes traditional for their sex.

The single most effective thing schools can do to ensure an equal representation of females in science and technology is to dispense with early specialization altogether. In countries where physical science is part of the core curriculum until 16 or school leaving age, girls apparently attain as well as boys, and have a better chance of continuing with science (Whyte, 1984). Most English schools require pupils to study only one science: many girls opt for biology alone, perhaps because they view it as the most 'human' science. It is not in their long-term interest to do so, for physical sciences are extremely diffficult to take up again later and dropping physical sciences closes the door on many interesting and well-paid careers. Even a number of traditionally female jobs, such as dietetics, fashion design and production, hairdressing, laundry and dry cleaning, physiotherapy and radiography require or use science qualifications. Even in primary teaching, that quintessentially feminine field, physical science specialists may be preferred in the future. At present most schools in the interests of balance counsel children to take only two science subjects, and it is unusual nowadays for either a boy or girl to be allowed to take all three sciences. Ultimately only moves towards an integrated secondary science curriculum including physical science for all pupils is the answer to the shortfall of girls, but the kind of science taught should be broad-based and humanistic if it is to retain pupils' interest.

Until that comes about, most English girls will have only three years of science education. Their foothold in technical crafts is even more tenuous. Two problems here are, first, the mini-options at the end of first or second year, when girls and boys are bound to revert to sex-segregated crafts, and second the structuring of options so that CDT and home economics are mutually exclusive. (They often appear in the same column as 'practical' or 'creative' subjects.) Both practices place clear barriers to non-traditional choices.

The sex split after mini-options is so predictable that one is led to suspect schools take it into their calculations when they arrange options. Many crafts staff dislike the 'circus' system which has operated in recent years, and often say that they now have to squeeze a former three-year syllabus into one and a half years. This is probably the reason for so many schools deciding to go for the mini-option system. But it is only in a rather traditional model of what's supposed to be the content of home economics and crafts that the problem of covering syllabus content really arises. It should not be necessary for children to work through the construction of a box, then a shelf, then a tray etc., acquiring all the different skills of woodwork. A craft, design and technology course can approach the same content by using exemplary projects which develop a range of skills, in a variety of materials, and offer in addition some intellectual goals, such as problem solving and assessment of design techniques.

The EOC's working party on craft, design and technology (chaired by John Catton, of GIST) recommends a move away from the rotation or circus system. Pupils would attend CDT, home economics and art areas every week throughout the whole academic year (EOC, 1983). This would avoid the duplication of teaching which seems to occur as pupils move round the materials area of a department. A core of experience would be identified, organized perhaps round a common design and a regular skills course, using fabrics as well as wood, metal and plastics.

Girls' absence from technical crafts after the third year has not been regarded as a serious problem because of the assumption that the traditional segregation of the sexes in the labour market is a permanent feature of our economy. Engineering and industrial design are seen as men's work, but tomorrow's women may want to contribute, too. It is mainly men who design houses, because they are the building technologists and architectural technicians, but these are jobs which might well appeal to a girl. Most children can be excited by the thought of contributing to the design and production of everyday things from telephones, children's toys, bicycles, cameras, food and drink to airports. If the approach begins from this angle, girls may be able to wait until later before deciding whether they want to go in for a career in mechanical, chemical or civil engineering. GIST girls were keen, as girls traditionally are, on 'helping people', but usually unaware that the jobs of many engineers can involve work of direct benefit to people.

Having studied CDT to exam level at school would make it easier for girls to enter engineering, because, more than boys, they have to prove themselves to potential employers, and one way to do this is to have followed a practical crafts course or to have some demonstrable technological awareness, problem-solving skill and design competency.

Home economics develops fundamentally different skills, defined nowadays as 'life skills', 'family studies', etc (see EOC, 1983). For pupils to be denied access to either home economics or CDT because of the structure of the option system is in each case to be denied a distinctive and important educational experience.

Implications of single-sex grouping

Single-sex grouping in mixed schools seems to have a positive influence on girls' attitudes to science. The evidence from other experiments with single-sex setting indicates its success in creating positive attitudes, for example of boys to modern languages (Powell and Littlewood, 1982). Given the extreme reluctance of schools to go along with any policy of positive discrimination to redress the balance against girls, single-sex groups may offer the next best alternative means of showing how powerfully girls are affected by the presence and pressure of their male peers.

The evidence of its power as a tool to help girls is most clear from the outcome of the crafts club run by a member of the GIST team at Green Park (see Chapter 9). Girls who had been involved on the 'woodpecker' project became so assured of their competence that they opted for woodwork in the fourth year. This was despite the fact that none of them had been permitted to take technical crafts as part of the 'official' provision in lower school, because of the segregated crafts curriculum still in operation for the GIST cohort.

The Green Park club faltered and stopped when John Catton returned to his main work on the team. The teachers, like some in other schools, were clearly reluctant to do anything 'just for girls', even when 'bending the stick the other way' would have seemed more fully justified than usual. At Moss Green, girls' attitudes and choices changed considerably, but the largest shift was at Edgehill, a school in which no single-sex grouping took place. This does not necessarily point to a causal effect of single-sex grouping. It is possible that Moss Green girls were responding as much to the visible concern of teaching staff about girls' progress, a concern which happened to be exhibited concretely through the institution of single-sex groups. Even here there is a possible trap awaiting the unwary teacher. If single-sex grouping in classes in the male-dominated subjects becomes a permanent feature in a mixed school, there is a danger that teachers, perhaps especially new teachers coming into the school, would interpret this as a need to offer a different curriculum to boys and girls. We are familiar already with the syndrome in crafts education of offering boys heavy metalwork while girls make ornamental jewellery. Similar things can happen in science classrooms; girls can study cosmetics while boys are investigating some other more theoretical branch of chemistry. This is a very real possibility so long as teachers continue, as most of us do, to carry in their heads the sex stereotypes which make all sorts of assumptions about girls and boys.

Single-sex teaching is certainly valuable as a measure to illuminate for teachers what is happening in the mixed classroom and how different things are when the girls are on their own. It can compensate girls for their more limited experience outside schools of the kinds of activities which help in the understanding of technology and science. It can also build up girls' confidence through the single-sex experience, to strengthen them for the return to the mixed classroom and the mixed world in which they must live.

There is a strong case for the introduction of single-sex classes in subjects such as science and technology, which have a powerful 'masculine' image. However it is an intervention which will work positively for girls only if that is the end at which teachers are aiming.

Caution is necessary before trying to link specific interventions in GIST schools with particular outcomes. Single-sex grouping was not the only possible cause of change at Moss Green; teachers were explicit in discussing with pupils their concern about girls' underachievement and this may have been of equal importance.

There are similar doubts about the wisdom of a widespread return to segregated schooling. Jan Harding's work indicates that girls are more likely to choose physical science in girls-only schools, but a recent report from the Equal Opportunity Commission (Bone, 1983) points out that, with the exception of grammar schools, girls' schools tend to be short of the resources needed to teach science and maths, and very few indeed offer craft, design and technology. When boys and girls are educated separately, there is always the danger that girls' schools will have inferior resources and staffing. Bone suggests the difference in physics stems not from a single-sex environment itself, but from a tradition of teaching which applies less in comprehensives, and she concludes that the 'real challenge would be to combine mixed schools with a feminist spirit'.

Creating the right climate

The GIST project was not limited to changing individual teachers' attitudes, but went beyond that to the attempt to alter school norms. The extent to which GIST was successful in particular schools appears to have been highly dependent on the existing school ethos and its consistency or otherwise with the provision of equal opportunities between boys and girls. For the teachers at Green Park, the school norm of highly determined sex segregation clearly clashed with the aims of the GIST initiative. The doubts about changes wrought by the project (desegregation of school crafts, participation in the engineering project) were most acutely felt by the teachers, of whom greater changes of belief, attitude and practice were demanded than in any of the other schools. Nonetheless, the school did change; more girls than ever before chose to take chemistry, and some girls who had joined the woodwork club chose to continue with the subject in fourth year. The real world is intrinsically complicated and contradictory, and the identification of the 'ingredients for success' is by no means simple. However, the variety of responses from the GIST schools does offer a number of clues about the forces which will facilitate change in the future.

A framework devised by Lippitt (1974) suggests that barriers to change in schools may occur in one or more of four areas: personal attitudes, the climate of the school, the innovative practice which is being advocated, and the physical/temporal arrangements made to encourage change.

They are considered in turn below.

(1) *Individual attitudes*
Although teachers were reluctant to admit to any changes in their own attitudes or practice, the evaluation interviews clearly show a development in awareness and a widespread interest in combating girls' underachievement in science and technology. The student survey of GIST teachers' attitudes found some important differences between the GIST group and other teachers. They were better informed about, and more inclined to accept, socialization rather than naturalistic explanations of sex difference, but also more aware of the effort involved in trying to

bring about change (Kelly *et al.*, 1984a). The evaluation report concludes that 'some teachers *did* point to changes for themselves, that some *did* point to changes in their colleagues and that there *were* organisational changes. . . . Given the general reluctance to refer to changes . . . these perceived changes stand out as important successes for the GIST project' (emphasis in original).

(2) *Characteristics of the innovative practice*
The development of a concept of girl friendly science is one of the achievements of the project and is now fully discussed in Smail, 1983a and 1984). Watching the VISTA visitors, many teachers saw their subject anew, and the positive response of the children confirmed that science taught in a 'girl friendly' way is good for boys too. Some teachers adapted their materials, but wholesale curriculum reform was beyond the resources or expertise of the project team, and would not necessarily have helped the teachers any more. Classroom observation and single-sex projects clarified the nature of the *process* of girl friendly schooling, and showed teachers that positive change was possible, and not too difficult to achieve. These aspects of the project worked well, opening up possibilities for change. However, Lippitt's other areas were more likely to raise barriers to change.

(3) *The 'climate' of the school*
If public recognition is given to innovators and adopters of the advocated change, one can expect the diffusion of innovation to be facilitated. At Tall Trees, the head was strongly supportive of GIST, and the head of science enhanced his professional standing by his involvement with the project. At Meadowvale and Edgehill, the heads allowed full-scale staff meetings (at Edgehill the best part of an in-service day) to discuss GIST issues, clearly signalling the professional value of participation in the project. At Moss Green, the arrival of a new head who himself carried out an intervention gave a boost to the project, and produced the best results overall. But at Sutton Hill, Hamlet and Green Park, teachers seemed to receive little encouragement to spend time or energy on GIST. The schools which assisted the innovation also seem to have been those where a progressive ethos and a democratic atmosphere prevailed. Support for GIST came from senior staff, and in some cases it seems that the presence of women staff in senior positions may have helped the project. According to Lippitt, innovation will be advanced if there are

good communications between teachers, if the head of the school supports the innovation activity, and if s/he creates a staff atmosphere of sharing and experimentation. As an outside team, we were unable to affect the climate for change in the schools, and it seems that those most closed to change in Lippitt's framework remained the least affected by GIST.

(4) *Time, space and energy*

In the early stages of the project, we sometimes said that changing schools to increase equality of opportunity need not necessarily cost very much. In monetary terms, this is true. The total cost of GIST is equivalent to the price of employing one teacher in each of the GIST action schools for less than six months.

Those who hoped for fundamental social change for such a small sum should not be surprised at the relative modesty of the outcomes. However, time and energy are something else. Development of curriculum materials, classroom observation, attendance at conferences, all required extra work and time from the teachers, many of whom provided it. But we did not reach the stage in any school where a permanent semi-formal sub-committee or working group was set up to monitor sex stereotyping and make recommendations for curriculum practice. Most teachers had no particular time or space, apart from the conferences, when they could discuss their own thoughts and feelings about GIST.

An Australian report of a discussion lesson between boys and male staff on 'male images, friendships and feelings' remarks that 'the biggest problem was our awkwardness in discussing the issue in an articulate manner. The reason . . . was obvious . . . we had never properly discussed it among ourselves.' The report goes on to recommend that teachers planning the same sort of work should have specific preliminary discussion of the issues amongst themselves (Equal Opportunity Newsletter, 1984).

In the GIST schools where such discussion *was* on the agenda in a semi-formal way (Edgehill: in-service day; Meadowvale: staff meeting and bulletin; Moss Green: teachers asked to keep diaries on progress of single-sex experiment), GIST was most successful. The implication is clear: this kind of innovation is more likely to succeed if teachers have 'quality' time and energy to carry it out.

Schools as a force for social change?

It is possible to identify four levels of difficulty in bringing about educational change. The easiest step is to advance our knowledge of the situation. Next comes the changing of attitudes, followed by changes in the behaviour of individuals. The final stage is change in group behaviour, or in the 'institutional ethos'.

Applying this model to GIST we would argue that the project has considerably increased our knowledge about girls' underachievement in science and technology and the reasons for this underachievement.

Attitudes have also changed: GIST has had some effect on children's attitudes, particularly with respect to sex stereotypes and what they consider it acceptable for girls and boys to do. Their attitudes to science altered less, but moved sufficiently in the desired direction to indicate how science would have to change to make it more attractive to girls – and boys.

However there has been less impact on children's behaviour when making their option choices, perhaps because these are determined much more by their daily experience of school subjects and by their perceptions of the existing sexual division of labour, in schools as well as in society.

Some teachers' attitudes, no less than their behaviour, altered in the desired direction. Teachers' attitudes are usually longer established than children's and their world-views are less fluid. Thus it is logical that the institutional ethos, as the collective manifestation of these world-views, should be most impervious to change; and so it proved to be in this project. But there is evidence that changes in group behaviour were more likely to occur in schools and departments where the prevailing ethos comfortably incorporated GIST concerns.

What are the implications for larger-scale attempts to institute changes in schools? Reynolds (1984) argues powerfully that schools have relative autonomy and can make real changes in pupils' lives. Many educational writers see teachers as key agents of change, an argument put in its strongest form, perhaps, by Gobbe and Porter (quoted in Robinson, 1981):

> Teachers are a critical factor in development; they are in a privileged position to break the circle of poverty, ignorance and prejudice in a manner likely to be accepted by the populations concerned; while the multiplier effect of their

occupation singles them out as a valuable investment at a time of crushing demand and limited resources.

We did – and do – believe that teachers have a powerful influence on their pupils. For this reason we put a lot of effort into working with teachers. Teachers in the more progressive and democratic institutions responded most positively to the GIST initiative, and these were the schools where most change occurred; their capacity to adapt to innovation confirms them as 'creative schools', in Hoyle's definition (Hoyle, 1975).

Yet it should be remembered that, overall, the measurable changes were very small, so small that one must assume the operation of extremely powerful factors which counterbalance even the influence of benign schools.

An alternative to the view of teachers as 'pioneers of change' sees sex differentiation as deeply embedded in the ethos and practice of schools, reproducing the sexual division of labour in the society at large. This implies a rather different model of school and society, based on a view of the school as a central agency of socialization into sex-differentiated society and a labour market segregated by sex.

Neither model seems exactly to fit the GIST outcomes. The teachers-as-liberators model seems over-optimistic in the light of the caution with which even sympathetic teachers approached the issue. We know that teachers as a group are conservative people, and Delamont has argued that in the past decade, schools have been more conservative about sex roles than either homes or wider society (Delamont, 1983). Yet our own feeling, after five years of working on GIST, is that a great deal has changed. If anything, the GIST programme was slightly, but only very slightly, ahead of its time. Already (in 1984) there are several local authorities, and a number of pronouncements and initiatives at governmental level, supporting similar goals to those with which we started. Even as short a time ago as 1979, the atmosphere was not quite so favourable to the notions that schoolgirls are underachieving, or that sex typing of subject choice is undesirable, as it seems to be now.

Part of the success of GIST, in national publicity terms, may be due to the rising tide of opinion in favour of widening opportunities, especially in employment, for women.

In a discussion of the sources of educational innovation, Zaltman *et al.* (1977) argue that a major source of demands for educational change corresponds to rising expectations for relevant groups of pupils. If the GIST intervention has brought about specific changes in schools, it may have been helped along by the social forces already demanding change, which we were able to harness to reflect those demands within the schools themselves. This is a less deterministic model of school and society. Schools have some freedom to change features of their own organization but actual outcomes will depend on how far the changes promoted by the school operate in conflict or in harmony with other social forces. It implies, however, that the prognosis for female equality in schools depends upon the strength of the social forces which are pushing in that direction. Here, some comparisons with the fate of similar interventions elsewhere may be instructive.

Despite early policies for educational equality in Sweden, dating back to 1971, there has been no significant change in the conventional choices made by girls and boys entering the upper secondary school. There *have* been changes in attitude; girls now 'think in terms of a job . . . they don't intend to be housewives for a future husband'; but there has been no change in their vocational choices (Scott, 1984). The barriers to change identified in the Swedish context are:

those resulting from conflicting priorities in the school system (especially the impact of youth unemployment);

those arising out of the structure of the economy (especially the reduction in demand for all but highly skilled workers, few of whom are women); and

the sex role concept itself.

Swedish efforts at bringing about equality made an assumption that evolutionary changes in sex role concepts would be to the benefit of men as much as women. The policies appear to have achieved formal equality, without producing the authentic changes hoped for. Women leaders, disappointed at the results, now argue that equality work has so far been conducted on terms dictated by men; they point out that there has been little advance on the promotion of women within educational structures themselves and conclude that the need now is for women to seize their share of the power, as men are unlikely to give it to them (Scott, 1984). A report on the effects of recent intervention projects in Australia says that 'evidence of achievements in terms of outcomes is rather more difficult to point to' and discusses the tensions which arise between different approaches and strategies (Yates, 1984).

Yet in the United States there is evidence, according to one commentator, of 'dramatic changes' in women's career preferences (Astin, 1978). Since the late 1960s, women have shown a steadily increasing interest in four occupations traditionally dominated by men: business, medicine, engineering and law. The period of this increase coincides with the growing impact of the women's movement in America. It may also be linked to the stronger legislation on equality in employment, whereby employers may actually be fined if they do not implement equal opportunity policies.

If there is a limit on how far schools can promote fundamental social change, it is almost certainly the division of labour by sex. Girls and boys in the GIST cohort agreed in putting jobs as the first consideration in choosing school subjects; their choices were no doubt coloured by their own perceptions of segregation in the labour market. Schools, as Delamont says, exaggerate and stereotype such divisions even beyond the reality. They may now at least begin to reflect the reality of women at work, and the kind of contribution they make to society outside the home. Schools have the possibility to provide girls with qualifications to enter new fields. But their efforts are bound to be limited by economic and political factors determining the degree to which change can occur within the labour force itself. And in the economic and industrial sphere, issues of power and control appear much more nakedly than in the world of education.

Science, technology and girls' values

Science

The GIST children were enthusiastic to know more about science when they first arrived at secondary school. In countries throughout the world, pupils in their first few years of secondary school appear to become disenchanted with science. They have been compared to a starving person, at first eager to sit down and eat, who after seven heavy courses becomes gorged and bored (Gardner, 1984). The phenomenon of pupils' decline in science interest is universal, and not confined to girls (Goodwin *et al.*, 1981; Gardner, 1984). One of the early hopes of the GIST project was that this decline in interest might be arrested, if new ways to teach and present science (especially physical science) could be implemented in the schools. Our suggestions and recommendations were taken up by some of the action schools and teachers, and these, together with the VISTA visits, do seem to have softened the negativism of children in the action schools towards science. In one or two schools (boys at Edgehill, girls at Moss Green), the response was against the negative and declining trend. That the GIST effect was not stronger is probably due to the piecemeal way GIST recommendations were incorporated in school syllabi. The effect on the total and daily experience of science at school was muted. The content and presentation of third year science in particular seems to depend largely – more than it should – on the downward pressure of examination requirements.

In all the schools, and despite their declining interest in science, both girls and boys became *more* interested in learning about human biology. This across-the-sexes enthusiasm about human biology was something mentioned to teachers as a key to stimulating children's involvement in physical science (see Chapter 6). The fact that both sexes became even more interested may of course be a feature of adolescence, and a growing concern with the changes in one's own body. Yet human biology often has the image of a 'soft science', and is frequently taught to 'less able' girls. If science teaching is to build on children's interests, then perhaps a review of the place of human biology in science education would contribute to reducing the development of negative attitudes to science in general.

Sex stereotypes

The GIST interventions do seem to have made a measurable and significant difference to children's sex role stereotypes. Not only did girls and boys in the action schools come to view science as more sex-neutral, they also became more liberal in their notions of 'men's' and 'women's' work, and more open to the possibility of aspiring to jobs non-traditional for their sex. Given that the programme was implemented by teachers, many of whom preferred an 'implicit' to an 'anti-sexist' approach, the changes which have occurred show that young people's sex stereotypes *are* subject to modification, and that the presentation of alternative views and lifestyles can assist the process.

Attitudes altered significantly, but behavioural change in the form of non-traditional subject choice was disappointingly small. There are clear signs of the impact of GIST, especially on girls, and especially on stereotypes of science and related occupations. These results suggest that the 'gender factor' is only one of the reasons for girls' dislike of science, and girls' stereotypes of jobs are only one element in the process of making subject choices. It is good to know that interventions will modify sex typed attitudes, but continuing problems remain. The day-to-day experience of school science, its contents and teaching methods, must have contributed to the negative attitudes so generally displayed, but were beyond the power of GIST to change. Sex typing in subject choice is the outcome of complex processes in which girls' motivations and aspirations are powerfully affected by the expectations of those around them.

Some other findings tend to confirm that this is the case, and provide food for thought. In the first year, science curiosity and personal liking for science were virtually unrelated to ability, but by the third year there was a clear trend for more able pupils to exhibit greater interest in learning about science.

Many teachers made the case to us that physical science is just too difficult for the majority of children, which in itself is sufficient explanation for the decline in science interest amongst all but the most able. This may be too complacent a view, especially as regards girls. The relationship between ability and liking for science was much more marked for girls than for boys. Girls are less confident about their performance, and only 'like' science if they think they are good at it. Ability and liking for science were correlated for them more than for boys. The decision to choose science in the fourth year may have less to do with ability and more to do with extrinsic motivation than many science teachers have hitherto realized. Boys like science, whether or not they are good at it. They apparently choose to do science, and say that they like it, for reasons other than their real or perceived ability in the subject. Instrumental factors such as the desire to enter masculine occupations may be just as important. That is a motivation not available to girls, so long as the masculine stereotypes of such jobs continue to be widely accepted.

Chapter 6 provides the framework for a 'girl friendly' science (see Smail, 1984) using examples from everyday life with which girls as well as boys can identify, highlighting the social and human benefits and implications of science and technology, creating a supportive classroom atmosphere for female pupils. The impact of GIST interventions, slight but significant, indicates that even small changes in the right direction can increase enjoyment of science, not just for girls but for boys too. On the obverse of the coin, a science which is antagonistic or tangential to girls' interests is one of the sources of girls' avoidance of science. It is not sufficient simply to change masculine examples and illustrations if the subject still appears irrelevant to everyday and social concerns, anti-humanistic and unattractively difficult.

Previous definitions of the 'problem' of girls and science had frequently focused on girls' unfortunate tendency to avoid a useful and valuable subject. GIST was intended to answer the questions, why are girls' attitudes so negative, and what can be done to make them more 'interested' in science? The answers to our questions in the second attitude survey about reasons for choosing a subject are quite clear. The three factors which most influence girls (and boys) are, first, 'usefulness for getting a job', second 'finding the subject interesting' and third, perceived ability in the subject. The second factor seems to bring us back again to the issue of 'interest'. Girls' answers, and choices, imply that they are not 'interested' in physical science. A critique of the concept of 'interest in science' (Van Aalst, 1984) makes the point that 'interest' is sometimes treated as if it were uni-dimensional. In fact, interest is composed of at least three dimensions:

subject matter;
the extent of (pupil) commitment; and
the pupil's 'purpose'.

'Purpose' is defined as 'intention to behave', i.e. 'interest' represents generalized curiosity, but also includes motivation: the willingness to engage in actions, and purpose: the intention to behave in specific situational contexts. Purposes develop from:

personal needs (including the understanding of the applications of science);
social issues (pollution, nuclear energy, etc.);
academic preparation, leading to academic work at tertiary level;
career education awareness and knowledge of relevant jobs and careers. (Van Aalst, 1984)

If interest and purpose are thus so intimately connected, the problem of making girls more 'interested' in science is clearer. No one measure – introducing social implications, offering information about non-traditional job opportunities – will be sufficient. To change choices, and not merely attitudes, all the conditions affecting interest and purpose must be favourable.

And for girls, one of the most important of these is their perception of their own performance in science. In the first attitude survey, we found that girls were less confident than boys about their ability in the future; the same was true two and a half years later. A study of civil engineering and chemistry students found that those who received low grades were more likely to change their course, but denied any relationship between their lower grades and lack of interest. But those who perceived they were not doing well subsequently made less effort to succeed, and entered into a vicious circle of failure, perception of failure, reduction of effort, repeated failure, and more negative attitudes (Drotz *et al.*, 1984). Something like this seems to have happened to the GIST girls. The finding that children who had chosen *not* to continue with physics or chemistry then did significantly *less* well in the end of term exams supports this analysis. The project's outcomes imply that girls' interest or otherwise in science is constructed on a complex basis of related purposes, motivation and perception of own performance. Our main achievement as an interventionist team was to increase, slightly, the appeal of science and therefore girls' motivation, and to reduce, considerably, the exclusively masculine image of science. These changes, however, proved insufficient to alter qualitatively the conditions structuring girls' choices.

Overtly, GIST aimed to change girls' attitudes but covertly the attempt was also to alter, radically, the image and practice of school science; in this latter aim, success was only meagre. Norwegian researchers have employed the term 'rationality of care' (*omsorgsrasjonalitet*) in connection with the kind of rationality underlying much of women's behaviour. In 'rejecting' a science which is still largely devoid of social and personal values, girls' choices of subject, course and occupation can be seen as entirely rational in this sense.

Arditti (1982) has argued that scientific 'objectivity' encourages scientists to approach problems in a way which attempts to ignore the human concerns and consequences of their work. As yet the scientific community is composed mainly of white males who have been socialized into this professional value system. If women, with their greater sensitivity to issues affecting people, enter science and technology in large enough numbers to make their presence felt, they are likely to challenge the separation of scientific enquiry from its social implications. But before girls will choose to become part of that community, schools need to present the human face of science and technology.

GIST was not a conventional research project: it was a deliberate intention that by using an 'action research' mode, we would be able to offer policy implications which would ultimately be of benefit to girls. The results of the interventions are not as clear-cut as some of those who supported our aims had hoped. But a linear model as a sequence of fundamental research, followed by applied research, development and finally application is inadequate to describe the impact of research on schools in any case. It is, moreover, inappropriate to the action research framework of the GIST programme. An alternative model, of a kind of 'glacial advance of human understanding', envisages educational research as influencing expectations and aspirations rather than specifically affecting practice in a causal network (Nisbet and Broadfoot, 1980). In this sense, it is to be hoped that GIST has demonstrated a shortfall between girls' potential and their actual achievement, and certainly that it has raised the aspirations and expectations of those responsible for girls' education. GIST challenges the traditional arguments in favour of a status quo in which girls have unduly lost out, and confirms the need for policies directed at countering female underachievement. The exact nature of those policies will need to be adapted and interpreted by interested teachers and schools: 'Action research is unlikely ever to yield neat and definitive prescriptions from field-tested plans. What it offers is an aid to intelligent decision-making rather than a substitute for it' (Halsey, 1972).

Appendix 1

GIST Questionnaire: VISTA visits

We wish to evaluate the impact of VISTA visits to GIST schools, and to improve as far as possible their organization. Your help in completing a questionnaire after each visit would be very much appreciated. Your answer will be read only by the GIST team. When the evaluation is complete, our summary will be made available to any interested teachers.

Please complete one questionnaire for each VISTA visitor

Teacher's name ______________________________

School ______________________________

Date ______________________________

Name of VISTA visitor ______________________________

Date of visit ______________________________

(1) How did you prepare the children for the visit? e.g. did you cover a related topic beforehand/talk about women in science or technology/simply inform them that a visitor was coming/other?

(2) In your opinion, was the children's response best described as:

extremely interested	☐
generally favourable	☐
mildly interested	☐
not interested	☐
hostile	☐
other (please specify)?	☐

(3) In your opinion, was the response of girls and boys the same, or different. If different, in what way?

(4) Was the VISTA visit helpful

	YES	NO
in developing children's understanding of the science topic concerned	☐	☐
in presenting a positive female role model in science/craft/technology	☐	☐
in increasing children's awareness of career opportunities in science/technology?	☐	☐

	YES	NO
(5) Was the VISTA speaker clearly audible?	☐	☐

	YES	NO
(6) Did the VISTA speaker use language at the right level for your class?	☐	☐

	YES	NO
(7) Did the VISTA speaker use A-V aids successfully?	☐	☐

	YES	NO
(8) Did the VISTA speaker demonstrate some part of her work?	☐	☐
Was this demonstration successful?	☐	☐

(9) Did she involve both sexes in answering questions, doing practicals, etc.?

(10) In retrospect, how do you think planning for visits might be improved, e.g. topic covered/A-V aids/seating arrangements/other?

(11) Have you any comments/advice to offer to the VISTA speaker for her next visit to other school(s)?

Appendix 2

Intervention strategies

First Year *September 1980-July 1981*

(1) *The Vista programme*
Incorporation into the scheme of work of visits by women scientists, technologists and craft workers with jobs relevant to lesson content.

(2) *Standardization of marking with other departments in the school*
So that marks given for homework, tests and examinations *cover the same range* for all subjects.

(3) *Use of teaching methods sensitive to the needs of girls*
I.e. positive encouragement. Pattern and routine of working with guided discovery methods, rather than open-ended questioning style. Co-operation rather than competition.

(4) *Compensatory background science experience sessions (BASE)*
A limited amount of this work could be done by the GIST team assisted by fourth year BEd students from Didsbury. A more extensive programme may be possible if GIST is successful in its applications for additional research personnel. Enthusiastic teachers may wish to follow the programme worked out by GIST themselves in after-school or lunchtime sessions with the pupils identified by initial testing as in need of extra background knowledge.

(5) *Modification of lesson materials*
   (a) to include more examples related to girls' interests;
   (b) to include more practical applications of theory;
   (c) to include more about the social implications of science;
   (d) to include material about women scientists and their achievements;

(e) to reduce the conceptual difficulty of the topics covered if necessary.

(6) *Discussions in science/craft lessons of women's roles and career opportunities*
To expand the girls' (and boys') views of their future lifestyles.

(7) *Spatial ability training sessions*
GIST hopes to monitor the effects on spatial-visualization skills of a series of technical drawing lessons already incorporated by one of the project schools into its first year crafts 'circus'. If a positive effect is found, then other schools may consider adopting a similar series of lessons in drawing simple three-dimensional objects in the first or later years.

(8) *Reconsideration of assessment methods* in the light of the evidence on multiple choice versus essay and extended answer questions. Scrutinizing the number of questions framed in 'masculine, feminine and neuter' contexts.

(9) *Sex-segregated teaching* for maths, science or technical crafts.

(10) *Work clinics*
Teachers may wish to set up after school or lunchtime sessions to sort out problems encountered in class.

Second and third years *September 1981-July 1983*

Strategies 1 to 10 above will continue to be used in the second and third years with the addition of the following:

(11) *Careers information*
Background information about subject choice for scientific and technical careers to be made explicit to pupils before the third year. Use of non-sexist careers materials to inform pupils of non-traditional as well as traditional options open to them and routes they will close if they opt out of certain subjects.

(12) *Links with local industry*
Visits by small groups of selected children to industrial sites. Possible inclusion in classwork of materials relating importance of industry to everyday life.

(13) *Reconsideration of timetabling and option systems*

(14) *Parents' evenings*
Giving information about girls'/boys' achievements in science, maths and technical crafts and careers which could be followed with qualifications in these subjects.

(15) *Direct parent counselling* for high female achievers in non-traditional subject areas.

Appendix 3

Action research

Judith Whyte

The term 'action research' has been used occasionally throughout this book, and in practical terms the reader may have a good idea what the GIST team meant by it. This appendix lays out in more depth the theoretical background to the concept and the ideas underlying the GIST form of action research, which was itself innovative within an innovative project. The portmanteau term of action research has a special appeal in the educational context because it promises to combine the respectability of research with the utility and relevance of school-based concerns. As defined and executed by GIST a strong research and evaluation base (the testing and evaluation) supported planned intervention in the schools, carried out collaboratively with the teachers. One of our ultimate goals was that teachers in the project schools would begin researching into their own classrooms to investigate further the 'underachievement' of girls in male-dominated school subjects.

Models of action research

There were elements of two previous forms of action research in this approach, one derived from social administration, the other from the idea of teachers as researchers. In the context of social administration, or perhaps it would more more accurate to say social engineering, attempts have been made to improve the lot of particular groups of people by action research. In the 1960s in Britain, the growth of comprehensive schooling was accompanied by target areas for action known as Educational Priority Areas, with the hope of bettering the achievement of working-class pupils in school. A similar programme in the United States, called Headstart, tried to do the same thing by offering poorer children from ethnic minorities extra educational resources before entry to formal schooling. In the States the effects of Headstart seemed to wear off after only a few years, and many commentators have demonstrated that working-class children are still failing to achieve their full potential in the UK. To some extent, the social engineering approach has been discredited as a result.

GIST was similarly motivated by the discrepancy, perceived in 1979 chiefly by feminists, between girls' potential and their actual achievement, not so much at school as after leaving school, when even able girls obtain considerably less than a fair share of further and higher education and training, in part, it seems, because of their lack of qualifications in science and technology. The idea of concentrating resources, or in the case of GIST, positive interventions, upon a specific group of girls with the hope of showing what might be done draws directly on the action research model in social administration.

A more recent definition of action research from the same field is offered by Elizabeth Newsom in *Seven Years Old in the Home Environment*. It is to:

(1) establish and identify where a special need exists and what innovatory procedures or services might meet that need.

GIST was intended to dramatize the shortfall of girls in science and technology as an unrecognized need, and to try out innovatory interventions to meet the need.

(2) to carry out those innovations in such a way
(a) that they provide a realistic model for future services which might be recommended as a result of this research.

Because GIST was intended to be a realistic exercise, we chose ordinary mixed comprehensive schools in the northern region where we lived and worked. With hindsight, one can see that much greater success might have been attained by working in girls' public schools, where a commitment to girls' interests can already be assumed. On the other hand, there seemed to be some value in locating the project in the kind of school where most children in Britain today are educated, to indicate what it is possible to do, not necessarily in the most promising circumstances.

(b) that their usefulness can be rationally evaluated, both in whole and in part.

Evaluation of GIST interventions was built in only very broadly, with a blunt comparison of action schools with control schools. Because we were committed to collaboration with teachers, we were not prepared to decide in advance which interventions individual schools should use, and therefore could not estimate the value of each part of the innovatory practice, only the overall effects. This aspect of the GIST research design makes it more difficult than otherwise to define exactly what measures are bound to be effective in encouraging girls.

(c) that the snags, problems, direct and indirect benefits and spin-offs can all be carefully monitored.

For GIST, this was one of the most interesting and appealing aspects of action research: the possibility that our ideas and the formulation of the GIST problem might change before our eyes, in unanticipated ways. This very uncertainty, characteristic of action research, was, in the event, double edged. The project has produced a rich crop of results, of data and of material for forming new hypotheses about girls in schools. But with the growth in our understanding of what discourages girls at school, we saw the hoped-for outcome of a substantial GIST cohort of 13-year-olds choosing to study physics, chemistry and technical crafts receding into the distance with each year of the project.

An important feature of GIST from the beginning has already been mentioned: the desire to create a collaborative relationship with teachers and to foster teachers' own research in classrooms. This commitment arose from a second strand of the action research tradition in education: the teachers-as-researchers kind of action research initiated largely by Lawrence Stenhouse, who believed that teachers' reflections on their own practice were at the heart of action research. As John Elliott, who worked with Stenhouse, has put it, this kind of action research 'aims to feed practical judgment in concrete situations, and the validity of the "theories" it generates depends not so much on "scientific" tests of truth, as on their usefulness in helping people to act more intelligently and skilfully.'

Certainly, GIST endeavoured to help teachers who wanted to make their classroom more 'girl friendly', and a booklet produced by one of the project team, Barbara Smail, testifies to the success of the strategy in producing valid, well-judged ideas of a practical nature which are based on direct classroom experience (Smail, 1984). GIST does not neatly fit the teacher-as-researcher model, however, essentially because the problem we perceived – girls underrepresented in science and technology – was not, at least at the outset of the project, recognized by teachers in the GIST schools as a serious professional issue. The wish to collaborate on an equal basis with the teachers was thus almost a handicap to a project set up to promote innovation on an issue not yet widely agreed to be of genuine concern.

These two models of action research are deeply embedded in the GIST approach, which was both a social experiment, rather a bold one as it emerges, and an attempt to help teachers improve their own professional consciousness and practice. Yet GIST is distinct from either: it was not really an experiment, with all that implies about rigorously controlled conditions, and subjects asked to conform to a predetermined research design; schools and teachers had perfect freedom to ignore or take up suggestions as we made them. It departed, too, from the teacher-as-researcher approach, of which the most important principle is that teachers themselves should identify and formulate the practical problem to be investigated. Far from seeing the lack of girls in fourth year physics as problematic, a few teachers were more worried, and said so, about what, as a practical matter, could be done if more girls wanted to take the subject and there were not sufficient teachers or laboratories to accommodate them. Not only for this reason, but also because of a team commitment to educational research, the perceptions of practitioners were not our only guide to action. We wished to use research methods to some extent traditional and scientific to advance the general knowledge and understanding of girls' reluctance to take science at school. Despite this apparent traditionalism, the design of the project revealed our impatience with the limitations of such traditional research, either in illuminating the real situation of girls in school, or in leading directly to changed school practice. For us, the overarching benefit of the action research method was that it combined rigorous research (to confound the 'sexist' pundits, to ensure the validity of any findings) with an interventionist, feminist desire to change schooling and make it more 'girl friendly', a term we adopted somewhere into the third year of GIST.

The GIST model of action research

THE GIST approach thus had a number of idiosyncratic elements in combination with what had been learned from these two models. We sought the straightforward goal of an advance in scientific knowledge about the roots of girls' avoidance of science and technology. The testing programme addressed all the available theories, from both educational and feminist literature, of the likely causes: that girls lose motivation because of the masculine image of science, that teacher attitudes play a part, that the lack of positive role models leads most girls to doubt the vocational relevance of science or technology for the occupations they may consider, and so on.

Figure A.1 indicates the cyclical process which is the central feature of the project. Research evidence generated hypotheses for the action programme: efforts to make science more girl friendly, in-service work with teachers, and the VISTA programme which brought live role models into the school. The battery of tests which constituted the GIST initial survey was designed to explore the explanatory power of each of these hypotheses, plus some more: the effects of maternal employment on girls' attitudes, the image of science children bring with them to secondary school, opinions about suitable activities and occupations for males and females, the impact of different assessment styles on girls and boys, etc. etc. In the next stage the results of the tests were fed back to schools, i.e. to groups of teachers, so that everyone would know how the GIST children viewed science and sex roles at the age of 11. The tests and interventions were 'done to' the teachers and pupils. But they, as social beings, also began to form hypotheses about the nature of the problem; indeed, this process of hypothesis forming was a hoped-for outcome of the interventions. That is, only when pupils came to regard their choices as at least partially determined by social factors

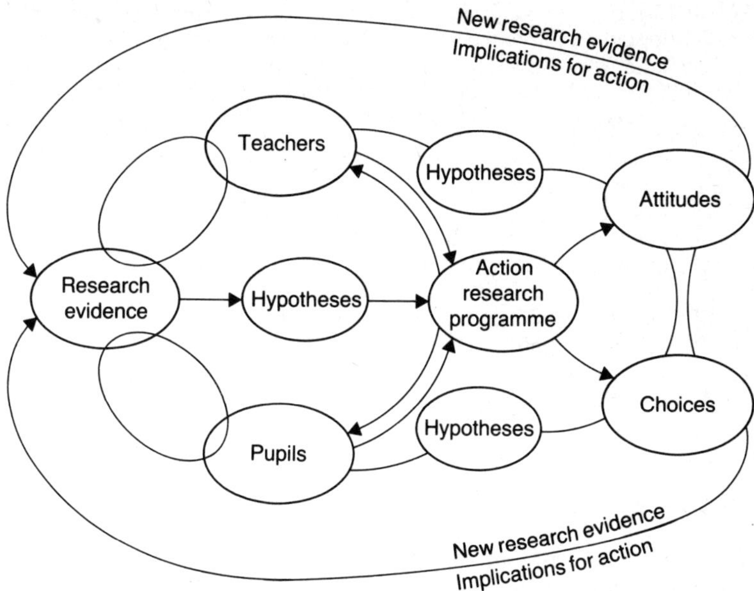

Figure A.1 The GIST model of action research

(stereotyping of jobs, sex role expectations, etc.) would they be free to alter their own attitudes and choices. Similarly, when the teachers adopted the GIST problem as their own, it was anticipated they would begin to experiment in their own classrooms with innovative teaching approaches designed to deal with the felt discrepancy between girls' abilities and their choices and performances at school.

Finally, the decisions made by each group, the teachers and the pupils, would then form, for the project team, the basis of new research evidence, and new hypotheses about how pupils, their teachers and their schools may change, generating further hypotheses about action research in a cyclical process. In this model of action research, the two activities are intertwined, occur simultaneously, and, at least in theory, are to be regarded as of equal value: no reluctance on our part to follow the paradigms of scientific research, and yet a willingness to become deeply involved in what has turned out to be a highly political issue – the treatment of girls by schools.

In a third context, that of organizational research, we have found a model which seems to correspond more closely with the GIST design than any other. Rapoport (1979) calls it an approach which 'aims to contribute both to the practical concerns of people in an immediate problematic situation and to the goals of social science by joint collaboration within a mutually acceptable ethical framework'.The GIST team adopted an extended form of this definition which we have called the 'simultaneous-integrated' model of action research (see Whyte and Smail, 1982; Kelly, 1985) developed by Hult and Lennung writing in the *Journal of Management Studies*: Action research:

(1) simultaneously assists in practical problem solving and expands scientific knowledge
(2) as well as enhances the competencies of the respective actors
(3) being performed collaboratively
(4) in an immediate situation
(5) using data feedback in a cyclical process
(6) aimed at increased understanding of a given social situation
(7) primarily applicable for the understanding of change processes in social systems
(8) and undertaken within a mutually acceptable ethical framework. (Hult and Lennung, 1980)

Productivity of GIST

In terms of the first part of this extended definition of action research: '(1) simultaneously assists in practical problem solving and expands scientific knowledge', GIST has been extremely productive. We know a great deal more than before about the factors in schooling which specifically discourage girls.

It has been suggested (Curran, 1980) that there are just three possible lines of investigation with regard to the girls and science problem:

(a) girls can't do science;
(b) they aren't allowed to (including covert prohibitions);
(c) they don't want to.

One way in which GIST has advanced research knowledge is by providing a strong prima facie case that (b) is the answer to the question and the other two possibilities are virtually eliminated. On (a), GIST has strongly indicated (see Smail, 1983 and Chapter 7, this volume) that demonstrated sex differences in spatial competence are unlikely to be innate, but have an acquired component. As this is the main plank of the genetic deficit argument, it is thereby considerably weakened. The greater enthusiasm (or lesser negativism) of the action children, both girls and boys, towards science suggests that girls will want to do science if they are not turned off by the subject's presentation as irrelevant and unduly masculine. The problem then is neither that girls cannot do science, nor that they don't want to, but that they are covertly discouraged by all those around them. In addition, as Alison Kelly remarks in her endpiece, there is an extensive and valuable database of longitudinal information about a large cohort of children, on which even more work and analysis remains to be done. On point (4), 'in an immediate situation', the decision to choose unremarkable schools probably created more interest in GIST than would otherwise have been the case. Possibly more female engineers could have been produced if we had started somewhere else, but by locating the project in not particularly sympathetic schools, in a northern environment, we were able to highlight the real problems which will attend national policies for the encouragement of girls. That is why GIST has been so instructive in elaborating understanding of the 'given social situation' (point 6): the subtle processes of teacher-pupil interaction and school atmosphere which, almost inevitably it seems, channel girls away from science and technology. The GIST action research framework has also allowed some new analysis of the barriers to change in schools (see Chapter 13) and pointed to the importance of a congruent school policy orientation and the presence of women staff in key positions (see Figure 13.6) as factors in making schools 'girl friendly'. This is a contribution to the understanding of change processes in the school as a social system (point 7).

The relationship between GIST and the teachers

The remaining points are more problematic, and deserve discussion.

(2) . . . 'enhances the competencies of the respective actors'
(3) 'being performed collaboratively'
(8) 'and undertaken within a mutually acceptable ethical framework'.

These were our intentions but, as we know, what actually happened was different from what might have been hoped. Of critical importance was the teachers' relationship with and reaction to GIST. Undoubtedly some teachers, unvaryingly polite as they were, felt hostility or at least ambivalence towards the aims of GIST. Yet others, as evidenced in the independent evaluation report and in a volume on classroom research edited by one of the evaluation team (Hustler, 1985), give witness to changes in consciousness and subsequent modifications of actual classroom practice. Readers of the GIST evaluation report, published in 1984, may be surprised when they read the chapter by the evaluators in Hustler's book, for there the project is represented as having had considerable success, quite the opposite of the conclusion reached by a *Times Educational Supplement* report at the time of its publication. In the book by Hustler, four GIST teachers, including the head of one of the schools, all write about their participation in the project in a way that suggests a positive reaction by staff who have begun to operate as classroom researchers in the field of gender in their own right, an intended outcome of the original action research design.

Reasons for the apparent discrepancy relate both to the context of action research in education, where changes seem to occur almost subliminally, and certainly slowly, and the specific nature of an innovative project focused on gender differences at school, an issue of high emotional and personal as well as professional significance.

The evaluation report itself is difficult for the ordinary reader who is trying to reach some conclusion about the effects of GIST. Although no overall judgment is arrived at, a central value judgment appears on page 76, where the authors remark that interviewees should be seen essentially in their role as biology teacher, head of department, headteacher, or whatever, i.e. that their individual professional concerns dominate their thinking and response to the GIST initiative:

> our respondents displayed identities with particular relevancies and professional interest. Heads, class teachers, heads of year, heads of department – all talk about GIST through reference to their positions which provide them with significant features of their identity within the interview and, presumably, within the school. In other words, their memories and perceptions are heavily structured around, or contextualised in terms of, these involved identities. In particular such concerns as 'What it's my job to do', 'What is my responsibility here' and 'How does GIST connect with my job as a problem or a resource' seem to underpin the talk.

On page 78, they go on to say, 'we do wonder to what extent in the initial stages of the project [the GIST team] took account of . . . teachers in professional contexts – as apart from teachers as just busy people.'

In fact, as a team, we were well aware not only that teachers needed convincing that the GIST problem was relevant to professional practice at all, but that for many individuals, the lack of any formal responsibility for girls and science and technology constituted the perfect excuse for doing nothing about it.

So in team discussion we sometimes questioned the value of limiting our work with teachers to what could be seen as matters of professional concern. It led in too many cases to the Schools Liaison Officers being burdened with a great deal of work which was tangential to the aims of the project: producing worksheets and discussing science and craft syllabuses in much the same way as any traditional curriculum developer. John Catton in particular complained that every conversation he started with the crafts men rapidly moved away from talking about girls to the perennial question of what the 'new' CDT teaching should really be, and how curricula should be adjusted to satisfy the demand for a more technological problem solving approach. Despite his commitment, John felt he was often having to talk for an hour about these issues in exchange for a brief five minutes on the issue of girls in technology.

On the other hand, during the three to four years of regular contact with schools, teachers would sometimes initiate highly personal conversations about their own experience of gender roles. As these conversations were recorded and discussed within the team, we soon noticed certain patterns emerging. We heard about wives who were perfectly happy to be at home full-time and/or daughters studying aeronautical engineering who had never encountered discrimination. One or two male teachers talked about the housework they shared, or didn't share, with their wives, the difficulty of making joint decisions when both partners have careers, the question of what sorts of toys one should buy for a baby girl, and so on. In the evaluators' terms, these were strictly 'non-professional' topics; for us, they were the meat and drink of the project. It is precisely the fusion of personal and professional understanding of gender issues that is required before teachers can be aware of the impact of gender stereotyping in the classroom. Teachers' responses, as teachers, to the project, were clearly linked to their own personal experience and attitudes towards the women in their lives (for the 75 per cent of the teachers who were men). It was when this became clear that we realized how useful it might be to have an independent evaluation (for our own predilections were obvious) of teachers' attitudes which could perhaps produce a typology of lifestyles and willingness to promote GIST aims.

Unfortunately, this is what the evaluation report, by focusing strictly on 'professional' concerns, signally failed to do, though, to be fair, the evaluators were not directly asked to do it.

The evaluation report suggested that GIST ought to have been more aware of teachers' professional concerns, with the implication that the teachers' responses would then have been more positive. An alternative interpretation is that in the context of the gender issue, the usual demarcation between personal and professional beliefs and practices is inappropriate, and that an essential determinant of teachers' response, unsurprisingly, is connected with their personal views and family experiences.

An interesting question is why so little, relatively, was said in the evaluation interviews about teachers' personal lives. Were they inhibited by the 'strictly professional' approach of the evaluators, or did they assume that, as males, they would share traditional beliefs about women's place, whereas such an assumption was clearly impossible with members of the GIST team?

In future action research projects where the sex of the team or of the evaluators is likely to be an issue, team composition may require careful thought. It seems possible that this evaluation of the GIST teachers' perceptions was characterized by a silence based on assumed consensus of views about the feminist aims of the project, not just because the evaluators were men, but because they were not prepared for the subtleties of interpersonal interactions when gender equality is part of the hidden agenda of a conversation.

For instance it was noticeable that many male teachers commended the one male member of the GIST team for his lack of aggression (Payne *et al.*, 1984, page 55) though he and we agree that what he said and did was no different from the approach of other members of the team. Almost certainly, males and females uttering the same words or carrying out the same actions are viewed differently. The asymmetrical power relations between the sexes mean that a woman who is described in some situations as forceful and verbally standing her ground, features commonly considered male qualities, may be seen as mannish or aggressive. Switch the forceful behaviour to a male, and he will be labelled as 'masculine', a positive appraisal (Eakins and Eakins, 1978, page 127).

Teachers resisted the message of GIST in an inventive variety of ways, which are remarkably similar to the reactions met with by feminists who talk about linguistic sexism. Smith, in an interesting book about language and gender (Smith, 1985) describes the usual lines of defence. First, it may be argued that sexist language does not exist; it is just feminists' perceptions that are the problem. In the same way, GIST teachers argued that as they did not mean to be discriminatory or unfair, there could be no discrimination in fact. Secondly, calls for linguistic change may be refuted on the grounds that feminists mistakenly think language *causes* sexism. Similarly, GIST teachers sometimes thought the GIST team ignored other non-school factors: parents, employers, the media, society in general. While these of course are influential, every agency could make the plea that sexism starts elsewhere. As Smith says, this is a vulgarization of the feminist claim that language (or in the case of GIST, schools) reflect, influence, reinforce and maintain stereotyping and sexism.

The charge is often made that a preoccupation with language is a trivial approach, diverting energy from more important issues. At least one teacher in the evaluation report indicated the same idea. Manchester feminists have long suffered from the 'Personchester' joke, and the title of the evaluation report 'GIST or PIST', the latter standing for 'persons' into science and technology, is a variant of the same kind of ridicule.

A final line of defence, already mentioned, and also described by Smith, is one of simply removing the discourse to another subject. GIST teachers often preferred to talk about science or craft curriculum issues, and perhaps the evaluation team preferred the safer ground of 'teachers' professional concerns' to the quicksands of assessing teachers' commitment to anti-sexism.

These are some of the factors which, in many of our relationships with teachers, inhibited the formation of a 'mutually acceptable ethical framework'. Research published since 1984 shows that the GIST teachers, as a group of mainly male and mainly science/craft staff, would have views tending towards the non-feminist end of the spectrum of teacher attitudes generally, views related as much to the subjects they taught as to gender (Pratt *et al.*, 1984; Pratt, 1985).

There has now been so much written about equal opportunities and gender in education, possibly more in volume than on any other educational topic in the last decade, yet the issue is far from being a priority at any level, national, local or school-based. Against this background, it is something of an achievement that the evidence about

GIST teachers indicates the project did raise their consciousness about girls' experiences at school, and some did begin to take independent action. So have a large number of science and craft teachers around the country, over a thousand of whom have written and continue to write to us about their efforts to encourage more girls into the sciences or crafts. The lack of strong governmental or local education authority initiatives or policies (with one or two honourable exceptions) suggests to me that the resistances encountered with the GIST teachers have their parallels elsewhere, and crucially, amongst educational policy makers.

Conclusion

The decision to employ an action research mode arose out of the twin aims of GIST for intervention and research, and out of a recognition that there are drawbacks to either 'pure' empirical research or unreflective activism. Enthusiasts may achieve a great deal in the short term, but there is the attendant danger that projects die when the moving force shifts elsewhere. Empirical research has the power only to tinker with various features of the 'real' world; it cannot address or consider as variables the complex interactions which take place in immediate situations. There are limits to the questions that a traditional research approach can answer, and the change programme we envisaged stepped well outside those limits. We were convinced that the causes of girls' avoidance of science/technology were not only complex but cumulative. We could have tried to use the schools as an experimental setting in which to manipulate variables, but the chances were that such minor bits of tinkering would simply be overwhelmed by the stronger pressures of school norms and stereotyped social expectations. By working within the unique and immediate context of each school to see what could be achieved the area of investigation has widened considerably.

Any research hypothesis contains hidden value judgments. By refusing to adopt a supposedly neutral research stance, GIST was able to call attention to the partial and biased nature of some traditional research on gender difference, without losing the perspective of educational research. Alerting teachers to gender stereotyping as a personal and professional issue was crucial to the programme. It also offered an opportunity to test out approaches and learn more about the attitudes teachers hold, and under what circumstances they will be prepared to reconsider them. This curiosity about the process of normative attitude change is a legitimate focus of reflective educational research, and could not have been addressed in a project with a purely action orientation.

As feminist educational researchers we have had two points of reference: the research world and the women's movement. MacDonald and Walker, writing about curriculum innovation, describe project teachers as being caught between, on the one hand, the practical demands of practitioners in schools looking for feasible solutions and, on the other, the academic world with its requirement that the innovation be described and analysed in a theoretically satisfactory way. They say that because projects are subordinate to the school system and can operate only with their permission, they tend to engage in 'image manipulation' to disguise discrepancies between their own educational convictions and those held by others, teachers and academic critics. Consequently there emerge two distinct and conflicting views about what the project really is (MacDonald and Walker, 1976).

The critics of GIST also operate from two camps: feminists wonder whether the commitment to research has not been a brake upon the possible achievements of a project designed to help girls, while others have criticized GIST for insufficient regard to teachers' professional concerns. The way these two groups see GIST is naturally different, and the team was highly aware of the divergent views. But attempting to maintain a double loyalty and double vision may in retrospect have been a strength, by focusing attention on the genuine differences of opinion about educational aims and priorities. If GIST has clarified and illuminated both the research and the action needs for gender equality in schools, future work on both fronts may be better informed and ultimately enriched.

References

Curran, L. (1980), 'Science education: did she drop out or was she pushed?' in L. Birke *et al.* (eds) (Brighton Women and Science Group), *Alice Through the Microscope: the Power of Science over Women's Lives*, London, Virago, pp. 22-41.

Eakins, B.W. and Eakins, R.G. (1978), *Sex Differences in Human Communication*, Boston, Houghton Mifflin.

Elliott, J. (undated), 'Action research: a framework for self-evaluation in schools', Schools Council Programme 2, 'Teacher-pupil interaction and the quality of learning' project, Working Paper no. 1 (mimeo).

Hult, M. and Lennung, S. (1980), 'Towards a definition of action research: a note and a bibliography', *Journal of Management Studies*, vol. 17, no. 2, pp. 241-50.

Hustler, D. (ed.) (1985), *Action Research in Classrooms and Schools*, London, Allen & Unwin (in press).

Kelly, A. (1985), 'Action research: what is it and what can it do?', in Burgess R. (ed.), *Issues in Educational Research: Qualitative Methods*, Brighton, Falmer Press

MacDonald, B and Walker, R. (1976), *Changing the Curriculum*, London, Open Books.

Newson, J. and Newson, E. (1976), *Seven Years Old in the Home Environment*, London, Allen & Unwin.

Payne, G., Cuff, E. and Hustler, D. (1984), 'GIST or PIST?' Teacher perceptions of the project "Girls Into Science and Technology" ', Manchester Polytechnic (mimeo).

Pratt, J. (1985), 'The attitudes of teachers', in Whyte, J. *et al.* (eds), *Girl Friendly Schooling*, London, Methuen.

Pratt, J., Bloomfield, J. and Seale, C. (1984), *Option Choice: A Question of Equal Opportunity*, Windsor, NFER-Nelson.

Rapoport, R.N. (1979), 'Three dilemmas in action research', *Human Relations*, vol. 23, pp. 499-513.

Smail, B. (1983), 'Spatial visualisation skills and technical crafts education, Research note', *Educational Research*, vol. 25, no. 3, November.

Smail, B. (1984), *Girl Friendly Science: Avoiding Sex Bias in the Curriculum*, Harlow, Longman, for the Schools Council/School Curriculum Development Committee.

Smith, P. (1985) *Language, the Sexes and Society*, Oxford, Basil Blackwell, pp. 179–81.

Whyte, J. and Smail, B. (1982), 'GIST as action research', *EOC Research Bulletin* no. 6, Spring, 'Gender and the secondary school curriculum'.

Endpiece

by Alison Kelly, Co-director with Judith Whyte of GIST

This book represents a landmark in the continuing history of the GIST project. It tells the story of what we did and why we did it; what seemed to work and what was less successful. But it is by no means the end of the story. All of us who worked on GIST, as well as others who were less centrally involved, and even people who only heard about it indirectly, continue to be influenced in our thinking and our actions by what we learned on the project.

My own approach to GIST, and my continuing work in this area, were strongly influenced by two factors. One was my membership of Women and Education, a small group of feminists, mainly teachers in secondary schools, who produced and distributed a termly newsletter. This experience in a collective, non-hierarchical organization gave me a strong sense of alternative ways of working and of the situation of feminist teachers, and their sense of isolation in the schools. The other was my background in educational research, particularly in the analysis of large-scale surveys of schooling. From the first, I felt it was important that GIST be more than an action project, that it also include a strong research component. Knowledge is power, and our efforts to change the world are more likely to succeed if based on a thorough understanding. The model of action-research that we adopted is based on these dual concerns with knowledge and social action.

Our work with teachers, as described in this book, was based on a softly softly approach which played down the feminist aspects of the project and worked through the hierarchy of the school. From the start, perhaps because of my experience in the Women and Education Group, I was unhappy with this approach. I felt that we should form alliances with feminist teachers and be more explicit about our purposes. In the event I am not sure that either strategy was correct. As I have argued elsewhere (Kelly, 1985a), the gentle approach was either ignored (only four of the thirty-four teachers interviewed by our evaluators saw the project as having anything to do with changing teachers) or rejected, despite our best efforts, as unacceptably radical. The explicit approach would inevitably have been rejected by all but a small minority of teachers.

Perhaps the main fault in the conceptualization of GIST was the attempt to effect change through working with ordinary teachers in ordinary schools. With hindsight I would run the project with committed, volunteer teachers, even if they were scattered thinly across schools. The aim would be to test out strategies, and examine how these worked in favourable conditions. Dissemination would concentrate on showing what could be done, and creating an educational climate where other, initially less committed teachers, felt that they could and should do the same.

The work with teachers was perhaps the most problematic aspect of the project. We were much more successful in organizing interventions, re-writing curricula, producing posters and advising on classroom practices, largely due to the untiring work of Barbara Smail and John Catton, our dedicated Schools Liaison Officers. In research terms too the project was productive. We employed both qualitative and quantitative methodologies, and have written the usual sort of academic reports. But perhaps the most innovative aspect of GIST was the way we intertwined action and research so that each utilized and stimulated the other. This has been discussed at length elsewhere (Kelly, 1985b), and it is a method which inevitably produces its own problems. Nevertheless it has the overwhelming advantage, to my mind, of breaking down the artificial barriers between teachers and researchers, and allowing them to co-operate on projects which have both practical and theoretical importance.

My experience in quantitative research led to my taking chief responsibility for the collection and analysis of quantitative data. This aspect of the project has been, and continues to be, highly productive. We have learned a considerable amount about the attitudes and achievements of 11-year-olds. With the addition of data from the same children three years later we now have a unique longitudinal data set tracing the development of children's attitudes during the early years of secondary school and linking attitudes to subject choices and career plans. So far this data has only been analysed in the most superficial way, and numerous questions remain. Were the GIST interventions more successful with some groups of girls (e.g. middle-class pupils, or those with low initial sex stereotyping) than with others? What is the relationship between attitudes to science and option choices? What is the relationship between sex stereotyping and option and career choices? Can option choices in the third year be predicted from children's attitudes and achievements in the first year? These questions have both theoretical and practical importance. The answers will suggest how and when we should intervene in schools for maximum effect; they will also tell us something about the structure of adolescents' thought. I hope to spend some time exploring some of these issues in greater detail than has been possible to date.

With longitudinal data the temptation is always to follow the subjects one step further, and this possibility exists for the GIST cohort. At the time of writing these pupils are preparing for their O-level and CSE examinations. Why not go back to the schools next October and find out how they got on? We could also enquire who left school and who returned, and what sort of jobs, training schemes or A-levels they went into. If this were done the longitudinal data would become even more impressive as a record of the development of specialization in science.

As a project GIST is completed. But as an idea, and as a resource, it continues. The issue of girls' underinvolvement in science and technology is now of widespread concern, and we are constantly asked to speak about the project, its interventions and its results. By doing so we hope to stimulate others to think about these issues and develop their own solutions. Disseminating the GIST approach, that peculiar combination of action and research, is more problematic. In too many minds these activities still exist in water-tight compartments. Yet this approach may, in the long run, turn out to be the most lasting achievement of GIST. At its best action research allows practitioners and researchers to co-operate as equals on problems of mutual interest. If such an approach becomes more widespread educational research may cease to be seen by most teachers as an expensive irrelevance, and become a useful tool which they can use to answer their own queries. This in turn may generate a problem solving attitude to change, which in the long run could liberate both teachers and pupils from the shackles of conventional thinking.

This of course is utopian thinking. But utopias do not emerge fully formed. They are built slowly and painstakingly. My hope is that GIST will be part of a continuing process of changing people's thinking about girls and science, and about educational research. This book is a crucial component of that process, as it reaches out to a wider audience than before. But it will only succeed in the spirit of GIST if it stimulates that audience to look for questions rather than answers, and to experiment in their own interactions as parents, teachers and learners.

References

Kelly, A. (1985a), 'Changing schools and changing society', in Arnot, M. (ed.), *Policy Making in Education*, Milton Keynes, Open University Press.

Kelly, A. (1985b), 'Action research: what is it and what can it do?', in Burgess, R. (ed.), *Issues in Educational Research: Qualitative Methods*, Brighton, Falmer Press.

Bibliography

Arditti, Rita (1982), 'Feminism and science', in *The Changing Experience of Women*, (ed.) W. Whitelegg *et al.*, Martin Robertson, Oxford in association with the Open University.

Astin, Alexander, W. (1978), 'The undergraduate woman', in *The Higher Education of Women*, ed. H.S. Astin and W.Z. Hirsch, Praeger, New York.

Baldwin, Jill (1979, 1980 and 1981), *Active Tutorial Work*, Books 1-5, Blackwell, Oxford, in association with Lancashire County Council.

Ball, B. (1984), *Careers Counselling in Practice*, Falmer Press, Brighton.

Belotti, E.G. (1975), *Little Girls: Social Conditioning and its Effect on the Stereotyped Role of Women during Infancy*, Writers' and Readers' Publishing Cooperative, London.

Bem, S.L. (1975), 'Sex role adaptability: one consequence of psychological androgyny', *Journal of Personal and Social Psychology*, 31, pp. 634-43.

Best, D.E., Williams, J.E., *et al.* (1977), 'Development of sex trait stereotypes among young children in the US, England and Ireland', *Child Development*, 48 (4), December, pp. 1375-85.

Bone, A./Equal Opportunities Commission (1983), *Girls and Girls-only Schools: A Review of the Evidence*, pamphlet, Equal Opportunities Commission, London.

Borley, Joan (1982), 'Equal opportunities in education: a follow up to the EOC's Publication, *Do You Provide Equal Opportunities?*', MA thesis, University of Manchester.

Catton, J. (1985), *Ways and Means: Girls in Craft, Design and Technology*, Longman, Harlow, for the Schools Council.

Catton, J. and Smail, B. (1983), 'Removing the blinkers', *Women and Education Newsletter*, no. 25, Summer.

Clarricoates, K. (1980), 'The importance of being Ernest . . . Emma . . . Tom . . . Jane: the perception and categorisation of gender conforming and gender deviation in primary schools', in *Schooling for Women's Work*, ed. R. Deem, Routledge & Kegan Paul, London.

Crossman, M. (1981), 'Sex differences and teacher-pupil interaction patterns in secondary school science', MEd dissertation, Manchester University.

Dale, R.R. (1969, 1971, 1974), *Mixed or Single Sex School?*, vols 1, 2 and 3, Routledge & Kegan Paul, London.

Davies, L. and Meighan, R. (1975), 'A review of schooling and sex roles, with particular reference to the experience of girls in secondary schools', *Educational Review*, 27 (3), pp. 165-78.

Delamont, Sara (1980), *Sex Roles and the School*, Methuen, London.

Delamont, Sara (1983), 'The conservative school? Sex roles at home, at work and at school', in *Gender, Class and Education*, ed. S. Walker and L. Barton, Falmer Press, Brighton.

Department of Education and Science (1975), *Curricular Differences for Boys and Girls*, Education Survey 21, HMSO, London.

Drotz, B.M., Sjoberg, L. and Dahlstaand, U. (1984), 'Achievement and interests in engineering education', paper presented at IPN/UNESCO International Symposium on Interests in Science and Technology Education, Kiel, 2-6 April 1984.

Equal Opportunities Commission (1983), '*Equal Opportunities in Craft, Design and Technology*', report of a working party convened by the Equal Opportunities Commission, London.

Equal Opportunities Commission (1984), *Girls and Engineering* (leaflet), EOC, London.

Equal Opportunity Newsletter (1984), 'Boy talk', *EON*, vol. 3, no. 1, March. Published by Equal Opportunity Unit, 3rd Floor, 2 Treasury Place, Melbourne, Australia.

Fennema, E. (1974), 'Sex differences in mathematics learning: why???', *The Elementary School Journal* 75, pp. 1183-90.

Fennema, E. and Sherman, J. (1977), 'Sex related differences in maths achievement, spatial visualisation and affective factors', *American Education Research Journal*, 14 (1), pp. 51-71.

Festinger, L. (1957), *A Theory of Cognitive Dissonance*, Stanford University Press, Stanford, Calif.

French, J. and French, P. (1983), 'Gender imbalances in the primary classroom: an interactional account' (unpublished).

Galton, M. (1981), 'Differential treatment of boy and girl pupils during science lessons', in A. Kelly (ed.) *The Missing Half: Girls and Science Education*, Manchester University Press, pp. 180-192.

Gardner, P.L. (1984), 'Summary and cross evaluation of national reports', paper presented at IPN/UNESCO International Symposium on Interests in Science and Technology Education, Kiel, 2-6 April 1984.

Garner, J. and Bing, M. (1973), 'The elusiveness of Pygmalion and differences in teacher-pupil contact', *Interchange*, 4 (1), pp. 34-43.

Golden, G. and Hunter, L. (1974), *In All Fairness: A Handbook on Sex Role Bias in Schools*, Far West Laboratory for Educational Research and Development, San Francisco.

Goodwin, A.J., Hardiman, B. and Rees, V. (1981), *An Investigation of the Attitudes to School, Science and Science Lessons of 10-13 Year Old Children*, mimeo, Manchester Polytechnic.

Grant, M. (1983), 'Craft design and technology', in *Sexism in the Secondary School Curriculum*, ed. Janie Whyld, Harper & Row, London.

Griffiths, D. and Saraga, S. (1979), 'Sex differences and cognitive abilities: a sterile field of enquiry?', in *Sex Role Stereotyping*, ed. O. Hartnett, G. Boden and M. Fuller, Tavistock, London.

Hall, Anthea (1983), 'Is your daughter getting a fair deal?', *Sunday Telegraph*, 4 December, p. 12.

Halsey, A.H. (1972), *Educational Priority, Vol. 1: EPA Problems and Policies*, HMSO, London.

Hanson, D and Herrington, M. (1976), *From College to Classroom: The Probationary Year*, Routledge & Kegan Paul, London.

Harding, J. (1980), 'Sex differences in performance in science examination', in *Schooling for Women's Work*, ed. R. Deem, Routledge & Kegan Paul, London.

Harding, J. (1981), 'Report on science examinations and the type of school', in Contributions: GASAT (Girls and Science and Technology) Conference, 1981, Eindhoven University of Technology.

Harding, J. (1981), 'Sex differences in science examinations', in *The Missing Half: Girls and Science Education*, ed. A. Kelly, Manchester University Press, pp. 192-204.

Harris, A., Lawn, M. and Prescott, W. (eds) (1975), *Curriculum Innovation*, Croom Helm, London, in association with the Open University Press.

Hartley, R.E. and Klein, A. (1959), 'Sex role concepts among elementary-school age girls', *Marriage and Family Living*, 21, pp. 59-64.

Her Majesty's Inspectorate (1980), *Girls and Science*, HMI Series: Matters for Discussion, 13, HMSO, London.

Her Majesty's Inspectorate (1979), *Aspects of Secondary Education*, HMSO, London.

Hoffman, L.W. (1974), 'Effects on child', in *Working Mothers*, ed. L.W. Hoffman and F.I. Nyes, Jossey-Bass, San Francisco.

Hoyle, E. (1975), 'The creativity of the school in Britain', in *Curriculum Innovation*, ed. A. Harris *et al.*, Croom Helm, London, in association with the Open University Press.

Hudson, L. (1967), *Contrary Imaginations*, Penguin, Harmondsworth.

Hudson, L. (1968), *Frames of Mind: Ability, Perception and Self-perception in the Arts and Sciences*, Methuen, London.

Ideal Home (1984), 'Female threads', *Ideal Home*, April.

Inner London Education Authority (ILEA) (1982), 'Female and male teaching staff in the ILEA: Equal Opportunity', RS883/82. Report written by Richard Martini, ILEA Research and Statistics, July.

Kahle, J.B. (1983), *Girls in School: Women in Science*, mimeo, National

Association of Biology Teachers, USA.

Kaminski, D.M. (1982), 'Girls and mathematics & science: an annotated bibliography of British work (1970-1981)', *Studies in Science Education*, 9, pp. 81-108.

Kelly, A. and Smail, B. (1983), 'Sex stereotyping and attitudes to science among 11 year old schoolchildren', *British Journal of Educational Psychology*.

Kelly, A., Whyte, J. and Smail, B. (1984a), 'Girls Into Science and Technology: Final Report', mimeo (available from the Department of Sociology, University of Manchester, or Judith Whyte, School of Education, Manchester Polytechnic.

Kelly, A. *et al.* (1982), 'Gender roles at home and school', *British Journal of Sociology of Education* 3, pp. 281-95.

Kelly, A., *et al.* (1984b), 'Traditionalists and trendies: teachers' attitudes to educational issues', unpublished paper.

Lee, P.C. and Gropper, N.B. (1974), 'Sex role culture and educational practice', *Harvard Educational Review*, 44, no. 3, August, pp. 369-410.

Levine, M. (1976), 'Identification of reasons why qualified women do not pursue mathematical careers', Report to the National Science Foundation, August, NSF Grant no. GY-11411 (US).

Lippitt, R.O. (1974), 'Identifying, documenting, evaluating and sharing innovative classroom practices', Final Report to the Office of Education, Department of Health, Education and Welfare (USA), cited in Zaltman *et al.* (1977).

McClelland, D. (1962), 'On the dynamics of creative physical scientists', in *The Ecology of Human Intelligence*, ed. L. Hudson, Penguin, Harmondsworth.

Mischel, W. (1966), 'A social learning view of sex differences in behaviour', in *The Development of Sex Differences*, ed. E.E. Maccoby, Stanford University Press.

Morrison, A. and McIntyre, D. (eds) (1969), *Teachers and Teaching*, Harmondsworth, Penguin.

Nagi, S.Z. (1974), 'Gatekeeping decisions in service organizations: when validity fails', *Human Organization* 33, no. 1, Spring, pp. 47-58.

Nickerson, E.T., *et al.* (1975), *Intervention Strategies for Changing Sex Role Stereotypes: A Procedural Guide*, Kendall Hunt, Dubuque, Iowa.

Nisbet, J. (1974), 'Innovation – bandwagon or hearse?', first published in *Bulletin of Victorian Institute of Educational Research*, 33, 1-14. Reprinted in *Curriculum Innovation*, ed. A. Harris, M. Lawn and W. Prescott, Croom Helm, London, 1975.

Nisbet, J. and Broadfoot, P. (1980), *The Impact of Research on Policy and Practice in Education*, University of Aberdeen Press.

Ormerod, M.B. (1971), 'The social implications factor in attitudes to science', *British Journal of Educational Psychology* 41, pp. 335-8.

Ormerod, M.B. (1973), 'Social and subject factors in attitudes to science', *School Science Review*, 54, no. 189, June, pp. 645-60.

Ormerod, M.B. (1975), 'Subject preference and choice in coeducational and single sex secondary schools', *British Journal of Educational Psychology*, 45, pp. 257-67.

Ormerod, M.B. (1981), 'Factors affecting the science subject preferences, choices and attitudes of girls and boys', in *The Missing Half: Girls and Science Education*, ed. A. Kelly, Manchester University Press, pp. 100-12.

Osgood, C.E. and Tannenbaum, P.H. (1955), 'The principle of congruity in the prediction of attitude change', *Psychology Review*, 62, January.

Patterson, A. (1980), 'You want physics for everything', *Education in Science*, April, pp. 14-15.

Payne, G., Hustler, D. and Cuff, T. (1984), *GIST or PIST: Teacher Perceptions of the Project 'Girls Into Science and Technology'*, mimeo, Manchester Polytechnic.

Powell, R. and Littlewood, P. (1982), 'Foreign languages: the avoidable options', *British Journal of Language Teaching*, 20, no. 3, Winter.

Pratt, J., Seale, C. and Bloomfield, J. (1984), *Option Choice: A Question of Equal Opportunity*, NFER, Slough/Nelson, Walton-on-Thames.

Reynolds, D. (1984), 'Relative autonomy', reconstructed paper, presented at Westhill Sociology of Education Conference, 1983.

Rhydderch, G. (1982), 'One for the girls', *Women and Education*, 24, Winter.

Ricks, F.A. and Pyke, S.W. (1969), 'Teacher perceptions and attitudes that foster or maintain sex-role differences', *Interchange*, 4.

Robinson, P. (1981), *Perspectives on the Sociology of Education: An Introduction*, Routledge & Kegan Paul, London.

Roe, A. (1951), 'A psychological study of eminent physical scientists', *Genetic Psychology Monographs*, 43, pp. 121-239.

Roe, A. (1952), *The Making of a Scientist*, Dodd Mead, New York.

Rokeach, M. (1968), *Beliefs, Attitudes and Values: A Theory of Organisation and Change*, Jossey-Bass, San Francisco.

Rudduck, J. (1976), 'Dissemination of innovation: the Humanities Curriculum Project', Evans/Methuen, London (Schools Council Working Paper 56).

Ryrie, A.C., Furst, A. and Lauder, M. (1979), 'Choices and chances: a study of pupils' subject choices and future career intentions', Hodder and Stoughton, London, for the Scottish Council for Research in Education.

Samuel, J. (1981), 'The teacher's viewpoint – Feminism and science teaching: some classroom observations', in *The Missing Half: Girls and Science Education*, ed. A. Kelly, Manchester University Press, pp. 247-57.

Sartin, P. (1978), 'Training for women', in *School and After: A European Symposium*, Council of Europe, NFER, Slough.

Schofield, B., Murphy, P., Johnson, S. and Black, P. (1982), *APU*

Science in Schools: Age 13, Report no. 1, HMSO, London.

Scott, H. (1984), 'Sweden's efforts at sex equality', in *World Yearbook of Education, 1984, Women and Education*, ed. S. Acker, J. Megarry, S. Nisbet and E. Hoyle, Kogan Page, London.

Serbin, L.A. (1978), 'Teachers, peers and play preferences: an environmental approach to sex typing in the pre-school', in *Perspectives on Non-Sexist Early Childhood Education*, ed. Barbara Spring, Teacher's College Press, Columbia University, New York.

Serbin, L.A., Connor, J.M. and Citron, C.C. (1978), 'Environmental control of independent and dependent behaviours in preschool girls and boys: a model for early independent training', *Sex Roles*, 4, no. 6.

Serbin, L.A., O'Leary, K. and Tonick, I.J. (1976), 'First lessons in equality', *Psychology Today*, 2, pp. 12-15.

Sharma, S. and Meighan, R. (1980), 'Schooling and sex roles: the case of GCE 'O' level mathematics', *British Journal of Sociology of Education*, 1, no. 2.

Shaw, Jennifer (1980), 'Education and the individual: schooling for girls, or Mixed schooling: a mixed blessing?', in *Schooling for Women's Work*, ed. R. Deem, Routledge & Kegan Paul, London, pp. 66-76.

Smail, B. (1982), 'Changing the image of women scientists', in *Women and Training News*, 9, Winter.

Smail, B. (1983a), *Women in Science*, illustrated by Kim Barrington, GIST booklet.

Smail, B. (1983b), 'Spatial visualisation skills and technical crafts education', *Educational Research*, November.

Smail, B. (1984), *Girl Friendly Science: Avoiding Sex Bias in the Curriculum*, Longman, Harlow, for the Schools Council.

Smail, B. and Kelly, A. (1984), 'Sex differences in science and technology among eleven year old schoolchildren: I Cognitive', *Research in Science and Technological Education*, vol. 2, pp. 61-76.

Smithers, A. and Collings, J. (1982), 'Coeducation and science choice', *British Journal of Educational Studies*, 30.

Spaulding, R.L. (1963), 'Achievement, creativity and self-concept correlates of teacher-pupil transactions in elementary schools', Co-operative Research Project no. 1352, Dept. of Health, Education and Welfare, Office of Education, Washington DC.

Spender, D. (1978), 'Don't talk, listen!', *The Times Educational Supplement*, 3 November.

Stanworth, M. (1981), *Gender and Schooling: A Study of Sexual Divisions in the Classroom*, first published by Women's Research and Resources Centre Publications Collective, London. Reprinted by Hutchinson, London, in association with the Explorations in Feminism Collective, 1983.

Taylor, J. (1970), 'Sexist bias in physics textbooks', *Physics Education*, 4, 5 July, pp. 277-80.

Thompson, J. (1982), 'GIST: Girls Into Science and Technology', in *Teaching London Kids*, 19.

Toft, P. and Catton, J. (1983), 'More than half-way there', *The Times Educational Supplement*, 7 October.

Triandis, H.C. (1971), *Attitude and Attitude Change*, John Wiley, Chichester.

Val Aalst, H.F. (1984), 'A model of interest-motivation-learning', paper presented at IPN/UNESCO International Symposium on Interests in Science and Technology Education, Kiel, 2-6 April 1984.

Vlemmicks, J. (1983), 'Girls in the Technology Club', *School Technology*, December.

Walford, G. (1980), 'Sex bias in physics textbooks', *School Science Review*, 62, pp. 220-7.

Weiss, I.R., Pace, C. and Conaway, L.E. (1978), Visiting Women Scientists Pilot Programme 1978, Final Report, Research Triangle Institute, North Carolina.

Wernersson, I. (1982), 'Sex differentiation and teacher-pupil interaction in Swedish compulsory schools', in *Sex Stereotyping in Schools*, ed. Council of Europe, Swets & Zeitlinger, Lisse, Netherlands.

Whyte, J. (1972), 'Study of factors affecting occupational aspirations of boys and girls', PGCE dissertation, University of Oxford.

Whyte, J. (1984), 'Observing sex stereotypes and interactions in the school lab and workshop', *Educational Review*, 36, no. 1.

Wilkins, P. (1983), 'Women and engineering in the Plymouth area: job segregation and training at company level', *EOC Research Bulletin*, no. 7, Summer, pp. 20-37 (available from the Equal Opportunities Commission).

Yates, L. (1984), 'Counter-sexist strategies in Australian schools', in *World Yearbook of Education 1984, Women and Education*, eds. S. Acker, J. Megarry, S. Nisbet and E. Hoyle, Kogan Page, London.

Zaltman, G., *et al.* (1977), *Dynamic Educational Change*, Free Press, New York and Collier Macmillan, London.

List of works relating to the GIST project

Several of these articles are now out of print, but copies of those where a price is shown may be obtained by sending a large stamped addressed envelope and the appropriate fee to GIST, Manchester Polytechnic, 9a Didsbury Park, Manchester M20 8RR. Cheques should be made payable to Manchester Polytechnic, GIST/Friends A/C.

1 Barbara Smail, Alison Kelly and Judith Whyte, *GIST Introductory Booklet*, mimeo, November 1979.

2 Judith Whyte, 'Integrating careers education to provide equal opportunities', *Careers and Guidance Teachers' Journal*, Summer 1981.

3 Alison Kelly, Barbara Smail and Judith Whyte, *Initial GIST Survey: Results and Implications*, mimeo, September 1981.

4 Barbara Smail, Judith Whyte and Alison Kelly, 'Girls into science and technology: the first two years', paper presented at Girls and Science and Technology Conference, Eindhoven, Holland, November 1981. Published in *School Science Review*, 63, 1982, pp. 620-30; *South Australia Science Teachers' Association Journal*, no. 813, 3-10, December 1981; and *EOC Research Review*, no. 6, Spring 1982. 20p.

5 Judith Whyte and Barbara Smail, 'GIST as action research', *EOC Research Bulletin*, Spring 1982.

6 Alison Kelly *et al.*, 'Gender roles at home and school', *British Journal of Sociology of Education*', 3, 1982, pp. 281-95.

7 Judith Whyte, Alison Kelly, Barbara Smail and John Catton, *GIST: Options and Careers*, mimeo, August 1982.

8 Barbara Smail and Judith Whyte, 'Girls' access to engineering: what can be done in schools?', published in the proceedings of the Equal Opportunities Commission Seminar on 'Women and Engineering' London, 2 December 1982.

9 Judith Whyte, 'The dominant male', *Times Educational Supplement*, 31 December 1982.

10 John Catton, 'Girls in CDT – some teacher strategies for mixed groups', *Studies in Design Education, Craft and Technology*, 15, no. 1, Winter 1982.

11 Barbara Smail, 'Changing the image of women scientists', *Women and Training News*, no. 9, Winter 1982.

12 Judith Whyte, 'The Girls Into Science and Technology project', *Schools Council News*, Summer 1983.

13 Judith Whyte, 'Courses for teachers on sex differences and sex typing', *Journal of Education for Teaching*, October 1983. 20p.

14 Alison Kelly and Barbara Smail, 'Sex stereotyping and attitudes to science among 11-year-old schoolchildren', *British Journal of Educational Psychology*, in press. 20p.

15 Barbara Smail, 'Spatial visualisation skills and technical crafts education', *Educational Research*, November 1983.

16 John Thompson, 'GIST: Girls Into Science and Technology', *Teaching London Kids*, no. 19, 1982.

17 Judith Whyte and Barbara Smail, 'Initial teachers' workshops in the GIST project: a tentative interim assessment', presented to British Educational Research Association Annual Conference, Cardiff, 1980.

18 Judith Whyte, 'Observing sex stereotypes and interactions in the school lab and workshop', *Educational Review*, 36, February 1984.

19 Barbara Smail and Alison Kelly, 'Sex differences in science and technology among eleven-year-old schoolchildren: I Cognitive', *Research in Science and Technological Education*, 2, no. 1, 1984, pp. 61-76. 20p.

20 Barbara Smail and Alison Kelly, 'Sex differences in science and technology among eleven-year-old schoolchildren: II Affective, *Research in Science and Technological Education*, 2, no. 2, 1984, pp. 87-106. 20p.

21 Barbara Smail, 'Getting science right for girls', paper prepared for the second International Conference on Girls and Science and Technology (GASAT), Oslo, September 1983.

22 Alison Kelly, 'Action research: some definitions and descriptions', paper prepared for Qualitative Methodology and the Study of Education Seminar, Whitelands College, London, July 1983. 20p.

23 Judith Whyte, 'How girls learn to be losers', *Primary Education Review*, June 1983.

24 Judith Whyte, 'GIST as action research', paper presented to Conference on Action Research at Didsbury School of Education, Manchester Polytechnic, April 1983.

25 Barbara Smail, *Women in Science*, illustrated by Kim Barrington, GIST booklet, mimeo.

26 John Catton and Barbara Smail, 'Removing the blinkers', *Women and Education Newsletter*, no. 25, Summer 1983.

27 Peter Toft and John Catton, 'More than half-way there', *Times Educational Supplement*, 7 October 1983.
28 Alison Kelly, 'The construction of masculine science', to be submitted to the *British Journal of Sociology of Education*.

Index

CANISIUS COLLEGE LIBRARY
Q183.4.G7 W48 1986 c. 1
Girls into science a
3 5084 00192 0688

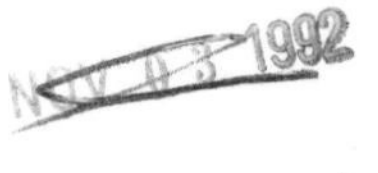